Prai
Beyond the (

"*Beyond the Good-Girl Jail* is a seminal book for both therapists and clients. Wise, accessible, and filled with illustrative case histories, it's more than just clear and instructive; it's a page-turner that's hard to put down. Each chapter feels like a revelation, adding depth and dimension to the perennial question of what it is to become whole, real, and rooted in one's essential self. The clear prose brings the reader to insight over and over again—'aha, I really get that!' The poetry deepens the insight and goes directly to the heart. This book is a treasure that is bound to become a classic for both therapists and their clients. Brava, Sandra!"

—Joan Borysenko, PhD
New York Times bestselling author,
Minding the Body, Mending the Mind

"This is a book every woman *must read*. Sandra Felt is correct, it has not been written before and it speaks to all of us women. I started reading it and didn't want to put it down. It is a book that you will keep and re-read. It is our 'get out of jail' card! It's not a free get out of jail card—we have to do the work—but Sandra offers the path."

—Claudia Black, PhD
author, *It Will Never Happen to Me, Repeat After Me*,
and co-author *The Missing Piece: Solving the Puzzle of Self*

"As Sandra Felt shows, the Good-Girl syndrome is a mask, a prison, a trap that limits people's lives, deadens their relationships, and drains them of energy. As I have often witnessed, it is also a major source of physical and mental pathology. Sandra has written a simple yet elegant guide to escaping the prison and finding the true self that has so long languished underneath the mask. This book will enhance your health."

—Gabor Maté, MD
author, *When the Body Says No: Exploring
the Stress-Disease Connection*

"There are not enough superlatives to describe *Beyond the Good-Girl Jail*. It is brilliant, well-written, practical, and user-friendly, whether the reader is a psychotherapy client, a therapist, or simply interested in bettering her life. The book reflects both Sandra Felt's therapeutic acumen as well as the transparent authenticity of her own healing process. This book is not formulaic self-help Pablum but a work of tremendous depth and complexity presented with remarkable clarity, wisdom, and compassion—a must read."

—**Lorie Dwinell, LCSW**
co-author, *After the Tears: Helping Adult Children
Heal Their Childhood Trauma*

"*Beyond the Good-Girl Jail* is a title at once provocative and hopeful. Therapist Sandra Felt has written a very wise and compassionate book for trauma survivors, many of whom struggle to identify with—or even like—who they are. Using vignettes from her own recovery, original poetry, and a depth of thoughtfulness, she provides readers with concrete suggestions and benchmarks for recovery that are founded on them as individuals rather than on the rules and the desires of others."

—**Christine A. Courtois, PhD, ABPP**
author, *It's Not You, It's What Happened to You:
Complex Trauma and Treatment*

"Sandra Felt extends an invitation that should *not* be missed to join her on a journey to examine and develop your 'true self.' She includes detailed guidelines on ways to recognize, reconnect with, rebuild, and return home to yourself. She demonstrates how to be open to awakening moments and how to take risks in order to invite aliveness and happiness into one's life. She creatively uses a combination of personal anecdotes, case studies, and poetry to demonstrate how to 're-story' one's life. Psychotherapists will find the practical suggestions offered a useful resource to use with their clients."

—**Don Meichenbaum, PhD**
distinguished professor emeritus, University of Waterloo
research director of the Melissa Institute for Violence Prevention

"The foundation of all healthy relationships is honest self-awareness. *Beyond the Good-Girl Jail* lays that foundation in concrete. It zeroes in on the heart of the matter."

—**Pat Love, EdD**
co-author, *Never Be Lonely Again: The Way Out of Emptiness, Isolation, and a Life Unfulfilled* and *You're Tearing Us Apart: Twenty Ways We Wreck Our Relationships and Strategies to Repair Them*

"This insightful and warmly written book provides the keys to unlock and free our muffled selves from our respective cages and thereby finally and fully respond to all of life's opportunities, challenges and joys . . . both inside and out."

—**Gregory Boothroyd, PhD, LPC**
professor emeritus, Western Michigan University
co-author, *Going Home: A Positive Emotional Guide for Promoting Life-Generating Behaviors*

"Sandra's book, *Beyond the Good Girl Jail* hits the target in understanding what happens to children from painful families. Her story is provocative, inspiring, and clear. Not only does it explain the depth of confusion and emotional pain suffered by children (and adult children) who are traumatized, it offers direct and easy to understand tools for moving from pain to comfort and from confusion to clarity. It is an empowering read. I highly recommend this book."

—**Sharon Wegscheider-Cruse, MS, CDC**
author, *Becoming a Sage: Discovering Life's Lessons One Story at a Time*, and founder of Onsite Workshops

"*Beyond the Good-Girl Jail* is an amazing book about the transformation of beliefs that were supposed to make one happy only to discover that they were meaningless. This is a book of self-exploration and the courage it takes to live the life that works for you. I highly recommend this well-written and thought-provoking book for everyone who wants to live a life of meaning and for those who truly want to find their true selves. You won't be disappointed.

—**Robert J. Ackerman, PhD**
author, *Perfect Daughters* and *Silent Sons*

"Sandra Felt has written a really valuable book. It is interesting, inspiring, practical, and wise, all rolled in one. I think readers will find it very helpful in their recovery from life's blows."

—**Colin A. Ross, MD**
co-author, *Trauma Model Therapy:*
A Treatment Approach for Trauma,
Dissociation and Complex Comorbidity

"I found this book to be comforting, personal, and supportive in many ways. It helped me reflect on my own life, and my efforts to be a whole person with a sense of self. I really appreciate how Sandra interweaves her personal story with client examples, useful information to expand core concepts, and her own poetry. What affected me most in Sandra's book was her honesty. Time and again, she shared about her choice points, revealing the depth of her personal integrity and how she was able to bring her values and her life choices into alignment.

"While the book includes some of Sandra's journey, I think her story is also every woman's story, that we each must confront the same issues that Sandra confronts. This book is a valuable tool for women finding their voice and seeking their lost Self. I found it very inspiring . . . I think you will, too."

—**Janae B. Weinhold, PhD LPC**
co-author, *Developmental Trauma: The Game*
Changer in the Mental Health Profession

Beyond the
Good-Girl Jail

When You Dare to Live
from Your True Self

Sandra Felt

Health Communications, Inc.
Deerfield Beach, Florida

www.hcibooks.com

Library of Congress Cataloging-in-Publication Data
is available through the Library of Congress

© 2016 Sandra Felt

ISBN-13: 978-07573-1845-0 (Paperback)
ISBN-10: 07573-1845-2 (Paperback)
ISBN-13: 978-07573- 1846-7 (ePub)
ISBN-10: 07573-1846-0 (ePub)

The stories in this book are true, representing what clients and others have presented. All names and identifying information have been changed, except for immediate family and a few close friends.

Publisher: Health Communications, Inc.
3201 S.W. 15th Street
Deerfield Beach, FL 33442–8190

"The Good Girl Jail," an original painting by Alice McClelland, used by permission. © *1981 Alice McClelland.*
Cover and interior design and formatting by Lawna Patterson Oldfield

For Eric and Sarah Bree,
who first taught me that it was impossible
to be a perfect mom and who then
taught me that it was more
important to be real.

What If?

What if there really is a me inside?
A self who is all me—and mine?
A unique set of quirks and qualities
To claim and develop?
To live from and through—and be?
What if I already have the right
And enough room
To be who I am?
What if I'm already here,
Capable of living my own life?
What if I'm actually meant to be
This me I already am—
My piece of the universal puzzle?
What if it's truly okay
To dance, to dance in daffodils,
Fully expressing all that is?
And all that oozes through my soul?
What if I refuse to miss
The possibilities of my own truth?

CONTENTS

"To live is the rarest thing in the world.
Most people exist, that is all."

—Oscar Wilde

Foreword xi

Acknowledgments xiii

Introduction 1

PART I: RECOGNIZING OUR TRUE SELF 7

Chapter 1   The Many Names of Self 9

Chapter 2   Daring to Listen to Our Self 27

Chapter 3   Listening Through the Fog of Fear 45

PART II: RECONNECTING WITH OUR TRUE SELF 65

Chapter 4   Creating Our Own Safety 67

Chapter 5   Hearing Our Physical Body 85

Chapter 6   Engaging Our Feelings......................................103

PART III: REBUILDING OUR TRUE SELF 123

Chapter 7 Emphasizing Choices 125

Chapter 8 Cherishing Time Alone 143

Chapter 9 Updating Core Beliefs 157

PART IV: RETURNING HOME TO OUR TRUE SELF 177

Chapter 10 Claiming What Fits Me 179

Chapter 11 Letting Go of What Is Not Me 197

Chapter 12 Honoring Our Own Boundaries 217

PART V: LIVING FROM OUR TRUE SELF 235

Chapter 13 Standing in Our Truth 237

Chapter 14 Uncorking Our Voice 257

Chapter 15 Dancing in Daffodils 279

Related Reading 295

Endnotes 297

FOREWORD

This is an extremely important book! Here's the reason why. With the advent of humans, a new form of evolution was begun. The archeologist Teilhard de Chardin called it the *noosphere*, the sphere of consciousness. Over time, our collective consciousness expanded to the point where we became acutely aware of the history of our consciousness.

We have now reached a moment in the evolution of human consciousness where many of us realize that for most of human history, we have been imprisoned by a life-limiting and vicious co-dependent reality. Co-dependency is dis-ease of the developing self, a failure to develop a true sense of our own reality. Dictatorships and religious patriarchies have kept us in the dark about what we truly think, feel, imagine, need, or want.

Women have been especially battered by these totalistic systems, but men have been damaged, too. I grew up believing that I was only lovable when I was not being *myself*. I now think that the greatest achievement of human evolution occurs when we develop an authentic sense of self.

In *Beyond the Good-Girl Jail*, Sandra Felt offers a practical guide for recovering and discovering yourself. She shares her poetry, her personal life events, and her insight formed from many years of listening to her clients' experiences. The result is pure gold—real wisdom.

In Part One, she offers us ways to become aware of our self. Part Two offers us three essential skills for self-reunion. Once we've begun to experience our own boundaries, be aware of our body's wisdom, and know what we are feeling, we can begin to expand and rebuild our true self. Sandra Felt emphasizes the critical importance of being fully aware of our choices. She urges us to reevaluate our core beliefs and enjoy ourselves in solitude.

Part Four reminds me of David Whyte's poem that urges us to realize that "anything that does not bring us alive is too small for us." Sandra shows us what it means to speak our own truth and spontaneously act out our own calling and destiny.

This book answers the question posed by the old African proverb, "When death finds you, hope it finds you alive!" Rather than going to your death never knowing who you are, join Sandra in finding your true calling and selfhood. Her poem asks "What if I refuse to miss the possibilities of my own truth?" Make what is perhaps one of the most important choices of your one and only life. Read this book. Who knows, you may soon be *dancing in the daffodils*.

—John E. Bradshaw, Sr.
New York Times best-selling author
author, *Post-Romantic Stress Disorder*
Voted by his peers as one of the most important
writers on emotional health in the twentieth century

ACKNOWLEDGMENTS

It has truly taken a village to foster my own personal growth sufficiently to write this book and then to also share it with others. *Beyond the Good-Girl Jail: When You Dare to Live from Your True Self* would not have become possible without the help and support of the following very special people:

First of all, the hundreds of clients and other trauma survivors I have been privileged to know who have shared their deepest fears, courage, stories, trust, and dogged determination to heal. I deeply respect each and every one of you and hold you dear to my heart.

My many teachers over the years who have provided numerous opportunities to learn to trust my own process and spiritual connection, especially: Ruth Kranzler, the college instructor who believed in me enough to teach me to trust my own observations and experiences; Bill O'Hanlon, who generously taught me the essentials of turning my writing into a book; and Greg Chenu, who truly knew what I was talking about and repeatedly challenged me to dig deeper still to find the essence of it all.

The Grass Hat Gals, and other bluegrass musicians, who have encouraged me to take wild risks to be playful and expressive—and laugh heartily.

Alice McClelland, the artist who gave visual form to what I had so often experienced viscerally. Thanks for permission to use your painting. My other precious women friends, too, who have provided the safety net I often need as I continue to grow. I think you know who you are.

My dear husband, Dan Barmettler, who has been consistently by my side through it all, ever ready with a comforting hug, dinner out, and a spot of humor when needed. Thanks for opening so many doors for me.

Peter Vegso, editor Christine Belleris, copy editor Tonya Woodworth, proofreader Laurie Taddonio, graphic designer Lawna Oldfield, public relations director Kim Weiss, and the other staff at Health Communications, Inc., who have taken this chance on a new author and then added their own strength and skills to make the book better.

The many other authors who have believed in the possibilities of this book enough to endorse it. I thank you so much for your generosity.

Others, too, who have provided honest input, encouragement, and assistance of many kinds along the way, especially Bernadette Prinster, Loretta Lewis, JM, RBW, RD, ARW, and my daughter-in-law, Sandy Wisch Felt.

The precious *daffodil spirits* who eagerly helped me find my way to write in the wee dark hours of dawn. And last but never least, life itself as it continues to provide the perfect awakening moments that invite me to feel fully alive.

INTRODUCTION

"Truth is like the sun.
You can shut it out for a time,
but it ain't goin' away."

—*Elvis Presley*

I was once a very good girl. I did what was expected of
me. I cleaned my room and got good grades. I kept quiet and didn't
brag. I tried to be nice, like everyone, and be cooperative. I thought
I was living life *right* and didn't yet realize I had already shut down
my precious aliveness. I didn't yet know that being good is not the
same as being fully alive. I didn't know I had already landed in the
Good-Girl Jail.

I expected to be a good wife and mother and live happily ever
after, but life had other lessons to teach me. By the age of thirty, I was
emotionally drained and painfully empty inside. I had done my best
to live life *right* and had found it impossible. I had so completely lost
my connection with my inner self that there was NO ME LEFT to
give anything to anyone.

When following the rules to be good and meeting the expectations of others didn't work, I didn't know what else to do. I didn't know where to turn for answers. Was there a different guideline for living life? Was there something more to life than being good? What was I missing? What was I doing wrong? These questions haunted me.

Many of us spend our life following the rules and expectations of parents, spouses, teachers, doctors, ministers, and other authority figures. Now I know that we cannot simply follow someone else's *right* way to live and expect to find our own unique, respective paths that bring us fully alive. Now I know that most of us are neither taught nor encouraged to utilize our own innate internal guidance system to find our own *right* way to live.

To be honest, being a good girl did feel *right*, but only until I discovered a passionate inner aliveness that felt more like dancing in fields of daffodils, my favorite flower. There simply is no one *right* way for us all to live life. That is a myth. No one else can know what our life is about or what we need. We each must find our own way to live our individual life; the path that best fits that *me* inside. There is no quick fix, and the journey can be full of distracting detours and challenging surprises. It is, however, also full of sanity, growth, meaning, spirituality, and hope—once we reconnect with our amazing true self.

Beyond the Good-Girl Jail will gently encourage you to find your own path, your own way to live your life. It is the idea that I wish had been mentioned to me at twenty to tell me that living from inside—from self—is actually possible. It is the lesson that I wish I had been taught at thirty, when I was parenting young children. It is the permission I wish I had received at forty to stretch toward my own aliveness. It is the encouragement I wish I could have trusted at fifty, when I wanted to know that so much more was possible. It is the validation I wish I had received throughout my life whenever I felt weird, numb, inferior, discouraged, or unacceptable.

Beyond the Good-Girl Jail is also the text I wish had been required reading in graduate school to teach me what is critical as a psychotherapist, especially when treating trauma survivors. I know now that coming home to self is the underbelly of healing from trauma. Perhaps it is the underlying issue of all psychotherapy, for when we learn to listen at a deeper level, we hear our own deeper truth. If you are a therapist and a client brings you this book, please pay close attention. You are being asked to listen very carefully. You may find these chapters helpful in more ways than you expect.

Beyond the Good-Girl Jail walks through the nooks and crannies on this sometimes bumpy and confusing journey home to self. It is not necessarily an easy book to read, as it may sometimes trigger uncomfortable feelings, questions, and memories, but it is an in-depth guide to discovering and claiming your inner truth. It describes simple steps and places to begin, as well as what lies ahead and what can become possible. While there seems also to be a good-boy jail, this book is written especially for the many women who have become exhausted and perhaps lost from endless futile attempts to live life *right*, as defined by other people. It is written for those who want to fully live their own lives. I suggest that you read it now and read it again a year from now. You will find yourself thinking about it. I believe you will notice considerable progress.

Beyond the Good-Girl Jail is not my memoir, but I utilize some of my own past learning experiences to describe what specific awakening moments feel like. I've included some original poetry written over the years, as some people tell me that these poems speak to them "in a different language." Additional examples from various clients and friends illustrate the common struggles we all encounter as we discover and begin to trust our own individual path. While some of the stories included involve childhood trauma, the pressure to obey the rules of powerful authority figures rather than listen inside to our true self is a lifelong issue for all of us.

Shutting down our aliveness to wear the good-girl mask is not the solution; it is the problem. Switching to the other extreme to rebel and become a bad girl is not the solution either. The solution that allows us each to grow beyond the Good-Girl Jail is to learn to listen to our own precious inner sense of self. When we live life from this deeper truth, we become who we honestly are—and we come fully alive.

There are four R's to growing beyond the Good-Girl Jail. First, we *Recognize* our sense of self and learn to listen to it through the fog of fear as described in Part I. Then, we *Reconnect* with and experience our self through our deep need for safety, our body, and our feelings as delineated in Part II. Specific strategies to *Rebuild* our self through emphasizing the choices we make, time alone, and updating core beliefs are discussed in Part III. In Part IV, we *Return* home to our true self by claiming what fits *me* and letting go of all that is *not me*, which clarifies our natural boundaries. Part V concludes with living from our true self, especially becoming more authentic as we stand in our deeper truth, "uncork" our own true voice, and tune in to our personal dance in daffodils.

I have struggled with the English language as I have written this book. Quite naturally reflecting the dualistic nature of our Western society, our language emphasizes opposites like good/bad, right/wrong, male/female, adult/child, and yours/mine. It has few words that include us all—words like *our*. When we each have more than one of something, using the word *our* works easily—"our boundaries," "our feelings," "our thoughts," "our core beliefs." But when I add "our lives" and "our selves," the complications surface quickly. While some of us may know other lives and many inner selves, this book focuses on this life with one core sense of self. Nevertheless, I have chosen to use the terms "our life," "our body," "our voice," and "our self" to emphasize the universality of this critical journey home to our true self. While my high school English teacher may roll over in her grave, I believe this solution works best to convey my message in the most accurate manner possible. This creative use of language may seem awkward at first, but I think you will settle into the intention behind it as you read.

The following picture is an original painting by my good friend Alice McClelland. She didn't title it. I call it *The Good-Girl Jail*. Do you find yourself hiding behind a zombie-like mask? Do you experience your butterfly wings squished into a box? Like the woman in this painting, do you feel gagged and shut down inside the relentless straitjacket I have come to call the Good-Girl Jail? If so, I invite you to join me now on this courageous but delightful adventure beyond the Good-Girl Jail into the vibrant inner world of the true self. I hope it leads you, too, toward dancing in daffodils.

The Good-Girl Jail
Original painting by Alice McClelland

Part I
Recognizing Our True Self

RECOGNIZE:
acknowledge the existence of
become aware of
perceive directly

Once we learn the language of our sense of self, we hear it beckoning to us. We remember what the self is and why we cannot come fully alive without it. We begin to understand how we may have hidden it in the Good-Girl Jail for safekeeping, perhaps at too young an age to even remember doing so. We begin to comprehend why our true self might be underdeveloped now and how what we have learned to fear tends to continue to shut us down.

"The greatest hazard of all,
losing one's self, can occur quietly
in the world, as if it were nothing at all.
No other loss can occur so quietly;
any other loss—an arm, a leg,
five dollars, a wife, etc.—
is sure to be noticed."

—Soren Kierkegaard

The Many Names of Self

What Do I Know about My Self?

"And what have *you* been doing lately, Sandy?"

There it is—that question. It sounds so simple, but it doesn't feel simple at all. It strikes some kind of raw, electrified nerve I don't even know I have. I drop my jaw. Nothing comes out. How am I to know that such a ridiculously simple question will change my life?

The past few years begin to flash through me. When my husband Tom returned safely from an endless year of military deployment, I felt relieved and most grateful. While quite naturally a stay-at-home mom, I had chosen to teach child development at my alma mater while he was gone, hoping to keep myself busy enough to preserve my sanity during a most confusing time. Leaving our one-year-old Eric every morning, though, was simply not my idea of being a good mom. I cried all the way to work on more than a few mornings, my heart aching for easier times.

I believed my life purpose had been renewed when I was once again able to stay home with our now two children, ages one and four. Decorating our home, taking the kids to the park, keeping up with the laundry, having dinner ready when Tom came home, and being ready to go camping on the weekends seemed to easily fulfill my naive but deep need to be a good wife and mother. Wasn't that what life was all about? That's why I'm not prepared for my friend Susan's confronting question.

As the typical Colorado afternoon thunderstorm passes, we finish eating burgers on the patio with our friends and tuck the kids in for the night. We wives migrate indoors to clean up after dinner and chat among ourselves. "Did I tell you what happened yesterday when my son locked himself in the bathroom?" "How is your baby doing with her new formula?" "Brandi's walking already?" And so forth.

As we finish talking through everything about our children, our husbands, our new purchases, and the weather, Susan turns to me to ask that simple-yet-profound, welcomed-yet-hated, innocent-yet-life-changing magical question: "And what have you been doing lately, Sandy?" How could she have found those amazingly perfect words?

In spite of the warm summer breeze, I freeze inside. I can't move. I can't change the subject. I can't even speak. In spite of the previous free-flowing casual conversation, I have no answer for that question, nothing at all to say. In spite of our seemingly solid friendship, I can't share my truth. Heck, I don't even know my truth! There is simply nothing to draw on to answer that question. I am numb—and suddenly trembling.

What *do* I do? *Nothing important . . . just take care of the kids,* I tell myself, but something won't stop gnawing at me. She had definitely said, "*you . . .* Sandy," with an emphasis on *you*. Who is *you*? Is there a *me*? Is there supposed to be a *me*? What is that, anyway?

With that one innocent question, Susan touches something I don't yet know. With that one innocent question, I realize my whole life is about being a good girl, a good wife, a good mother. Isn't caring for others the only thing that matters? Isn't that my job? That is what I have been taught. That is what I have learned. While it is important to me to care for my family, I begin to grasp that it is also all that I know. Simply stated, there is NO ME LEFT inside to be doing things. There is no *me* to have my own interests and no *me* to have my own opinions and needs. No room exists for me to have any personal life at all. I don't even *dare*! That isn't even allowed, is it?

I have always said that if there are only three pieces of cake left for the four of us in our little family, I would be the one who didn't take any. Others always come first. In some very significant way, I understand that I don't really count. I am supposed to be behind the scenes, invisible, and supportive of the more important others. I am the secretary, never the president. I am the stage hand, never the director.

My world starts to close in on me. I feel the lid closing tightly on the too-small box I find myself in. I'm forgotten in the back of some dark closet with the door shut. Or is it a jail? Yes, it feels like jail. I suddenly hear the metal door clanging shut, locking me in.

The sudden chill I feel in this moment hardens my flesh into a metallic shell, hiding the giant, dark, and silent hollow I now notice within. Clearly, there is nobody home in Sandyville.

With that one question in that one awakening moment on that one warm summer evening, I discover utter emptiness inside and ask myself, "Is this all there is?" For the first time, I begin to comprehend that there *might* be ... there *must* be something more to life. My heart aches. I can barely breathe. I want to cry. Something is missing and I don't even know what it is, and I can't stop thinking about that jail door slamming shut!

REIGNITING OUR TRUE SELF

Somewhere deep within each and every one of us lies a fiery ball of energy. It may feel as big as the sun that lights our entire universe or as tiny as a glowing ember barely surviving and hiding, but it is there. It may be damaged by years of horrendous experiences, criticism, judgments, neglect, and the possible misuse of life's apparent pleasures, but it is there. It may never have had a genuine opportunity to grow forth and fully blossom but nothing has ever been able to completely destroy it either.

That fiery ball of energy is our true self. It is universal in each and every one of us and in every culture. It is completely normal, natural, human, and organic to our nature. Experiencing our sense of self is how we know for certain that we are alive, both as unique individuals belonging in this universe and also as one connecting with all others.

Our true self, our precious *me*, is that authentic little voice deep within that naturally drives us to keep growing ever deeper and more real, experiencing every moment of our life as we flow onward toward coming fully alive.

Our true self is our light that shines, radiating aliveness in all directions. It is the source of all creative expression. It is the solid mass that fills that hungry, hollow emptiness I first acknowledged when Susan asked me that magical question. It is everything authentic about us.

Our true self can feel safe living in an unsafe world. It is the rock that holds us steady when the hurricanes come and the sunshine that feels warm and clear after the depths of depression and confusion have passed. Our true self is home. It knows our purpose. It knows what's what. It cares and knows what is important. It is our reason to get out of bed in the morning and our reason to rear our children lovingly.

Unfortunately, many of us don't know our precious true self very well. If we haven't listened to it for years, it tends to be elusive and underdeveloped. It may even feel like a stranger.

This first chapter reintroduces us to our true self and helps us to recognize the common characteristics of an underdeveloped sense of self. It dispels the common beliefs that have led us to mistakenly see the self as some kind of negative quality that must be avoided and kept under control.

Beyond the Good-Girl Jail: When You Dare to Live from Your True Self is an invitation to come to know and claim this true sense of self that is deep within each and every one of us—the *me* that fills the aching emptiness I discovered that day with my friend Susan.

Do you feel that same aching emptiness inside that I did? Do you wonder if there could be more to your life? Are you ready to thoroughly enjoy being the precious one you genuinely are? Most of all, do you want to know your truth—no matter what it is?

A CENTER WITH MANY NAMES

The sense of self is an internal energy with numerous names. Many other authors have named and described it from their own point of view.

Sue Monk Kidd, describing her own journey, writes about our *Deepest Self* and "the voice of soul in the solar plexus that spins the thread of our own truth."[1]

Thomas Moore, a former Catholic monk and professor of religion and psychology, refers to the original self as the "one who lives from the burning core of our heart."[2]

Gerald G. May, MD, author of *The Dark Night of the Soul*, describes an inner wilderness he calls "the untamed truth of who you really are."[3]

Gail Larsen speaks lovingly about activating "your inner Holy Fool."[4]

James F. Masterson, MD, distinguishes the real self from the false self and suggests that "no matter how much we change, something basic in us holds its own."[5]

Louise J. Kaplan, PhD, one of the pioneer infant researchers, talks about *constancy* as "the enduring inner conviction of being me and nobody else."[6]

Heinz Kohut calls the nuclear or healthy self "the sense of our being the same person throughout life."[7]

Tara Mohr refers to an "inner mentor" in her book *Playing Big*.[8]

Carl Jung wrote extensively about an inner center he calls the "Self," with a capital S.[9]

Dan Siegel, MD, an attachment researcher, uses the simple image of returning to the hub of a wheel.[10]

Martha Beck titled her book *Finding Your Own North Star* and refers to the "essential self."[11]

Oriah Mountain Dreamer, a visionary writer, describes "the deep stillness at the center of what we are."[12]

Joan Borysenko, PhD, a cell biologist as well as a psychologist, uses the term *Fire in the Soul* to title one of her books.[13]

Jean Shinoda Bolen, MD, a Jungian analyst and professor of psychiatry, uses the term "heart fire."[14]

Tara Brach, PhD, a Buddhist, has coined the term "true refuge."[15]

Finally, Quakers listen for "the still small voice within."[16]

So, is our true self the real *me*, our authentic self, or our sacred self? Is it our inner being, our higher self, or our grounded core? How about our intuition, our soul, our will to live, or the writer's muse? Is it what some of us experience as God's will or perhaps a higher power actively continuing to create us?

All of these terms seem to fit, depending on the varied language we each have learned as well as the varied nuances of our different perspectives and training. Apparently, we each experience this phenomenon somewhat differently. Perhaps there is no need to come to a common language and definition to explore our own personal, internal experiences. Maybe the true self is simply that which goes by many names. Whatever name works best for you is certainly the one to use.

I have come to call this persistent little voice inside that refuses to be completely ignored the "sense of self," "self," "true self," or "*me*," and I use these terms interchangeably. I have found this simple language to be neutral and the most readily accepted by my clients as it seems untainted by both past religious experiences and psychological jargon. The language of heart and love sometimes gets entangled with romance and sex, and the language of God and spirituality sometimes becomes confusing and offensive.

Whatever we call it, many of us experience an energy deeper than our thoughts that drives us not only to survive but also to keep growing to fully live life. We have our own perceptions and experiences that we identify as our own personal truth. We can tell what feels real and right for us from the inside, and we experience some sort of an internal, constant essence that no one else can ever take from us.

SETTLING THE CONFUSION

Perhaps because of the many names used over the years, our sense of self has often been seriously misunderstood. Before we proceed further, let's answer some common questions.

Do we really have a right to a strong sense of self? Yes, we do. Simply because we were born and are alive, we have a right to fully grow into the splendid creatures we truly are, just as all other living plants and animals do.

Isn't the current trend to let go of self to become one with all rather than to claim our individual self? Yes, that is the current trend, but oneness does not mean to dissolve our boundaries to merge with others. Oneness refers to becoming aware of what we have in common with others, aware that we are all equally valued. As our true self strengthens, differences become less threatening. We see that we all have needs, feelings, and bodies and that these similarities are more significant than the differences regarding what language we speak, how educated or wealthy we might be, and who we worship and vote for. Once our sense of self is well developed, we naturally grow toward this genuine oneness with others.

Does calling our sense of self "God in action" limit us to being part of a particular religion? There are many religions and twelve-step programs for recovery from addiction that honor a higher power. Many of them call that higher power God or Goddess. God, as we each understand and know God, is a very personal experience aside from any particular religious persuasion. Sometimes our personal spiritual experiences fit a particular religion and sometimes they don't. Our true self is our spiritual core in this generic sense and is neither part of any particular religion nor opposed to any particular religion.

Does emphasizing the sense of self make me selfish and self-centered? No. The word *selfish* is often misused to imply that we completely disregard the needs and interests of others. There are, of course, some people who do not consider the needs of others, but many of us have adapted to the other extreme. Having been taught to be good girls, we have learned to put the needs of others ahead of our own to be other-centered. We focus too much on the needs of others. When our sense of self is well-developed, we are aware of our own needs *as well as* the needs of others. Everyone's needs are equally valued. Strengthening our sense of self thus allows us to grow beyond being either self-centered or other-centered to live from a centered self.

Isn't the sense of self the same as ego? No, not in the way the term is commonly used today. In the early 1900s, Sigmund Freud adopted the Latin word *ego* to describe what he called the "I" or "soul." His description of ego included our core abilities to think, reason, make decisions, and be aware—valuable parts of our makeup. Freud also identified *ego defenses*—the behaviors and masks we utilize to protect our core.[17] I believe it is these ways of protecting the ego that have become confused with the ego itself over the years. Perhaps the two are most aptly described today as the true self and the false self. The more developed our sense of self becomes, the easier it is to let go of these protective defenses when we no longer need them so that we can return to our "I" to live.

Is the self a sense, a part of the brain, or what? Like tasting, hearing, touching, smelling, and seeing, the self is a source of information about our environment and about how we are responding to changes in our environment. Perhaps it is an additional sense, but the self is more like *who* smells the flowers? *Who* hears the music? *Who* enjoys that music? Or *who* doesn't want to go to yoga today? Perhaps it is not so much a specific part of the brain but instead the glue that ties together our feelings, thoughts, and senses—the missing link that integrates body, mind, and spirit.

Can we really trust our inner sense of self? Absolutely! We have learned to put our trust in external forces more than in our internal self. Sometimes we have been helped and guided wonderfully by others, but some of us have also been hurt, misinformed, lied to, and manipulated. Our own inner guidance is indeed more trustworthy than the rules and expectations of others—once we learn to listen to and understand the language of our sense of self.

Sonia, for example, tried hard to be a good patient when her first baby was born. She took her doctor's instruction to feed her baby every four hours literally, but her nursing baby was hungry in only two hours. She tried to make him wait until the *right* time to eat, but he cried inconsolably when he was hungry and nothing else soothed him. It was clear to her that her little fellow was hungry. After struggling a few days with both her inner knowing and trying to be a good patient, she finally decided to feed her baby when he was hungry. Only later did she learn that nursing babies need to be fed in two hours, not four. Looking back as she told me this story, she said, "It seems like an obvious choice." But it had not been obvious to her at the time. She had been well trained to follow authoritative advice "to a T" so that she could be a good girl, a good mother, and a good patient. She had landed in the Good-Girl Jail, but when she had to choose between being a good girl for the doctor and feeding her hungry baby, she chose to follow what fit her sense of self inside. She said, "I just *had* to feed him." It was indeed a wise choice for both her and her baby, and that choice came directly from trusting her true self.

Doesn't trusting our sense of self lead us to being impulsive and ultimately self-destructive? No. Our sense of self will always lead us toward being fully alive. Anything destructive is something else. Even when our choices seem unusual or surprising, if they are coming from *me*, they also feel right deep down inside. A sensation of relief usually provides excellent feedback that suggests we are on track.

Eva needed to escape from an abusive cult-like situation to create a safer environment for herself and her young children. She quit her job without notice and quickly sold what she could to raise some money. Then she packed her most valued belongings and children into her car and drove away. Eventually, she selected another town in a different state as her new home. She knew no one there and had no specific plans. She only wanted to hide out for a while to be safe. She said her behavior may have seemed crazy, irresponsible, and perhaps even self-destructive to others, but she knew she had to leave in that particular abrupt manner to have the freedom and safety she needed. She "trusted her gut" for insight and direction more than she trusted the cult, and she never regretted that choice. While life was hard for months, she was aware of the relief she experienced every day knowing she had made the choice that best fit her and her children.

Isn't this drive to be fully alive basically evil? Never. While we might refer to our sense of self as our inner "brat" or even our "bitch" or "witch" because it has been unacceptable to important people in our life, it is never innately bad or evil. It is never wicked, morally reprehensible, vicious, or hurtful to others. Listening to our sense of self is never about intentionally hurting ourself or others—never! Still, others may want or expect us to meet their needs more than our own. They might try to convince us that our choices are wrong—particularly if they think we inconvenience them, play too much, make too much noise, rebel against unreasonable rules, don't keep secrets, or do something unacceptable.

Is it easy to recognize and rebuild our true self? Not necessarily. Strengthening our sense of self often seems to take longer than we think it should, but it remains easier than living the rest of our life with an underdeveloped and undernourished *me*. Living from our core is a different way of living, not merely something else to put on our to-do list. It is more a process of becoming than a decision to do so or learning how to do so. No, it is not always easy to learn to live from our true self, but it is tremendously rewarding and certainly worth the effort.

Do we have to reconnect with our sense of self? Of course not. Doing so is 100 percent a personal choice. However, a solid state-of-the-art self is not available for purchase at the nearest discount store or even on the Internet. It cannot be borrowed from friends, and it doesn't rub off on us when we cling to others who may already have a stronger sense of self. We can't simply go to India or follow a guru to find it. A therapist cannot create it for us, nor can it be given to us by those who love us most. Reconnecting with our true self is personal growth work. It can only be further developed and strengthened by each of us when we are ready, when we become aware of the possibility of doing so, and if we want to. It is always our choice.

Why would we want to live from our sense of self? To some, this evolution into aliveness may just sound like a lot of unnecessary work. This path may not be for them, at least not now. But others of us discover that something we may not completely understand is inviting us onward to a simpler way to live, a way that includes integrity, peace, and aliveness. Some of us absolutely must find a better way to live. We can do no other.

HOW WE EXPERIENCE OUR TRUE SELF

When I ask others how they know their sense of self exists, I get a wide variety of answers.

June knew she liked the color green. It was the only thing she said she knew about herself for certain. Green was what kept her solid and sane whenever she felt overwhelmed and confused by her stressful life situation.

Anna said hers felt both calm like floating on water and free like the wind blowing through her hair.

Olivia said her sense of self was what gave her hope.

Jenny called her sense of self her "freedom," and she just knew she had to have it.

Sonia said she knew her sense of self was there because it wanted to wear hats and she couldn't yet allow that.

Rubianne distinguished between the much quieter, loving voice inside that told her the truth and the loud taskmaster voice that told her how wrong and bad she was and what she had to do to make herself right and good. She said her loving "soulself" nudged her gently when she needed to do something different. "These nudges felt like the phone ringing," she said, and she always had a choice whether or not to answer the call.

Eva, who experienced many alter parts inside of herself, knew for certain which one was her true self—the one who was tiny, young, protected by many of the other older internal parts and anchored solidly in the trunk of the tree she visualized herself to be. She stayed close to that part and always kept it with her. At one point in her healing, she wrote to me with considerable emphasis:

> I remember being elated when I could at least say I AM. I didn't have a lot of answers as to WHAT I AM at the time, but I could claim I was here. That might seem odd to many, but I don't believe it is odd at all in the realm of healing from trauma. I poignantly remember the day I could claim, I HAVE myself!

Where we experience our self also varies widely, although most of us seem to experience our sense of self somewhere within our body. June said that hers was in her feet. That was an important place to be because her family had frequently "pulled the rug out from under her," catching her off-guard. Anna knew her sense of self was in her heart, although she admitted she couldn't yet always feel it. Olivia said hers sat in her solar plexus, and Raven felt hers inside her pelvis. Rubianne recognized her sense of self as a rock in her tailbone. Interestingly, mine seemed to hide in my armpit, hoping no one would notice.

AN UNDERNOURISHED SENSE OF SELF

The primary defining symptom of an undernourished sense of self is feeling empty inside, as if there is nothing real or solid inside, as if there is NO ME LEFT. That is what I became aware of when my friend Susan asked that magical question.

When we can't find something internal to trust, we don't know who we are. We don't trust our own perceptions and judgment. We may feel abandoned, rejected, neglected, or judged by others—even when we haven't been. We may wonder if we really exist. Life itself might appear meaningless or cruel, and death may seem terrifying.

As a result of feeling invisible and empty inside, we tend to turn outward to others for everything—our identity, our purpose, our decisions, our safety, and assurance that we do indeed exist and are okay. When we focus this much on someone or something else to get these basic needs met, we become unnecessarily vulnerable to the ways in which those others treat us. Even when others take advantage of us, we tend to be reluctant to leave or stand up to them because we cannot tolerate being left alone with our emptiness. And when we see others as powerful and defer to their authority for too many things, that other person (or group, activity, religion, addiction, or object) may even serve the function of a higher power in our life, making genuine spiritual connection difficult and confusing.

With an undernourished sense of self, we tend to experience many day-to-day difficulties. Changes may seem devastating, especially when they are sudden or initiated by other people. Another person's disapproval or different opinion can feel threatening. We have difficulty saying "no" to honor our own needs and boundaries. Relationships become more complex than they need to be, sometimes involving ferocious power struggles. Intimacy frequently means enmeshment, and we might become lost in another person's life rather than live our own. Good-byes are often painful and thus avoided. We may view others as being mean to us when they are simply making the choices that best fit them. We may be exhausted because focusing so much on others demands a great deal of energy. These descriptions may sound extreme, but I see these examples frequently in both my psychotherapy practice and in interactions with others.

Answering the following questions will help you to assess how undernourished or affected by life experiences your own sense of self may be:

+ Do you feel empty inside?
+ Do you keep wondering, *is this all there is?*

* Do you have difficulty feeling like the same person in different situations?
* Do you feel lonely, even around other people?
* Do you say "yes" when you need to say "no" or "no" when you want to say "yes"?
* Do you feel used or abused by others?
* Are you uncomfortable being home alone?
* Do you feel invisible, ignored, or not listened to?
* Do you frequently say, "It doesn't matter" or "I don't care"?
* Do you "disappear" into relationships, work, your children, or addictions?
* Do you have difficulty letting go of other people?
* Do you feel undeniably exhausted for no apparent reason?
* Do you long for a spiritual connection but have difficulty keeping it?
* Would you rather focus on someone or something else than live your own life?
* Do you wish someone else would take care of you?
* Do you compare yourself to others and end up feeling inadequate or worthless?
* Are you easily influenced by others?
* Are you frightened by another's anger?
* Do you pretend to be okay when you are not?
* Do you have difficulty finding purpose and meaning in your life?
* Do you have difficulty allowing pleasure and fun in your life?

NOURISHING OUR SENSE OF SELF

We are not crazy if we experience many of the items on this list. There is no specific psychiatric diagnosis for this state of being and no medication or medical treatment to relieve the symptoms. An undernourished sense of self is not a mental illness even though it may exacerbate many different mental health issues. Instead, an undernourished self is a *developmental* issue, which simply means that we have not fully developed our sense of self yet.

Nourishing our sense of self is therefore a growth process rather than a cure for illness. No matter how tiny or fragile we may find our self to be, once we recognize it and begin to nourish it, our self begins to flourish. We can choose to nourish our true self at any age by listening to it until we become as strong and solid inside as we want to be.

Nourishing our sense of self means to grow deeper rather than merely older. It is an invitation to live rather than merely exist. It means growing forward in life rather than just accomplishing more. It means claiming our self more than our possessions. It means claiming purpose and meaning more than power and control. It means developing a stronger inner home anchor to return to when life's challenges temporarily blow us off course. Nourishing our true self is a process of becoming more fully who we genuinely are and who we want to be in this lifetime. I'm talking about a deeper, richer place of truth from which to live.

CONSIDERING THE POSSIBILITIES

As our true self strengthens, we grow to feel solid in our body, knowing our own feelings, needs, wants, thoughts, beliefs, and hopes for the future. We claim what fits us and let go of the things that do not fit us or no longer fit us. We keep thinking for our self and make the choices that best fit *me*. Even when others disagree, we remain true to our self.

As our sense of self grows stronger, we begin to appreciate the quiet inner peacefulness that time alone can bring. We become more able to cope with changes and transitions of all kinds, including aging, loss, disappointment, death, and physical pain. We grow through even the most difficult experiences life brings our way.

A strengthened sense of self makes it possible to say "no" without feeling guilty, express different opinions, feel acceptable when someone is angry with us, and take action to stop being mistreated. We feel generally safe in the world. We become able to genuinely connect with others. We express our love for those we care about and know that we are loved simply for being the precious beings we naturally are.

With a more solid sense of self inside, the point of reference from which we live shifts from what we believe others expect of us or need from us to what we know fits our own integrity. When there is no need to prove our worth, we become surprisingly more generous, creative, and loving. We likely feel more comfortable and peaceful. We definitely feel more alive. Perhaps we all want to feel comfortable, loving, peaceful, and alive.

RECOGNIZING OUR TRUE SELF

Most of us genuinely want to grow deeper, not just older. We may have needed to shut down our sense of self in order to please others in our particular family or community, but it is still in there somewhere, waiting for the right nourishing conditions—just the way daffodils wait for absolutely the best spring conditions to bloom. Deep down we all want to bloom, and nourishing our true self ultimately means thriving and blooming as an adult.

I believe it is possible to live happily ever after. It just doesn't happen the way we were told it would. It doesn't happen because we marry Prince Charming, live in a palace, have babies, and acquire wealth. Those are the fairy tales. In real life, genuine happiness and meaning result when we recognize and honor our continually-evolving true self. A solid sense of self inside allows joy to flow and reminds us every day that we will be okay—no matter what.

I hope that you already know your true self and that you never needed to abandon it or hide it for safekeeping. I hope you have never experienced NO ME LEFT, as I did when Susan asked me that powerful magical question. If you have, though, I invite you to keep reading to learn the 4 R's—to Recognize, Reconnect with, Rebuild, and Return home to the natural wisdom of your true self so that you, too, come fully alive.

The Cave

I walk past that cave
Maybe several times a day,
Wondering what's in there
But feeling too afraid to find out.
It's the closet for those secrets
I must keep buried and never, ever tell—
The underground river
That must never see sunshine.
It's the grave for my dreams,
Locked forever beneath the earth—
The ones my heart must never live.
It keeps the lid on that mysterious fire
That promises so much more—
But might be wild and tumultuous.
That cave,
Oh, how she mysteriously invites,
Yet terrifies,
And surreptitiously seduces
Yet prohibits.
Can I at least take a peek?

Chapter 2

Daring to Listen to Our Self

Am I Listening to My Awakening Moments?

It is quiet, so utterly quiet, like the very early morning before the birds begin to chirp their precious wake-up tunes—and I am alone. What, then, is this voice I am hearing? Who is it? Where is it coming from? Am I going crazy?

I have come to the hot springs today with a group of friends, all women. It is a cave with several pools with different temperatures, and most of us have migrated to the warmer, larger pool to be together. We have been sharing stories and talking about all kinds of things, completely relaxing in the unique privacy of this cave. Those who get too hot sit on the edge of the pool, staying close to be part of our group. As unique as each body is in color and shape, our commonality is paramount today. We each have a face, hair, breasts, legs, and a butt, so the other details don't seem to matter much. Having rarely been naked with other women before, I welcome the surprising safety I feel in the midst of this new experience.

I want to stay with the others, but I am getting too hot to simply sit on the edge of the pool. Wandering in search of a coolness break, I find a massage table in another smaller cave nearby. Climbing onto it, I breathe freely once again and quickly begin to cool comfortably.

I notice my utterly limp body now drooping heavily on the table. The cooler air against my warm, wet skin somehow softens the light and exaggerates the utter silence the cave walls create, leaving only one occasional drip somewhere in the distance. I gently close my eyes to absorb the full experience. I long for a massage therapist but then realize that I don't even need one. My breathing slows even more. Have I ever been this relaxed before? I cherish this sacred moment to myself, not even wanting to move.

No, I don't want to move, but suddenly I feel as if I *can't* move— not even a single toe! Startled, I open my eyes, planning to sit up. I tell myself that I certainly can get off this table and go back to my friends if I want to. But . . . can I? Nothing seems willing to move. Am I frozen, tied down by some invisible force?

In this quick moment of confusion before I completely panic, I hear this voice I have never heard before. I check to be sure I am still alone. Yes, I am alone. I close my eyes again, fearing that I might be hallucinating but still choosing to pay attention as that unfamiliar, androgynous voice begins to converse with me.

> *"Is this what you want?"*
>
> "Are you kidding? I can't move. What *is* this?"
>
> *"Ah, you notice. This is the path you are on."*
>
> "Huh?"
>
> *"You are on a path that will take you to rheumatoid arthritis in the years ahead. This is how it will feel."*

"But I feel frozen. I can't move. No, of course I don't want that."

"Well, you have a choice about it."

"I have a choice? What choice?"

"Yes, a choice. You keep shutting down your anger. Would you rather deal with your anger or develop rheumatoid arthritis in the years ahead? It's that simple. It's your choice."

"But ..."

The voice is gone. That's it, no details?

I want more information, but no, the voice of the cave has delivered its message and is suddenly gone for good. I am confused. Numerous questions and doubts about my sanity fill my mind, but I am intensely aware that a life-changing choice has been dramatically brought to my attention.

I don't want to develop rheumatoid arthritis. Certainly not! Rheumatoid arthritis is the dreaded disease in my family. I have always wondered if I would get it. My grandmother had it. Several aunts and at least one cousin have it. I never believed I had any choice about it. It's genetic, isn't it? How could I have a choice about it? And why would dealing with my anger make any difference?

While this whole experience isn't making any sense to me, I am vaguely aware of the anger I have shut down inside myself—mountains of it, I'm reluctant to admit. I believe anger is a bad thing. It will make me a bad person. It will certainly get me into trouble—maybe even send me to a real jail. Anger is not part of being a good girl! No, anger is something I should never acknowledge or feel at all, so I have hidden it deep within where no one else can ever see it—or so I have believed.

Now here seems to be some kind of strange guidance urging me to find a different way to deal with my anger. What? How? I truly don't know, but I somehow trust the guidance I have just received in this most unusual manner. It makes sense in a way that I can't completely understand. I know I don't want to develop rheumatoid arthritis, so I will somehow have to find a way to deal with my anger. My choice is clear, though the path to get there is not clear at all.

I discover that I can now easily get off the massage table. I wander back to my friends in the big pool, aware that my hips are walking in just a slightly different manner. Something significant has shifted.

THE Y IN THE ROAD

There is what I have come to call the *Y in the road*. It exists for each of us every day. Sometimes it is more obvious than at other times. Some of us see it more clearly than others do. It is invisible to the ordinary eye, but nevertheless, it is real.

This Y in the road is a choice, a life-changing, deep-level choice between a numbing path of *shutting-down moments* and a healing, growing path of *awakening moments* that invite us to come fully alive. Coming alive, healing past trauma, and strengthening our sense of self all involve this essential choice to grow.

This chapter describes the Y in the road. There are actually three distinct possibilities we can choose when we reach such a crossroads—the shutting down path, the awakening path, and sitting at the crossroads in ambivalence and confusion as long as we need to. Learning to listen to that ever-present inner wisdom I call our true self helps us make these fundamental choices we want to make wisely and consciously.

I didn't have to choose to learn to deal with my anger that day in the cave. I could have rebuked the voice coming to me as crazy, evil, or simply irrelevant. I could have chosen to stay with the shutting down pattern I had already adopted rather than open to this invitation to grow. No one else would likely have known. I could probably have kept my anger secret and hidden for yet a very long time. Instead,

I chose to open to this new possibility that had come to me in this mysterious manner. I chose to listen to my sense of self.

This choice at the Y in the road is ours, always and completely ours. In order to choose the awakening path to our deeper truth, we need to know that we have a free and complete choice to do so. We cannot surrender to coming fully alive unless we know that we also have the free choice to shut down. The Y in the road gives us that choice. While the choice may sound simple and obvious, it is often full of ambivalence, detours, confusion, fear, and stubborn resistance—all of which keep us shut down in the Good-Girl Jail.

Clues We Are at a Y in the Road

Here we are, cruising along in life and minding our own business, when something catches our attention. It has to be something unusual, of course, or it won't catch our attention. It is odd and out of the ordinary, at least in that particular moment. It can be anything or anybody, but it tends to challenge our usual pattern of thinking and our habitual behaviors, just as the voice of the cave challenged me. This strange something seems to ask, "Have you ever thought about *this?*"

We are at a Y in the road experiencing an invitation to take the healing, growing path to come more alive whenever we experience any of these common clues:

+ Losing control
   "I'm going crazy!"
   "I feel as if I'm completely falling apart."
   "These memories (or dreams or feelings) just won't go away."
   "I keep crying and can't stop."
+ "But" thinking
   "I hate this job *but* I can't quit."

"I know I need to leave this marriage, *but* I don't want to hurt my spouse."

"I don't want to go, *but* I know I should."

"I want to find a way to deal with my anger, *but* I don't know how."

♦ Ignoring body signals

"I just don't want to do what I have planned for today."

"I wish my gut would quit hurting every time I am around that woman."

"I keep getting sick (or injured or having surgery)."

"I feel uncomfortable. Something is just not right."

♦ Relapsing into addictions and old habits

"Why can't I end this relationship?"

"I can dip into my addiction just this once."

"Why are all my addictions acting up at the same time?"

"I was doing so well, but now I'm relapsing again."

♦ Reaching our personal limits

"No more! I quit!"

"I just can't do this anymore and you can't make me!"

"If this doesn't stop, I'm going to die."

"Enough! This is just plain wrong!"

If you recognize any of these ways of thinking, you have been invited to listen to your sense of self. You have been invited to come more fully alive—if you want to.

Shutting-Down Moments

Down one fork of the Y in the road lie the same old patterns most of us have always followed. These are the habits we learned when we were young, the safety patterns that have helped us survive over the years, the rules and roles we learned in order to get along well with others. This is usually our automatic path, the one we take without thinking because we know it so well and have taken it so many times. Even if this path repeatedly creates pain and chaos in our life, it is often the most comfortable path because it is familiar. It is the path we seem to have known forever and, indeed, we may have learned these behavior patterns before we can remember why or how we learned them. This shutting-down path is nearly always our choice when we are afraid or uncertain. For some, it appears to be the only path. Shutting down is the path *away* from our true self.

We all have our favorite ways to shut down when we can't cope with life—or don't want to. At these times, we get busy. We eat. We isolate. We sleep. We say we need a drink or a cigarette. We have sex. We get high. We do *something* to lessen and avoid whatever makes us uncomfortable. These avoidance activities tend to work well for a while, perhaps even for many years. Some of us might call them effective coping skills, but in the extreme and over the years, these avoidance patterns sometimes take us where we don't want to go. They shut down our aliveness. They may become dominating patterns that result in a state of chronic numbness so that we merely exist day to day, perhaps stirring up that nagging question that arose in my NO ME LEFT moment many years ago that day with Susan: "Is this all there is?"

Rubianne simply retreated to intense "busy thinking" whenever she got uncomfortable. She was intelligent and read a lot, so thinking came quite naturally to her. It was socially acceptable and others found her thoughts interesting, so her use of busy thinking didn't seem problematic—until she realized she used thinking to numb out her feelings and shut down her aliveness.

Elissa started drinking as a teenager. Getting drunk was fun, she thought, and distracted her from her painful home life. Drinking seemed normal and functional to her—until she lost her job for drinking at work. It cost her thousands of dollars and caused a great deal of humiliation. Her occasional coping skill had become a dominating addiction that created chaos in her life. Only then did she begin to comprehend how much she had chosen the shutting-down path at the Y in the road.

It's not that there is anything innately bad or wrong about choosing the shutting-down path. We all shut down at times and will continue to choose to do so, at least to be appropriate in social situations. Being respectful of others, though, doesn't have to mean shutting down our own aliveness to become numb.

The questions to ask are these: Is the shutting-down path the one you want? Is numbness what fits best for you at this point in your life?

Some people want the shutting-down path in life and appear to be quite content, but others of us feel barely half alive when we are shutting down. We will never be satisfied with simply existing. We know that the numbing path at the Y in the road is what creates the emptiness we feel inside—and we want something different.

Awakening Moments

An alternative to shutting down is to choose the other fork at the Y in the road. Although it is a path that may feel uncomfortable at first because it is less familiar, this is the path of healing from any trauma we may have experienced. This is the path of listening to our self and completing the developmental process of growing up emotionally. This is the path of awakening moments that leads to our true self coming fully alive.

Awakening moments are those brief seconds when something taps us on the shoulder to get our attention. They often catch our attention while we are looking the other way. They are not necessarily logical or rational, and they don't usually get everyone's attention. Sometimes these breakthroughs seem even more trustworthy because they are surprising, illogical, and personal. The voice I was surprised to hear in that cave wasn't telling me that everyone who shuts down anger will develop rheumatoid arthritis—not at all. It was a message specifically for me that came in language that made sense perhaps only to me. It came in a way that insured I would receive the message I needed to hear, which was to learn to deal with my anger. And indeed, I did receive the message. I listened.

Awakening moments take us directly to our truth, whatever our deeper truth may be. They connect us with what we can trust. While this awakening path may sometimes seem more like an invitation to an earthquake than a dance in daffodils, choosing to know our personal truth always reconnects us with our sense of self and vice versa; choosing to reconnect with our true self always leads to knowing our personal truth.

When Elissa had successfully quit drinking alcohol for several months, she experienced a vivid new awareness. She had been on vacation and had loved being awake at 6:00 AM to be outdoors in the mountains—something she had never been able to do while she was drinking. Then Elissa really wanted a cold beer the following weekend on a hot summer night at a friend's party. She chose to allow herself two beers, thoroughly enjoying every swallow, and then stopped, quite proud that she could quit. But the next morning she didn't want to get out of bed. She didn't want to do anything. Her thinking was different and reminiscent of her drinking days. She was surprised these negative effects from only two beers lasted several days, and she didn't like these side effects at all! The dramatic contrast between the two experiences so close together was an awakening moment for her. The experience motivated her to more solidly choose her aliveness over her numbing, shutting-down pattern of drinking.

Numbness feels like a wall that prevents us from being fully alive. It can be thin and flexible like a sheer curtain, noticeable but not serving to completely stop us, or it can feel solid and rigid like cement, created to keep us safe every moment from all danger. Awakening moments are cracks in that wall that allow us to suddenly see things differently and much more clearly.

Some of us expect this path of awakening moments to be overwhelming and terrifying. Some of us are not sure we dare to take this path toward aliveness even when we learn that others have successfully navigated it. These expectations tell us how well-trained we are to shut down. It may be comforting to know that as we choose this growing path more and more frequently, we learn to more easily recognize our awakening moments. We learn what to trust. We learn that we can survive growth and change. The choice to take the risk comes from the natural wisdom of our true self, and the relief we experience in the long run often overshadows any fear involved.

While we cannot control awakening moments to make them occur whenever we want, we can invite them by formulating the precise questions we want answered. While asking many questions invites a *yes* or *no* answer, when we ask an open-ended question, we seem to invite a full paragraph of information.

When you are ready, you can invite awakening moments by asking relevant open-ended questions like these:

- If I was not afraid, what would I do?
- If I had enough money, time, and support, what would I *really* want to do?
- When I am dying and looking back on my life, what will I wish I had done?
- Where would I love to live?
- Who or what is important?
- What is *more* important than that?
- And what is *even more* important than that?

Don't dismiss these questions too quickly. Don't worry about practicalities like money, fear, current obligations, and ambivalence at this point. Open to all possibilities, allow your honest answers to come forth, hold them tenderly, and relish the process of learning to listen internally.

Pausing at the Juncture

Coming alive is a gradual process and more than simply a decision or choice to grow. Even when it is our chosen path, it will likely involve some ambivalence on our part. The third possible choice at the Y in the road is to pause at the juncture—that point before the two paths split. We can sit there as long as we need to, aware of the options in front of us.

Ambivalence at the Y in the road means a temporary inability to choose between the awakening path and the shutting-down path. Perhaps we feel uncertainty or confusion about making the choice or fluctuate back and forth between the two options. We may need more information to make our choice. Perhaps the timing isn't quite right yet. Perhaps we sit there until we simply reach our personal limits regarding our own indecision. Or perhaps we are drawn toward the growing path but also experience fear or shame about wanting to make that choice.

I can remember times when I believed that if I grew one more inch, my family would reject me for certain. I was afraid I was breaking old family rules in completely unacceptable ways. I thought I wasn't being a good girl, so I would sit there at that juncture actually trying not to grow. In spite of my best efforts, my growth would usually erupt anyway in some refusing-to-be-ignored manner, pulling me onward in spite of the risks. I learned to take my time. I also learned to trust that I would keep growing.

Shutting down our growth is akin to shutting down the energy in an atomic bomb. The more we shut down our aliveness, the more pressure it develops to later explode, perhaps sideways in some unexpected manner that we may not want. Shutting down our aliveness doesn't work very well, as our inner push to come fully alive is strong indeed. Still, invitations to the shutting-down path can be quite seductive. In our ambivalence, we sometimes experience detours from our awakening path for months or even years at a time.

Marsha felt pressured to marry a man even when she knew inside that he didn't feel right for her. Four children and twenty years later, she was able to leave him. She struggled to regain her ability to think for herself after years of being dominated. She said she felt grateful to finally experience another opportunity to grow and create her own life. She described herself as having been on a very long detour.

It may be reassuring to know that even when we start down one path, we can change our mind and shift over to the other path at any time. It always remains a free choice. It is only when we believe we have no choice that we are trapped in the Good-Girl Jail, and if we feel trapped, we are not seeing the Y in the road. We may already be on that automatic shutting-down path we learned so well so long ago.

Honoring our ambivalence is part of learning to listen to our self. We need to be patient and see our ambivalence as a part of the overall process of choosing to recognize what fits *me*. We can stay with our ambivalence as long as we need to.

Moving from ambivalence into choosing awakening moments may feel scary, unfamiliar, and even out of control at times. Choosing a path of awakening, though, also feels exciting, freeing, and right when we are ready. Sometimes we experience all these feelings mixed together.

The bottom line is that no one else can tell us what feels true and right for us. We are the only ones who can notice our own awakening moments. We are the only ones who can learn to listen to our true self.

THE POWER OF LISTENING INTERNALLY

The antidote to shutting down our aliveness is learning to listen internally to our true self. Even becoming willing to listen opens us to the possibility of learning the language of the self so that we know how our self speaks to us, what to listen to, and what to trust.

Listening includes noticing, observing, and being alert to the changes we experience inside us. It means to pay attention to our internal responses to changes in our external environment. It means no longer ignoring and disregarding that persistent little voice within.

Listening internally involves opening all our senses and utilizing them fully to receive information on an experiential level. We physically hear with our ears, but we also receive a great deal of information through touching, seeing, tasting, and smelling—as well as through that vague intuitive sensing level when we simply know something but are unable to explain exactly how we know it.

Theodor Reik adapted the Nietzsche term of listening "with the third ear"[18] to brilliantly describe a deeper level of listening with which we listen carefully past the words said to what another person is genuinely expressing—usually the more accurate message. When a friend is complaining endlessly, we might hear and respond to the hopelessness she feels, rather than merely the specific complaints. When she is laughing hysterically, we might hear the underlying emotional pain regarding a recent tragic event. When a child worries about her mommy dying, we might hear how frightened and vulnerable she feels.

Similarly, we can learn to listen to our own inner voice at this deeper level. We might hear the fear we feel for our self when we choose to stay with an addiction rather than take the risk of recovery. We might learn to hear how powerless we feel when thoughts of suicide arise. We may hear how our increasing physical pain is causing us to be overly impatient with our children. We might hear the joy and pleasure we can't yet allow that lead us to numb our feelings with work or perfectionism. We might hear that we have a choice to deal with anger rather than develop rheumatoid arthritis.

Sheila M. Reindl agrees that it is by *sensing* our experience that we develop and recognize our sense of self.[19] Interestingly, she further adds that women in particular tend to use metaphors of listening to describe how they know their truth, rather than knowing it through sight and observation.[20]

Listening to our deeper truth is what fills the holes left by neglect and thousands of shutting-down moments over the years. When we listen at this deeper level, we feel the connection we yearned for as children. It is what my clients often ask for when they seek help. They may say, "Nobody believes me," "Nobody hears what I say," "I feel invisible (or ignored or alone)," "I need to be heard," "My mother thinks I'm crazy," or "No one wants to help me," but they are all forms of "Please listen to me!" We all have a very deep need to be seen, heard, acknowledged, valued, and validated.

In my experience, our sense of self *requires* acknowledgement to grow, and listening internally is the primary building block to Recognize, Reconnect with, Rebuild, and Return home to our true self. Whenever *me* is ignored or neglected, it simply cannot grow. It has no nourishing soil, no fertilizer, no sun, and no water. When we choose to listen internally now, however, our sense of self grows rapidly, strongly, and eagerly—as if making up for lost time.

Listening to our sense of self in the awakening moments through which our true self expresses itself is something we can all learn to do. It is a choice we are able to make—whenever we are ready.

What we are listening for is our own truth, the things we cannot honestly deny any longer. While there may be different voices inside competing for our attention, our truth won't go away. It keeps nudging us to pay attention. It keeps coming back. It makes sense of our life.

Our truth is always life-affirming. It cheers us onward and feels right deep in our gut. When our truth finally comes through to awareness, our mind calms and our body relaxes. We often experience relief.

NEVER TOO LATE

The natural pattern of our true self is to gradually emerge and grow to become increasingly more solid as years pass. Yours may have been ignored, suppressed, and even damaged by your environment. It may have become covered over by multiple layers of protection from trauma or other unreasonable expectations from others. The gradual transition of peeling off these layers of no-longer-needed protection to reclaim and listen to your true self will bring you fully alive.

In one sense, returning to our sense of self is an easy transition, because it is a return to what has been previously known and because our guidance comes primarily from within. Yet, we are also complex social creatures, never living in complete isolation. We respond and react to others and they likewise respond and react to us, perhaps helping but sometimes hindering this return to our true self. Both the reactions of others to our growth and dealing with our own ambivalence as we grow can make awakening moments challenging and awkward.

It is almost as if the universe plays with us a bit, as the challenges along the way often have the overall effect of repeatedly asking, "Are you *sure* you want to reconnect with your sense of self? Are you *sure* you want to know your truth?"

While sometimes frustrating, answering these questions repeatedly also has the long-term effect of magnifying our determination to grow and evolve. Even when we answer "no" or "not sure," we can sit for a moment, a month, or even a year at the juncture of the Y in the road if we need to. Awakening moments will continue to come. If we don't like one, we can pass it by and choose another. If we aren't ready today, we can proceed tomorrow, next week, or next year. There is no judgment. It is always a free choice whether or not to grow, when and how to grow, and which path to take.

As my client Olivia asks, "Do we judge the flower that has not yet bloomed?" No, we don't. It is never too late to choose to grow and bloom, never too late to learn to listen to our self, never too late to remember who we are deep down inside.

Evelyn, in her sixties, had to make some serious choices about cancer treatment, which confronted her with the reality of her mortality. When she experienced a Y in the road, she chose to face her fears about dying. As she became less afraid to die, she became more able to fully live the time she had left. According to Evelyn, she also became more real. She began to claim more time for herself, focused her days on activities she enjoyed, and left her abusive husband. "Life is too short to mess around," she said.

Maddie, also in her sixties, is just now beginning to heal from severe childhood trauma, which she says could take years. She is courageously determined to "get well" and to know who she is—no matter what it takes. She is fully aware that it is never too late to choose to grow at the Y in the road.

My mother painted her front door bright red when she was eighty and started a wonderfully warm and loving relationship at the ripe age of ninety! As these women demonstrate, it is never too late to choose to listen to our true self to come fully alive.

RECOGNIZING OUR TRUE SELF

There are many different paths toward coming fully alive, but each includes recognizing and listening to our true self. No one way is always right and certainly no one way fits us all. We each need to find our own specific path. Our task is to learn to recognize what fits *me* as an individual, and we do this by learning to listen attentively to the powerful natural wisdom of our inner true self.

Listening Inside

What is that I hear?
A bell? A groan?
An ouch? A giggle?
Sometimes I wince
And hear the pain—
A rib, my back, my throat,
Perhaps a headache—
Talking in some unknown language.
"What are you saying today?"
Other times I freeze suddenly,
Hardening in fear of what
I believe might be coming.
"Oh no, no, no, not again!"
Or I melt in pleasure,
Warming to something—
But what?
I'm not sure . . .
But then I smile,
Hearing only an amused surprise.
Whew! Such relief!
Feelings, thoughts, memories,
Merging with body and light,
Creating a guiding language
I am learning to tend.
I seem to hear it now
As if with fourteen ears
And seventeen eyes.

Chapter 3

Listening Through the Fog of Fear

*What Am I Afraid Might Happen
If I Come Fully Alive?*

Three good women friends and I are sitting on the grass by the lake just jabbering and laughing as we love to do whenever we can grab a few minutes together. The picnic lunch we have hastily put together is tasty, and the warm sun feels soothing in the spring breeze. The ducks seem to wonder if we plan to feed them anytime soon.

Barbara is sharing about her new job and how intimidated she feels around her new boss. Her voice is shaky, her face is a bit too pale, and her shoulders are hunched up closer to her ears than we usually notice. Tears silently sneak into the corners of her eyes.

"What am I going to do? I get so nervous that I'm doing something wrong. I don't know how to do all these things he is already demanding of me."

We offer suggestions about how to deal with her new boss—talk louder, stand tall, avoid him, be more assertive—the usual varied assortment when we aren't sure what to do in an awkward situation. While we are trying hard to help our friend succeed in her new job, she has a "Yes, but . . ." answer for every suggestion we make.

"Yes, but it doesn't work that way in this office."

"Yes, but he's so scary to talk to."

"Yes, but I'm not supposed to ask for help. I'm supposed to already know how to do things."

We are trying to solve the problem of how to best relate to her new boss without even acknowledging Barbara's fear—the cement wall that I suddenly realize we can't get past.

My mind begins to wander. Fear has always been right here next to me, forever on guard for what seems like the next inevitable, terrible thing that is about to happen. I wonder if it is meant to be some kind of weird but consistent protective friend.

I remember watching the doorway as I fell asleep as a child. That seemed normal to me. Doesn't everyone watch the door to feel safe falling asleep? I remember watching my shadow to see if anyone was sneaking up behind me as I walked home alone after a Friday night movie with friends. I remember being scared of our babysitter's husband. He was big and gruff and loud—and he offered to buy me for a nickel. I was afraid my dad would prefer the nickel.

I remember being scared to give speeches in school, scared I would hit the wrong notes at piano recitals, and generally scared of men. I was certainly scared of everyone else's anger and what they might do to me. Well, I was just plain scared of doing anything wrong, of breaking any rules. After all, good girls don't break rules—period.

In this pensive moment at the lake, I now realize that I have believed that fear keeps me on track, out of trouble, and safe. I have believed that if I feel scared, I must be doing something wrong and need to stop—until this moment of truth, this flash of clarity, this awakening moment as I watch Barbara feeling scared. For some reason, it seems easier to see fear's effects in my friend than in myself.

Yes, Barbara is scared and I can clearly see that she isn't doing anything wrong. She isn't being bad. No one is mad at her or trying to hurt her. She hasn't broken any rules. I don't think she has any reason to feel humiliated. She is feeling scared simply because she is in a new situation and doesn't feel confident yet. She is scared that she might not be able to please other people. What is that fear anyway? It feels familiar.

When I bring my new awareness to Barbara's attention and acknowledge how scared she must feel, she bursts into tears, surprising us all. She gratefully and openly admits her fear of all the worst possible outcomes.

"I'm not sure I'm capable of learning some of the tasks he has hired me to do. What if I can't learn them fast enough? What if I'm not good enough for this job? What if I'm not smart enough? What if he gets mad at me? What if I lose this job?"

Barbara cries hard, her sobbing shoulders shaking, but when she cautiously looks up a few minutes later, she smiles at us and starts laughing! While we are confused about the sudden shift in her mood, she is now nearly bubbling with excitement about this new job—and full of confidence!

"Hey, how can I possibly already know I will do well? I've only been there two days!"

She laughs again and we laugh with her, my own shoulders dropping with relief.

"It may take some effort, but the office manager has offered to help me. I really think it will work out great. I've just been scared of a new situation—again. How normal is that? Hey, thanks, my friends, for reminding me that I'm normal."

Her fear has melted. She feels like herself again. She is ready to go on. We all laugh together as we share other times we have felt scared in new situations.

And I have a surprising new way to look at my own fear.

THE NATURE OF FEAR

No one welcomes fear sneaking around the corner. Fear is uncomfortable, so most of us do our best to overcome it—or to pretend it isn't there. There are just these times when the world tends to look a bit fuzzy as fear surreptitiously surrounds us with fog, confusing us and cautiously slowing us down for at least a moment. That fog is part of the Good-Girl Jail.

This chapter examines what childhood is meant to be and how the need to protect our precious, vulnerable core interrupts the natural development of our true self. At some point, many of us disconnected from our sense of self to focus on others instead. As we acknowledge our fear and learn to listen through and beyond the fog it creates, reconnecting with our true self becomes possible.

Fear is that distressing emotion aroused in us whenever we perceive danger. Our body tenses, preparing for whatever action may become necessary. Our mind becomes extra alert to our surroundings. Our adrenalin automatically flows and we focus on the best way to keep our self safe.

It is the anticipation of danger that awakens fear within us. Maybe the danger is not real but we think it is real—or might become real. Maybe something in the present reminds us of a scary moment from the past. Maybe fear surfaces long after some scary event has passed. Maybe we feel fear when we anticipate reactions from others that are not physically dangerous but that might leave us feeling humiliated, overwhelmed, powerless, or confused. Maybe we fear that our life will change.

Whatever the specific fears, my concern is that a state of chronic fear greatly impedes the development of our sense of self. Chronic fear stops us from taking risks. It hinders our ability to feel, ask questions, express opinions, and ask for help when we need it. It suppresses playing, loving, creativity, and joy. A need to keep *me* in hiding to prevent the constant possibility of doing something bad or wrong prevents us from even knowing our true self. It often keeps us surrendering to meet the expectations of others rather than choosing to grow at the Y in the road. In other words, chronic fear keeps us in the Good-Girl Jail.

Let's take a look at what might have happened.

WHAT CHILDHOOD IS MEANT TO BE

Childhood is where we have come from. It is our launchpad, our history from before the earliest time we can remember. It includes the circumstances into which we were conceived and born and the roots from which we quite literally have grown. It tells us who fed us and kept us warm until we became capable of doing these things. It is the first place we walked and talked. It is where we learned to do all the basic things in life—eat, sleep, use the toilet, read, write, play, and relate to other people. It is where we learned about attitudes, spirituality, holidays, and values—and about our self.

Once upon a time, we were each a newborn baby fresh out of the womb. Even though our sense of self was not yet fully developed, it was present. We were innocent, precious, and purely *me*. In fact, we could not have done babyhood any other way.

What we needed most at that tender infant age was at least one caregiver who genuinely wanted and welcomed us, who cared about us, who reliably helped us meet our basic needs, and who provided a nourishing environment that encouraged us to grow. Yes, we needed to feel safe, but we also needed more than safety to keep our true self developing. We needed someone's arms to crawl into when life felt too big to handle alone. We needed someone to stand with us, somebody to acknowledge our existence and connect with us—someone else who listened to *me*.

Ideally, our caregivers would have been available to us whenever we needed security, assistance, or encouragement. Ideally, our caregivers would have been emotionally available for an appropriately intimate, nurturing relationship with us in our early years and then also secure enough to let us gradually grow up and go on our own way as we became able to do so. Ideally, our caregivers would have provided both some consistent structure and security for us and also generous amounts of room to roam—*freedom channels*, I call them. Freedom channels are those times and activities that allow us to play and explore our sense of self outside of the usual expectations of rules and roles.

It's not that we needed to always have our own way, as we certainly needed to learn from our particular environment, but freedom channels, comfort when needed, and inclusion as an equally valued individual are the gifts that most support the development of a solid sense of self during childhood.

I once attended someone else's family reunion. The family matriarch at this reunion had eight grown children, twenty-three grandchildren, and a handful of great-grandchildren, so this was a large gathering with children of all ages everywhere. At one point, I was standing close to two men who were commenting on the baby asleep in her infant seat on the dining room table. I noticed that this baby had not been tucked away in a back room somewhere. She was right there, included in all the family activities. One man leaned over to the other, "Have you seen the latest arrival?" I wasn't sure they even knew her name or which relatives were her parents. They just stood there in silence for a few moments, arms folded across their chests, smiling, and tenderly noticing—truly seeing—that tiny baby.

I had never seen a baby so appreciated in this manner! Perhaps they were acknowledging the miracle of life that an innocent newborn represents. Perhaps they wondered who she would grow into and what she would choose to do with her life. While I could only imagine what they were thinking, the softness in their smiles showed me that no matter how tiny she was at this point in her life, she was welcomed and valued in that family. There was room for her. The tenderness I saw in these two men brought tears to my eyes as I appreciated her unusual welcoming committee. Perhaps we all longed for such a warm reception.

If our childhood included caring people like these men who saw us as a separate individual person with our own life to live, our own needs to meet, our own personality, our own wisdom, our own perspectives and preferences, our own experiences, our own particular lessons to learn, our own feelings that could get hurt, our own wounds to comfort, and yes, even our own fears, our sense of self probably developed quite solidly over the years—because we were allowed to *differentiate* from the others in our family.

DIFFERENTIATION

Differentiation is "a state of self-knowledge and self-definition that does not rely on others."[21] It is the developmental process of gradually leaving our childhood nest to independently take responsibility for our own needs as we become able to do so. It includes the privileges of becoming able to meet our needs in the ways that best fit us and acknowledging the ways in which we are different from other family members.

To differentiate means to have enough room to be with family and like family—and also to be separate and different from other family members without any judgment that we are bad or wrong just because we are different in some way. Claiming our self in this manner requires both having our basic needs consistently met over a long period of time and feeling safe enough physically and emotionally to risk living our own life. It is a long, gradual developmental process that starts very early in life.

Toddlers venture away from Mom and Dad to explore their world, playing for a while but returning every few minutes to be sure everything is still okay. They do this over and over, back and forth, going away from parental safety yet coming back whenever they need reassurance. When children leave home for daycare and then school, this pattern continues in an expanded version. Children stay away for the school day and then return. Adolescents and young adults stay away even longer as they become increasingly independent. Yet, Mom and Dad had still better be there, ready and willing to respond whenever needed for security and reassurance, perhaps at a moment's notice.

We tend to believe that differentiation is completed once we physically separate to live independently from family, but moving out to live on our own is only the most obvious symbol of differentiating. Moving away from family is not automatically enough to fully differentiate our sense of self.

A second significant level of differentiation is experienced when we grow to feel *equal in value to* other family and community members. This distinction means that we become less reactive to both praise and criticism from others[22] so we can make our own choices more easily. It means we can choose the ways in which we want to meet our own needs. It means we can explore different ideas, sort out what we believe to be true, and honor our own integrity, whether or not our values match those of others. It means there is room for us in this world in the way there was room for that baby at the family reunion I visited.

Most importantly, differentiation means living from our true self more than from the perceived expectations of others. The primary challenge of differentiating is to adopt the specific family and cultural ways that fit *me* while letting go of the specific family and cultural ways that do not fit. The more we live from our true self in this differentiating manner, the more we come fully alive.

This second level of differentiation is certainly more difficult if our family didn't fit us very well.[23] Differentiation is always more difficult if we have not been permitted to have our own perceptions, if we can't trust our own memories more than what others say happened, or if we have been severely controlled by violence, abandonment, manipulation, smothering, or humiliation.

THE TRAUMATIC DISCONNECT FROM SELF

My current husband Dan and I were once packing our suitcases to check out of a hotel room. Our three-year-old grandson had spent the night with us and was doing his best to carry things over to the door to help us get ready to leave. When I turned around, I saw him attempting to lift my very heavy suitcase off the bed. Panicking at the possibility of him getting squished on the floor beneath that heavy load, I yelled "No! Stop! That's too heavy for you!"

He immediately stopped, but then his head hung low and soon his little tears quietly began to flow. He was reacting to my loud voice, possibly believing he had done something terribly wrong when he was simply trying to help.

I went to him, invited him to sit on my lap, and comforted him with gentle touch as I thanked him for helping us. I explained how heavy the suitcase was and how scared I had been that it would hurt him. I let him sit there as long as he needed to. He slowly calmed and when he moved to get down, I put the suitcase on the floor to show him how heavy it was. He grunted and then laughed as he attempted unsuccessfully to lift it from the floor and quickly went on his way to find smaller things to put by the door.

He was very sensitive to how I treated him, which is normal and appropriate for a three-year-old. Sadly, I have seen children who no longer show this sensitive response.

When I was director of a child abuse treatment program, a little girl not yet three years old had to wait with me, a stranger to her, until the police came to pick her up to take her to foster care. Mariah sat on the floor near me for more than an hour, never looking at me and never making a sound. She never asked, "Who are you?" She never whined for her mommy. She didn't drink the water I placed near her. She didn't fidget and she didn't cry. When the big uniformed policeman arrived, she quietly walked away with him and climbed into the patrol car, never questioning or resisting what strangers were doing with her.

While Mariah may have been considered a good girl because she was so quiet and cooperative, such intense passive behavior meant that she had already learned to hide her feelings. She had already learned to quit asking for what she needed. She had already learned to surrender to whatever more powerful adults did to her. She most likely had already disconnected from her sense of self. She was certainly already familiar with the constraints of the Good-Girl Jail.

While, as young children, we may not understand why scary things happen, we definitely know fear. When we fear enough from our vulnerable position compared to the giant adults in our life, we may have to make a terrible, nearly impossible choice. Are we going to stay intact with our true self, continuing to ask for what we need even though we may get hurt or are we going to surrender to the will of those more powerful?

This is indeed an unfortunate choice to have to make, but given such a desperate situation, nearly all of us surrender to doing our best to please others. We shift our natural point of reference from our internal sense of self to that big dangerous external world. It is as if we hide our true self in a safe deposit box at the bank, hoping to be able to bring it out again on another safer day when we can once again grow and blossom. I call this shift the *traumatic disconnect*. It takes us directly to the Good-Girl Jail.

While disconnecting from our true self became a necessary choice for many of us, the price is high—shutting down the growth of our sense of self. I would hope that all young children could both live from their sense of self and please adults, but life doesn't always work that way. Sometimes we have to choose.

My grandson and Mariah illustrate the difference this traumatic disconnect makes. My grandson felt scared when I yelled at him, but he rather quickly responded to comforting and returned to the usual solid home base inside himself. Mariah, on the other hand, had already completely shifted her point of reference to the danger in her external world. I doubt if she felt there was room for her in this world. I doubt if she felt any home base inside herself anymore. She may have forgotten her true self even existed.

RECOGNIZING OUR OWN POINT OF REFERENCE

Our point of reference is the center point from which we experience life. We may have gone back and forth between focusing internally and externally during our early years, as needed. I believe, though, that those of us who now identify and experience our sense of self as underdeveloped likely shifted our focus to the external world to be considered good and to be safe.

I can often hear whether or not adults have made this traumatic disconnect in the language they use. Those who have already shifted from their internal sense of self to an external point of reference tend to make comments like these about their childhood experiences:

- "I don't remember much about my childhood."
- "I felt trapped; I had no choice."
- "I couldn't stop her. There was nothing I could do."
- "I died inside—every time."
- "I just curled up. I thought I was going to die."
- "I wasn't even there. I watched it happen but I didn't feel it."
- "He *got* me."

Yes, something got *me*. That is what they describe.

These same clients sometimes also describe dreams about feeling lost, unable to find their way home.

Evelyn had an image of herself as lost and floating around in outer space. Jenny saw herself alone on a tiny island in the middle of the vast Pacific Ocean. Olivia once described her loss of self to me as "utter nothingness, scary, unnerving, sort of like being totally lost at sea with perpetual darkness and no stars to navigate by, with no idea of direction, up or down, right or left and being tossed hither and yon by the relentless waves, never sure what will come next."

My own image of this desperate aloneness was a nighttime blizzard somewhere near the North Pole. I was alone. It was very cold. Even now as I write about this vivid image I had as a child, I feel a bit chilly. My body shudders just a little to remind me of that NO ME LEFT feeling I used to experience.

Alone, lost, dying. These are powerful descriptions of what it feels like to have disconnected from our essential internal anchor. In contrast, others who still know and live from their sense of self may respond as follows:

- "I always knew what she did was wrong."
- "I don't know how I dealt with it; I just did."
- "That was just the way it was. I didn't like it, but . . ."
- "Fortunately, I had my dog. He was always there."

- ♦ "I would go to my grandma's when I could. She knew what Mom was like."
- ♦ "You know, through it all, I never lost God. He was always there for me."

I hear in these words some sort of anchor—someone or something to return to after a frightening experience. It could have been a parent, of course. It could also have been an older sibling, a teacher, a spirit helper, an imaginary friend, a teddy bear—or their own sense of self. They didn't completely and permanently disconnect from their sense of self to survive. Perhaps they didn't land in the Good-Girl Jail.

I have come to believe that having no one there with us and for us during the times we most desperately needed help and comforting is the specific experience that contributes most significantly to a traumatic disconnect. Our sense of self cannot grow and develop without acknowledgment. It needs attention. It needs listening. Being ignored is a silent, usually hidden trauma created by significant omissions. Listening is what we *didn't* get that we truly needed. It is the missing piece we cannot identify when we ask, "Is this all there is?" We may not know what we are missing even when we can tell we are missing something.

We may never know precisely what happened, and attempting to figure it all out often keeps us focused outside our self. *Something* happened. That is the bottom line. We can tell by the results. The following examples may help you to know if you have shifted your point of reference from your sense of self to the external world:

- ♦ I give so much to others that there is NO ME LEFT.
- ♦ I violate my own integrity in order to please others.
- ♦ I would rather focus on someone else than live my own life.
- ♦ I attach to others to adopt their power or identity.
- ♦ I am afraid even when there is no current danger.
- ♦ I experience a need to be the one in control.

- I believe getting my needs met depends on getting others to take care of me.
- I believe what others think of me is more important than what I think of myself.
- I can never seem to get enough of what I need from others.
- I believe meeting the needs of others is more important than meeting my own needs.

If we have disconnected, we no longer live from the powerful, natural wisdom of our true self. We live instead from the soldier's point of view, as if protecting the moat around the castle, focusing outward on the needs and expectations of others. When something good happens, we expect something bad to happen afterward. We expect danger or evil to be lurking around the corner just waiting to *get* us. We watch everyone to see who might try to hurt us in some way. We watch everything all the time, hoping that if we anticipate danger, we will be okay. In other words, we live day-to-day in chronic fear.

LIVING IN CHRONIC FEAR

We are not meant to live in constant fear. I remember a simple awakening moment that showed me how we are meant to deal with fear.

Early one crisp spring morning, my dog Elliott and I went for our usual morning walk in the foothills. This particular walk, however, was abruptly interrupted when she raced back, breathless and terrified—with a coyote on her tail. I could see the coyote's teeth marks already in her back side.

Fortunately, the coyote also stopped and stood there all fluffed up, looking absolutely huge and menacing to us both. I took a deep breath and fluffed myself up as big as possible to see if I could scare him away. No luck. It was time to head for the car. I kept Elliott close on her leash and walked that long mile as quickly as possible, keeping a wary eye on that determined coyote as he followed us.

When we finally got inside the car, I sighed in relief—and locked the doors, as if to be sure to keep out the danger. I drove very carefully, aware that my heart was still pounding with adrenalin, and we were soon home safe and sound. Ten minutes later, however, I was sobbing and shaking all over. We were both safe at this point, but here came the fear, surging through my body and releasing itself without any effort on my part.

We have an amazing capacity to set aside fear to be able to effectively take action during threatening experiences, but we are meant to return to safety and release our fear when the threat is over.[24] If we cannot return to a safe anchor after danger or don't release our fear for some reason when we do, the fear collects and builds up inside us over the years. It is this leftover fear, perhaps accumulated from thousands of shutting down moments, that keeps us now living in chronic fear and worried that "it" (whatever "it" may be) might happen again.

❁ ❁ ❁

June came into therapy because of her depression, which had been a struggle for much of her adult life. She described days when she was "really depressed." When I asked about those times, she said she stayed in bed under the covers all day feeling scared. Scared is not the same thing as depressed, so we explored further.

What June discovered was a deep underlying fear, especially of being left alone. She could still feel the intense panic she had felt when her father had left her at day care when she was four years old. She also remembered feeling terrified many years later when her husband left their marriage. She had run hysterically after her daughter when she had appropriately left home as a young adult. Now she was centering her life on her grown children and grandchildren, already worried about her ten-year-old grandson leaving home for college.

When I asked June what happened inside her when people left, she described an unbearable big hole, a desperate emptiness inside that she said she could not tolerate. That gave us something to work with. Recognizing that this fear of being left had been her experience nearly forever put her current panic more at ease. It wasn't about the present. Becoming able to acknowledge her underlying chronic fear and observe its current effects helped her reconnect with her true self and begin to learn that she can now feel safe when she is alone. She listened through the fog of fear to hear her deeper truth.

Perhaps we all experience old fear like this to some extent. My concern, though, is that this leftover fear can keep us from choosing to continue to grow. Leftover fear keeps us focused outside rather than inside. It keeps us focused on what used to be rather than on what is now. It can lead us toward shutting down more and more over the years rather than accepting the invitations of awakening moments to come more fully alive when we reach a Y in the road.

The promise of listening through the fog of fear is reconnecting with our sense of self so that we can again feel whole, alive, safe, and anchored. For many of us, it is now easier to move through this underlying chronic fear and let it go than it is to remain frozen in its grip.

My challenge to you is to carefully notice this dynamic regarding fear in your own life. Question it, carefully distinguishing leftover past fear from fear concerning present danger. Doing so may help you listen through the fog that leftover fear tends to create so that you can more clearly focus on current possibilities.

THE OTHER SIDE OF FOG

As I learned that day with my friend Barbara when she shared her fear regarding her new job, being afraid does not always mean that we are in danger of getting hurt. Being afraid does not always mean that we are doing something wrong. It does not mean we are bad. Being afraid doesn't have to stop us from doing what feels right for us. If we feel afraid without any present danger, it is reasonable to assume that we are experiencing an old, underlying chronic fear that is leftover from earlier times. This fear is not the enemy. It is not bad. It is simply the point at which what we learned earlier in life rubs up against our current life.

When we experience this kind of fear, we are at a Y in the road. We have a choice to shut down once again because of it or to learn to listen through the fog it has created to our true self. We can even pause at that juncture at the Y in the road, remember, until we feel ready to make the choice.

Many times this old fear arises when we are entering new territory in our life. When Barbara stopped problem-solving what to do regarding her new job long enough to acknowledge her fear, she realized quickly that she was in a new situation that was not dangerous. The fear she was feeling was an old underlying fear about being in any new situation in which she could neither foresee nor control the outcome. Of course she felt some fear, but when she acknowledged it, she became able to see it for the past fear it was. She became able to listen through the fog to know her deeper truth.

Awakening moments, by definition, mean that we are in new territory. We are seeing something new. We are recognizing that we have choices we didn't realize we had. These are moments when we cannot possibly know what is next. We cannot already know who we are becoming. We cannot already have confidence that we will be able to do a new chapter of our life well. It is not possible for any of us, but choosing to acknowledge and listen to these powerful awakening moments helps us to refocus inward to recognize our true self.

Eva grew up with an alcoholic mother who did not adequately protect and comfort her. She says she never knew safety and comfort as a child. She disconnected from her sense of self and did whatever adults expected her to do.

As a young adult, she married a man who genuinely cared about her. He listened to her and was kind to her. She says she had never before experienced love like that. His acceptance and responsive attentiveness softened her inside. That same feeling occurred again for her when her first child was born. Her baby connected with her so intensely that her cement walls just melted. When she held her baby in her arms, she said she just knew something had to give. Eva needed to be there for her son, but she also, as she put it, "began to fall apart" emotionally.

Rather than falling apart, I would describe Eva's experience as an awakening moment. Something got her attention. Something significant shifted. She experienced something new and different. She was thus entering new territory. Eva listened through the fog of fear, became able to work through the feelings she had experienced as a child, and also became able to provide for both herself and her child what she had long been missing.

RECOGNIZING OUR TRUE SELF

Perhaps you, too, have experienced awakening moments—maybe a call to learn to deal with your fear of being alone or to "be there" for a baby you love. They are your true self calling you. Are you going to answer the call?

Awakening moments are connecting you with what's important. They are showing you that you can participate in your own development—to learn, to grow, to be *me*. The fog of fear is lifting in these precious moments. The sun is shining through. You are being invited to recognize your true self. I hope you notice these awakening moments. See them. Hear them. Open to them. Go toward them. Let yourself "just know," as Barbara, June, and Eva did. And yes, listen!

While there is no guarantee that we will never be hurt again, once we recognize that *me* deep down inside and begin to reconnect with our true self as our anchor, we can feel afraid and also safe enough to keep growing—at the same time.

Curiosity gradually begins to replace our fear. To be curious means to wonder without knowing for certain. It means to be open to all possibilities. It means to become willing to see what might happen without expecting or attempting to control any specific outcome.

Curious is neutral. It does not imply good or bad. It does not make us either good or bad. It does not stir up greater fear, nor does it make fear completely go away. Developing a curious attitude gives us a chance to grow beyond what we have already learned so that we can stretch toward what we really want and need. It encourages us to take the risk to stay open to new things coming into our life—whatever they may be.

When I asked my mother if she was afraid of dying, she paused in silence for a really long time as she pondered my question. Then she slowly answered, "No, I'm not scared . . . but I'm really curious. I just don't know what to expect." In two short sentences, she described being completely open to a future she knew she could not control. I couldn't imagine a more open attitude toward entering new territory. At the time, I felt relieved to know that my mother was okay about dying. Since then, I have silently thanked her many times for the valuable life lesson.

Chronic Fear

Oh she's there all right—
Forever just around the corner.
She silently sneaks in to shut me down
Again and again
When I get "too big for my britches"
Or too loud
Or maybe too uppity and sassy
Or too giggly,
Possibly having way too much fun.
Fear keeps me in line
Like a cattle whip
Cracking over my head
Or with terrifying images
Of some dank, dark foreign prison
Or dying from the cold.
I'm tired of the fear.
Can't I just live my life in peace?
Can't I just live?

PART II
RECONNECTING WITH OUR TRUE SELF

RECONNECT:
link or unite
come to know
reestablish communication with

Three essential self-skills show us the path toward reconnecting with the true self we once naturally knew and lived from. Learning any one makes a difference. Listening internally to all three—our safety, our body, and our feelings—changes how we experience our life. When we listen from a deeper level, we hear a deeper truth.

"Change occurs when one becomes what she is, not when she tries to become what she is not."

—Karen Casey, author of
Each Day a New Beginning

Chapter **4**

Creating Our Own Safety

What Would Help Me Feel Safer?

The looks coming back at me stop me in my tracks. There is no way to lie my way out of this one, no way to hide any longer. I am attending a weekend workshop for women healing their own emotional issues, and they can obviously see my black eye.

Miles hadn't wanted me to come to this weekend. When it came time for me to leave, he whined and complained. He invited me to go to the movies instead. He offered to help me clean the basement, which was long overdue. He hinted for me not to go, asked me not to go, and finally ordered me not to go. I left anyway.

If this had happened earlier, when I was still married to Tom, I would have stayed home, believing that my primary job in life was to please my man. But several years have passed since that NO ME LEFT moment when Susan had asked that magical question, "And what have *you* been doing lately, Sandy?"

I have grown a lot in these past few years. I survived an unwanted divorce that shook my beliefs about how life works. I returned to work, learned to balance work with caring for two young children, and moved to a different house. I started to run, play soccer, and cross-country ski. And I developed some wonderfully strong, supportive friendships. I was cruising and felt on top of the world. I knew who I was and what life was all about—at least I thought I did.

"And then . . ." I always said it this way. "And then I met this man. . . ."

Miles was delightful in the beginning and very different from my former husband. He let me know what he was feeling and wasn't afraid of anger, which I found refreshing. He laughed and encouraged me to lighten up and play. I felt alive with him, confident, and yes, certain that I was ready for a new relationship.

Well, Miles was different from Tom in more ways than I wanted to admit, and I was the same old scared me more than I could believe was possible. I still "stood by my man" way too much, trying to please him so he wouldn't get angry.

Yes, Miles has been violent at times and I have adapted much too easily. I violate my own integrity over and over with him—because I love him. He repeatedly pushes me to choose between him and my friends, between him and my children, between him and my true self—to prove how much I love him. I let him move in long before our relationship was secure and before we were ready to live together because he couldn't pay his rent. Now I am spending my meager salary from working at a childcare center to support him, gradually putting myself in debt. I rarely drink, but I am drinking more now because he likes his beer. I even eat more meat, just because he does.

Miles isn't violent every moment, of course. In between incidents, he is wonderfully fun and loving. I hunger for those loving times like a puppy waiting eagerly under the dinner table for a few tasty crumbs.

That's me—patiently waiting, overly tolerant, and ever-hopeful. If I just love him enough, if I can just do this relationship right, if I can just please him sufficiently, maybe, maybe, maybe he will change. Anyway, I keep hoping for what may prove to be impossible.

All that hoping and wishing has seemed quite normal and surprisingly acceptable to me—until tonight. Tonight I was determined not to give up my precious weekend just because he didn't want me to attend this retreat. My dad recently died, and I have needed help dealing with this significant loss. I just *had* to get here! So I stubbornly planted my heels, pulled all the strength I could from deep inside, stood up tall, and said something relatively adult and sane, like "I'm sorry you don't like it, but I really need to go."

Well, he couldn't tolerate my independence in that way at all, and we were suddenly off and running in another ferocious screaming power struggle. I ended up with a black eye ... but I left.

So here I am, now facing a whole circle of women I don't know who have come to examine themselves honestly, and my black eye is right out there on the surface unable to be hidden.

In spite of the overwhelming shame creeping hot up around my ears, I know immediately that my work for this weekend is not to deal with my father's death. My more urgent work is to acknowledge the glaring truth that I am a battered woman. I am having enormous difficulty keeping myself safe at this very primal level. I desperately need help.

I just don't want it to be true. I want to curl up in a tiny ball and hide in the back corner away from everyone. After all, Miles loves me ... doesn't he? I don't want the violence to be real. I want that part of our relationship to just go away.

How did I get into this mess? And why can't I get out of it? How could I be so far off base about what is safe? Why can't I figure this out? Where is *me* when I need her? I have a right to keep myself safe

... don't I? I have apparently lost contact with my sense of self once again—and I don't like it.

I am the last one to introduce myself. I look at the floor, even though I feel certain they have already seen my black eye. The others sit in complete silence, as if wondering what I will do. I wonder, too.

Slowly and cautiously I lift my head and look around the room. Something inside me *just knows* the time has come. I have to speak my truth—whatever it takes. I don't know how and I am painfully terrified to try, but I make my choice at the Y in the road to leave the Good-Girl Jail.

I begin by acknowledging my truth that Miles has been violent on many occasions. I am having enormous difficulty leaving him. I am terrified to go back home. Sobbing with raw humiliation and trembling in anticipation of their criticism, I spill it all out loud for the first time ever. It isn't easy, but I do what I *just know* deep down in my core I have to do, not having any idea where it will take me.

ASSESSING OUR OWN SAFETY

Sometimes we don't realize how much danger we are in. We get used to the way things are—or the way they have always been. We believe we have to simply take what others dish out. We think we can't do anything about what others do anyway, so why try? We tolerate inexcusable behavior because we love these people and believe that if we love them enough, they will eventually change. Sometimes we are not certain we could survive leaving a dangerous situation.

Honoring our deep need for safety is the first essential self-skill that takes us toward reconnecting with our true self. This chapter reminds us what it is like to feel safe. When we made that *traumatic disconnect* to an external reference point, we adopted a pattern of behaviors to keep safe that focused outward on others. We discover that we are now safer listening to our internal clues than shutting them down to meet the needs and expectations of others.

There is a lot of danger in our vast world. Whenever we watch the news, whether local, national, or international, we see frequent examples of war, natural disasters, catastrophic accidents, terrorism, poverty, and interpersonal violence of all kinds. Sometimes the danger is nearby. Sometimes it is even in our own home. When we feel vulnerable and unsure how to keep ourselves safe, the threats can seem overwhelming and terrifying.

How do we find a way to feel safe in a world that is full of danger? How do we meet our deep need for safety once we have learned that others who are bigger and stronger and more demanding might hurt us? How can little Mariah, the girl on her way to foster care, feel safe again once she has found it necessary to constantly watch for danger?

Safety is one of our most basic needs. We cannot stay alive without at least a minimal level of safety, and we certainly cannot blossom and enjoy life without feeling safe. Our sense of self cannot grow without safety, and we cannot possibly reconnect with our true self until we feel safe enough to do so.

To feel safe means to trust that we are beyond the reach of danger both physically and emotionally, at least for this moment. Our body is relaxed and feels solid. Our thoughts are calm. We sleep peacefully. We feel a wide range of feelings. We find most others are reasonable to deal with, readily take action to meet our needs, and can be asked for help when we need assistance. We smile freely and laugh joyfully. We know deep down that we are okay.

We might remember feeling safe sometimes as a child, perhaps when we rode our bicycle, played with a particular friend, visited Grandma, or got comforted when we cried. What creates this same sensation of safety now, as adults, varies tremendously from person to person. Some of us feel safe when we are able to pay the rent and have enough gas in the car. Some of us feel safe when we are home and our children are safely tucked into bed at night. I always feel safe in the calm silence of the early morning.

EXTERNAL CLUES FOR SAFETY

It would be nice to feel safe all the time, wouldn't it? But most of us don't. Many of us hid our true self long ago as described in the last chapter, vowing never to let *it* happen again, whatever *it* was. With that vow came the traumatic disconnect and a focus outward to watch for the next danger. We came to live in chronic fear, wondering when the next bad thing would come our way. Perhaps we began to rely on external clues to tell us whether or not we were safe: What kind of mood is he in? What does she do when she gets angry? Has she been drinking? Is he mad at me? Does she have a weapon? Does this man get violent? In other words, the behavior of others thus determined whether we felt safe or in danger.

When we shifted to focus outward to rely on external clues for our safety, we necessarily developed a *safety pattern*. The specific behaviors we adopted depended on what we believed would keep us safe. This safety pattern now tends to be our automatic response at the Y in the road. It keeps us focused on external clues and living in chronic fear. It keeps us in the Good-Girl Jail. While our safety pattern may provide only an illusion of safety, it might be the only way we have known to try to be safe.

More than the usual fight-or-flight response, I observe five general safety patterns commonly adopted to keep safe. We run away, hide, fight physically, freeze, or prove our worth. No one safety pattern is better or worse than another. They all work—but only to a point.

Raven's safety pattern, for example, is *running from danger*. She talks fast, quickly shifting from one topic to the next, and fidgets constantly. She has had many sexual partners but no long-term relationships. She has tried a variety of religions, doing each one wholeheartedly but only for a while. She is a skilled worker but leaves to find a new job whenever she can no longer tolerate the current job. She keeps herself ready and able to leave any situation whenever she sees danger. Her behavior says, "You can't hurt me if you can't catch me!"

In contrast, Iris's safety pattern is *hiding from danger*. She has a long history of employment for the same small company without any promotions. She has been married for twenty years and clings to her husband—a strong, reliable man who tells her what to do. She is a good mom, always there for her kids but otherwise avoids attention and other people. She feels safest at home alone. She prefers to be invisible, never needing anything from others. She doesn't want to bother me, her therapist, even when she feels suicidal. She lays low to stay out of trouble and avoid the possibility of any danger. Her behavior says, "You can't hurt me if you can't find me!"

Physical fighting is Annalee's safety pattern. She was a good soldier in the Army and now works light construction. She has a strong voice and speaks up readily whenever she feels mistreated. She fought physically when she was younger and says she would still "take somebody's head off" if she needed to. She says others are either for her or against her; there are no neutral parties. She doesn't have many friends but she, her spouse, her children, and her siblings "have each other's back." She keeps herself ready and able to fight physically to keep herself feeling safe. Annalee's behavior clearly says, "Don't you *dare* try to hurt me!"

Ryder's safety pattern is *freezing*. She stays home feeling utterly exhausted nearly all the time, and unable to hold any job. She spends much of her time lying down or just sitting, not even watching TV or reading. She doesn't participate in social activities and cannot go to the grocery store by herself. She shakes uncontrollably in terror when her teenage son brings friends home or when loud cars drive by. She sees danger everywhere and safety as impossible. She can't see options, make decisions, or ask for help. She has become immobilized and unable to take any kind of action to feel safe. Her behavior says, "I just have to take whatever others do to me."

And lastly, Connie's safety pattern is proving her worth. She is a competitive manager who has worked hard to climb the corporate ladder to earn enough money and status to feel safe and equal to the men in her office. She often takes on more tasks than she can reasonably handle to prove how capable she is. She is in the process, though, of quietly consulting an attorney about filing a lawsuit against her employer for gender discrimination. She clearly fights danger to feel safe, but she fights using legal and socially acceptable strategies. Her behavior says, "I refuse to get hurt."

Safety patterns are limited by the fact that they rely on external clues to anticipate danger. As long as we believe our safety depends on other people, our reference point will be external. We will spend our energy trying to manipulate others to be nice to us rather than hurt us. Safety patterns necessarily keep us focused externally on others, and focusing externally on others necessarily keeps us living from our safety pattern. The two go together and limit us to the Good-Girl Jail.

The need for a safety pattern is based on an underlying core belief that there are only two possible options: (1) get hurt by others or (2) be the one in control. Being in control, however, is not the same as feeling safe. Being in control does not guarantee safety. This does not mean that we must permit others to continually victimize us. It means there is an alternative at the Y in the road, a way to feel safe that also allows us to reconnect with our true self.

This alternative way to feel safe is listening internally. It means continuing to meet our deep need to feel safe but doing so from an internal reference point, from our sense of self. The two ways of keeping safe are very different.

INTERNAL CLUES FOR SAFETY

When we listen internally, we discover that there is a second aspect of safety beyond our physical safety—feeling emotionally secure. Things like snuggling with a teddy bear or a special blanket, sleeping with a light on, hiding under the covers, sitting next to the door at public events, and perhaps even wearing purple on Mondays may nurture our emotional safety. What the activity is or how silly it might seem to others doesn't matter if the activity helps us *feel* safer. I call it the *teddy-bear phenomenon*.

Children know this second aspect of safety well and naturally honor their own need for it. We might think children are just being cute when they cling to their teddy bear, but they feel safer even when their simple actions do not appear to adults to create any *real* safety. Unless they have already made the traumatic shift away from their true self, children naturally listen inside for what helps them feel safer and then take action to create their own safety.

My son Eric kept a beanbag frog on top of his headboard. He said it slept all day while he was at school so that it could stay awake all night to protect him. His frog helped him feel safe falling asleep at bedtime and whenever he awoke during the night—and that safe feeling was real.

My daughter Sarah woke up one night feeling scared. She had dreamed that some people were trying to climb in through her bedroom window while she was sleeping. When I asked what would help her feel safer, she bounded out of bed, opened her closet, grabbed her baton, and placed it right beside her pillow. She then easily went back to sleep. As an adult, I was amused. I found it difficult to believe that her baton would keep out the intruders in her dream, but I didn't argue. She seemed so sure of her own reality.

In the morning, she said they had come back, but she "just kicked them all the way to Texas" in her dream. The issue was over. Her fear was gone. She hadn't even needed her baton, but acknowledging her fear and taking action based on what felt safe to her had apparently given her what she needed to deal with the situation in her sleep. She felt safe again, and that safe feeling was indeed real.

Adults also know this teddy-bear phenomenon. June carries a special rock in her pocket to feel protected. Olivia wears a particular ring for good luck. Annalee took her St. Christopher's medal when she deployed overseas. Sirena hugs a special tree every morning to start her day on the right foot. Nora wears a *chamsah*, a Middle Eastern good luck charm that shields her from the evil eye.

Taking action to feel safer based on our internal clues is an essential self-skill that leads directly to reconnecting with our true self. I'm not suggesting that we quit watching our environment for danger. I'm saying that internal clues regarding our safety are also always readily available, and they may be even more accurate than relying on external clues.

I once walked into a meeting that had already started and took an available seat between two men I didn't know. After a few minutes, I noticed that I was leaning toward the man on my right. I pulled myself back, wondering why I had done that. When it happened a second time, I paid more attention. When it happened a third time, I got up and moved to a different chair, aware that the same thing had not happened with the man on my left.

Who was this man? He still appeared perfectly safe to me. He smiled. He made eye contact. He was calm and appropriate. He talked softly and courteously. He seemed to do everything right, but something kept warning me. I felt very uncomfortable around him. I avoided eye contact with him. My stomach tightened. I thought he wanted something from me, but I couldn't tell what it was. I wanted to get away from the "vacuum cleaner guy," as I came to call him. I chose to trust my internal clues of discomfort more than the external clues.

Had I experienced that same internal awareness when I first met Miles? I honestly don't know. If I had learned earlier to listen inside, I may never have had that black eye. I may never have experienced that battering relationship.

Honoring Our Internal Clues

When we listen to internal clues regarding safety, we are listening to our sense of self. We are reconnecting with our deeper truth. It is our true self, after all, that creates that gnawing little unsettled feeling in our stomach to caution us. It is our true self that nudges us to *just know* when something is right—or not right.

As we listen more and more, honoring our internal clues, we strengthen the clarity of these clues. We recognize them sooner and respond more quickly, thus feeling safe more and more of the time.

One way to practice this listening skill is to walk through your home. Notice what areas feel the safest and which feel the least safe. Consider rearranging the furniture to feel safer, so that the places you sit most often feel as safe as possible. If you feel safer in sunshine, for example, consider placing that chair you love to curl up in near a south window.

Especially notice where you sleep. Does your bedroom feel safe? Is the bed arranged in the safest position? Do the covers feel safe? Do you feel safest sleeping alone or with something or someone, during the day or at night, with a light on or off, or with background noise or when it's quiet? The safer you feel falling asleep, the easier it will be to sleep peacefully and the more rested you will feel upon waking, so your bedroom is an important place to feel as safe as possible.

Notice, too, what specific things in your home feel safe to you— or not so safe. Perhaps you can't look at that picture your mother-in-law gave you six years ago that you never liked anyway. Maybe your child's monster toy with the creepy eyes gives you an eerie unsettled feeling. Whatever the reasons they do not feel safe, consider putting these things out of sight or giving them away. Consider replacing the things that do not feel safe with things that help you feel safer. Be sure to keep whatever feels like a nurturing teddy bear.

Notice whether the people who come into your home feel safe or not so safe. Notice if your car feels safe. What would help you feel safer while driving? Notice if your workplace feels safe to you. What would help you feel safer at work? What other places feel safe to you or not safe?

Using this approach, you can gradually expand the percentage of the time you feel safe and do so from your internal reference point, reconnecting with and experiencing your true self. When we listen internally, we honor our need for emotional safety *in addition to* our physical safety. Our logical brain may say these seemingly silly things will not keep us safe, but they help us feel safer and feeling safe is very real. Our need for emotional safety is real at any age. Whatever works is what works.

✿　✿　✿

Evelyn had been molested throughout her childhood and then had been raped as an adult by an acquaintance. Her experience was that all men wanted to use her sexually. She had never found a way to stop a man who wanted to have sex with her.

One day she accepted a job going door-to-door to raise money for a cause she strongly believed in—rape awareness. I was surprised that she was able to even consider what seemed to me to be such a risky activity. When I asked how she could feel safe going door to door, she said she wore sneakers to be able to run away and always covered her body with an oversized shirt and long baggy pants so that men could not look at her body sexually. Her trauma had always occurred when she was alone in a room with a man she knew, never outdoors with strangers. She felt safe as long as she never went inside anyone's house.

Evelyn listened to her internal clues regarding safety. She knew what she needed to feel safe in that particular situation and she took the precautions she needed to feel safe. It worked for her.

Trusting Our Internal Clues

So, are we safe—or aren't we? How can we tell for sure? Sometimes we are actually safer than we feel, like when my friend Barbara started her new job. And sometimes we are in more danger than we realize, as I was in my relationship with Miles.

While some of us find it extremely difficult and confusing to know what to trust, I have come to believe that our own internal clues, especially physical and intuitive sensations, are precisely the best thing to trust to tell us if we are safe. These internal clues come directly from our sense of self, and listening to internal clues regarding our safety has the added advantage of reconnecting us with our true self.

Ryder's experience was that no place and no other person was safe. She barely slept and never left home alone. She lived in chronic fear and was scared all the time. Reconnecting with her true self—what I call *the underbelly of healing from trauma*—was critical for her. We needed to find ways she could begin to listen inside and then take action based on those internal clues to feel safe.

Together, we found several simple things she could do at home to feel safer, even if only for minutes at a time in the beginning. Listening to her internal cues, she rearranged her bedroom to feel safer and added warmer covers. She learned to sleep during the day when she was the only one in the house. She kept her protective dog close and asked her daughter to go with her when she needed to see a doctor or dentist. She rarely let outsiders into her home.

Gradually, as she practiced listening internally more and more, Ryder moved beyond the paralysis of chronic fear and waiting for the next bad thing to happen. She moved beyond her adopted safety pattern of freezing as the only way to keep herself feeling safe. Ryder discovered that taking action to meet her deep need for safety by listening to her own internal clues kept her feeling safe both physically and emotionally. And as she did so, she also reconnected with her precious self.

OUR CHOICE AT THE Y IN THE ROAD

When our physical safety is seriously threatened, our old automatic safety patterns may always take over to protect us from physical harm, as those little soldiers are very well trained. The rest of the time, though, when there is little or no present danger, turning our focus inward to listen to our internal clues regarding our deep need for both physical and emotional safety offers an effective alternative to chronic fear.

When we listen internally, noticing that pit in our stomach, our slight trembling, the tightness in our throat, a dry mouth, a sudden tension, or perhaps an urge to run, we know when something isn't quite right. We know when we are not feeling safe, and if we listen a little more attentively from that deeper place, we know what we can do to feel safer in that moment. In this way, we choose to participate in creating our own safety.

On one of my early morning hikes, I came to a literal Y in the road. Without thinking much about the choice, I took the left path. Within twenty feet, I suddenly stopped. Something brought me to an abrupt halt. I didn't know what it was, but my breathing suddenly got faster. I felt considerable tension in my body. I didn't want to move, much less go farther. I looked around for some kind of danger. I didn't see any. Neither could I hear any, but I lived in bear country and knew that a bear would see me long before I saw him. Or was it a person or a mountain lion? I had no external clues, but the internal clues were very clear. I slowly backed up, trusting my internal cues completely. I chose the other path instead, feeling perfectly safe the rest of my hike.

I believe our internal clues are trustworthy. They reliably bring us the information we need. Instead of fearing what is outside of us, we come to trust our internal sensations to help us know when we are not safe and what action to take to feel safe again. Most importantly, we come to trust our own perceptions.

RECONNECTING WITH OUR TRUE SELF

Relying completely upon others to protect and rescue us rarely works. We are the only ones who know what feels safe to us. We are thus becoming our own safe person, our own anchor to return to and trust. Maybe we weren't adequately and appropriately protected as children, but now we can take action to create our own safety. We don't have to, but now we finally can.

When I listened to my internal clues that day as I sat in the circle of women with my black eye, I remembered that my safety was important. I knew deep down that I needed to break away from Miles and quit expecting him to miraculously change his violent nature. Looking back on that awakening moment now, I can see that my sense of self was signaling me from inside in every way she could.

In case you have doubts about your right to take action for your own safety, remember that full-term babies are born with a solid ability to cry when they need something. Then when their needs become reliably met time after time, they become increasingly more specific about what they need. That is, they cry in different ways—long before they learn to speak words. It is only when no one has listened to a child's needs consistently and repeatedly that she quits asking and gives up—as Mariah so clearly demonstrated that day she went to foster care.

While we cannot make the world safe, when we reconnect with our internal awareness regarding safety, the world begins to feel safer. Those awful abuses no longer seem to just happen to us. It no longer takes six months (or three years) to get out of an unsafe situation or relationship. We recognize that we have a right to need safety and to take the initiative to meet this need.

Listening is what our true self has always needed to grow and flourish. When we listen internally to our safety now, no matter how small that first step might be, we begin to reconnect with *me*. And as we continue to listen internally on this deeper level and consistently respond to honor our internal cues, we become safe at that deepest level no one else can destroy. Being completely at the mercy of others is over. We no longer feel left alone in an overwhelming world. If we get hurt, our self is with us to help heal the wounds. If we become terrified, our self helps us ride through the fear and take action to feel safer once again. By listening internally, we are taking initiative for our safety to the upper limits of what is possible for us. We are stepping forward at the Y in the road to do the maximum we can do to feel safe. And in doing so, we reconnect with our true self.

Safe

I want to run!

I want to hide!

Escape—where can I be safe?

Is there no place safe at all?

Crawl out of my skin?

Explode? Implode?

Die? Lie?

How ironic that I already am safe.

I am safe.

I am safe.

I am safe. . . .

There is no longer any need to disappear.

It is safer now to be me.

I breathe.

I am calm.

Being me, I am safe.

Chapter **5**

Hearing Our Physical Body

What body sensations am I experiencing?

I am sitting here on our deck, the sun a brilliant orange glow through the trees. A couple of deer are casually munching away, oblivious to my quiet presence. The birds are twittering a full chorus of morning joy. Two squirrels are dancing from tree to tree, challenging themselves with tiny limbs that bow ever so deeply toward the earth as they land on their tiny feet. I'm wondering if a bear might amble through.

I am embarrassed—not that I broke my foot, but about how I've been handling it. This is my first experience with real physical pain, and I have not been graceful.

At first, my foot was just swollen. I could live with swollen. It hurt, but I kept walking on it, somehow hoping it would get better on its own. Denial is wonderful as long as it lasts, isn't it?

Three dreadfully long days later, I admitted that my foot really, really hurt. On the fourth day, I finally went to see a doctor and an X-ray confirmed a stress fracture. I went home on crutches. Yes, I had a broken foot and would be in a cast for six weeks.

As you might expect, severe pain brought an abrupt end to my denial. "This isn't so bad" grew into "This really hurts" and then "This is *pain!*" Sure, go ahead and live in your body, but what about when it really, really hurts?

As my denial dissolved, I plunged into despair mixed with generous doses of anger, resentment, and self-pity. I bounced off the walls for three days, jumping from one intense feeling and thought to another and then to another and yet another.

What about my morning walks? How will I keep my sanity without them? What about taking care of my flowerbeds—and working? What about the other trips we have planned for this summer? I can't have a broken foot! I don't break bones. I need to do more important things. I need to live my life. Oh, this must be the beginning of the end. First the feet go, right? Then everything else falls apart. Then you die. . . .

I couldn't seem to ask for help. I wallowed, embarrassed and desperate. I ate ice cream and escaped into daytime TV for hours before I became certain I wasn't likely to die from a broken foot. "This is ruining my summer!" got me nowhere, and everyone simply laughed when I said, "This is ridiculous!"

But something began gently nudging me to adapt to this new situation and, surprisingly, my body seemed to be leading the way. My muscles, already strengthening, began to say, "We can do this." My foot, even while screaming at me, also quietly whispered, "I can heal if you take care of me." The pain itself began to tell me when to take another pain pill. My tears began to relieve the fear of being immobilized. My trembling belly calmed. Sleep began to sneak back in more easily. Television gave way to sitting out on our deck, chatting with these eternally peaceful deer. I began to realize that this wasn't so bad after all. No, this life isn't over yet. There is more. I kept hearing, "There is more. . . ."

I can see that my thoughts have been scrambling to make sense of this new body experience. They couldn't stop until they landed on something that held some kind of meaning to that core part of me that helps me listen beyond the fog of fear. Yes, my busy brain is softly settling down, beginning to find some gifts in this new situation.

My irritation about being inconvenienced by my body has now become the reality of canceling four summer trips, not weeding my garden for half the summer, and just generally stopping the merry-go-round of my ordinary life to let my body heal. My usually ferocious self-sufficiency is necessarily morphing into a reluctant willingness to accept the generous offers of assistance I receive from others, even though I still hate admitting that I need help.

This morning, as I sit here on our deck, once again communing with the deer, I realize that I actually *like* staying home all summer! I enjoy these quiet mornings, reading and writing on our deck. Now that I am listening to my body, I am getting my priorities clear and discovering a deep determination to keep my body strong and healthy to avoid more pain in the future. And with much more time to be honest with myself, I realize that I didn't want to take one of those trips anyway.

OUR BODY—NOT THE ENEMY

Some of us have spent much of our life avoiding the reality that we are, in part, our body. We may see our body as something other than *me*, something that periodically attacks us, making us inconveniently ill or injured. Many of us see our body as something that necessarily takes more time and energy than we want to give it—and rarely looks the way we want it to. Some of us go even one step further. We see our body as an enemy that needs to be wrenched under control to work harder and serve us better. We push our body hard to work overtime—as if it were a machine and could actually do that. Or we see our body as sinful and bad, perhaps as a source of evil to be punished and deprived.

This chapter focuses on learning the specific language of our body. Acknowledging that our body is an essential and valuable part of *me* is very different from viewing it as an enemy to be controlled and perhaps even punished. While staying in our body through pain can be a challenge, our body also brings us considerable pleasure. Listening to our body is the second essential self-skill that leads to reconnecting with our true self.

When we hide our self for safekeeping and adopt an external reference point instead, we tend to also detach from our body. We view our body from the outside, as if looking at it in a mirror, rather than experiencing it from the inside. We set aside what is important to us to listen to the rules of life's teachers telling us what we *should* look like, what we *should* want, and what we *should* do. The *shoulds* replace the *coulds*. We forget what is possible and settle for what seems to have to be. We find ways to numb our body, shutting down pleasure as well as both physical and emotional pain.

What we have learned may be a long way from living inside our body in peace with our physical being. Let's reconsider how we think about our body. There is a vastly different and friendlier viewpoint.

ACKNOWLEDGING OUR BODY

Our body gently holds the physical space in which our sense of self lives. Our body is the concrete part of us that tells us we are solid and real. It is never the enemy and neither is it a machine. Our body is soft. It is warm and sensitive. It moves. We don't even have to like our body to know that we need it. Of course we need our body. It is the only body we get for this entire lifetime.

This miraculous creature we call our body is working constantly to support us and help us in every way it possibly can. Most injuries and illnesses heal all by themselves. Even while we are sleeping, our body works to rebuild our muscles, digest the nutrients we have eaten, and process our feelings and memories through dreams to help us function better the next day.

Through our senses—hearing, seeing, smelling, touching, tasting, and also our sense of self—we have an amazing ability to fully experience the world around us. We can appreciate beauty and love as well as protect our self from cold and danger.

We can move big objects like ants do. We can roar the way lions do. We can swim like fish do. We can love and snuggle like dogs and cats do. We can eat leaves the way giraffes do. We can feel warmth from the sun like rattlesnakes do. We can even have babies, and we can do all of these things . . . because we have a body.

Of course, not everything about having a body is wonderful. We have bodily needs like eating, sleeping, keeping warm, drinking water, and keeping safe from physical harm that take time and energy. We also have bodily functions like urinating, defecating, burping, passing gas, sweating, yawning, vomiting, breathing, menstruating, and giving birth—essential activities that are often inconvenient, messy, uncomfortable, and sometimes even embarrassing. And it is through our body that we feel pain, which both warns us that something is wrong and stops us from pushing too hard.

Our body can also bring us much pleasure—feeling safe and loved, smelling a roasting turkey on Thanksgiving, laughing out loud with a friend, dancing, holding a sleeping baby, and much, much more.

So, we have this thing we call a body. It is an essential part of being physically alive. Let's make peace with it. Let's learn to live with it.

Let's learn to listen to what it has to say to us. After all, it is a free gift to do with as we wish throughout this lifetime, and as you may have noticed, we can't simply return it to the store for a different model.

THE LANGUAGE OF PHYSICAL SENSATIONS

Our body talks to us nearly all the time, but it doesn't speak to us in words. It speaks to us in the language of physical sensations. We feel hungry when we need to eat and tired when we need to rest. We feel sore or get sick when we overdo. We get tense when we are stressed or threatened. We feel all kinds of emotions including fear, sadness, anger, joy, powerlessness, and confusion that tell us how we are responding to our environment. We feel pain when some part of our body is more aggressively screaming for attention. Yes, there are many ways our body speaks to us.

When we listen, we become able to catch a small injury or the beginning stages of an illness so that we can tend to these challenges earlier and more effectively. We become aware of how different factors affect our body. We become able to give it what it needs to be able to serve us well in return. We listen, we hear, we interact . . . and our body responds.

Now, are you listening? Do you hear the little hurts? Do you eat when you are hungry and quit when you are full? Do you rest when you are tired? Do you let yourself cry freely when tears come into your eyes? Do you respond to your body's pleas for assistance to meet your own needs?

Not hearing our body's cues can be part of shunning our body.

SHUNNING OUR BODY

Some of us don't know where we live in our body or even if we are inside our body. A general lack of body awareness, the use of any addiction, or a history of traumatic experiences of any kind can readily contribute to not knowing where we live in relationship to our body.

Iris stumbles a lot and accidentally bumps into things, frequently giving herself small injuries because she has so little awareness of where her body is. She once had a car accident because she was daydreaming when she drove through an intersection. Anna describes being up on the ceiling looking down on her little girl body when her uncle was molesting her. These are examples of not being fully in our body.

Some of us may remember times when we were emotionally numb, didn't remember something that happened, used addictions to escape, or couldn't feel all parts of our body. There are thousands of creative ways to shun our body and a very long continuum of degrees of separation.

Dissociation is the clinical term for not being fully present in our body. Dissociation means to separate our conscious awareness from our physical body, to leave *me* and go somewhere else while our physical body stays where it is. It is a powerful coping skill, a way to protect our precious self and certainly a valuable survival skill for dealing with traumatic experiences. Dissociating helps us feel safe even if we cannot physically run away, hide from danger, fight off an attacker, or prove our worth in socially acceptable ways. Dissociation is part of a freeze response to a threatening situation. It may be part of your safety pattern.

All of us dissociate at least occasionally. We might drive somewhere and not remember major milestones we know we had to have driven past along the way. We might miss what someone just said to us or what just happened because we were absentminded. Perhaps we feel weird or just generally not our usual self. Maybe we lose track of time or forget what we are saying.

Everyday situations that make it easier to dissociate include hurrying, multitasking, getting overwhelmed with too much to do, feeling pressured by work deadlines, being exhausted, getting injured or ill, being in pain, feeling scared or threatened, and experiencing flashbacks to previous trauma. Doing anything compulsively, intensely, or in a very particular manner—such as an addiction or a ritual—also makes it easier to dissociate and leave our body.

Remember the traumatic disconnect many of us have experienced? Anyone who has experienced a traumatic disconnect has dissociated, at least temporarily. That disconnect is a form of dissociation. If we have separated from our sense of self, we may have also separated from our body. The two often go together. It is this separation that makes it possible to view our body as something other—something that can attack us, get in our way, hurt us, humiliate us, betray us, or be inconvenient. Without this separation, we probably wouldn't judge or attempt to control our body. We wouldn't be so scared of its physical sensations. We would simply experience our body as a valued part of our true self instead.

RETURNING HOME TO OUR BODY

When we are ready to reconnect with our sense of self, we can choose a different path at the Y in the road. We can choose to return home to our precious body.

I find the following exercise to be particularly helpful when we choose to return. It is my own variation of an old standby. It can be recorded in your own voice, another can slowly read it to you, or you can simply memorize the basic idea and go through it quietly at your own pace. You may want to lie down, cover yourself with a blanket, and close your eyes—whatever feels safest and most comfortable. Go as slowly as you need to. Perhaps you will feel something warm and fluid like syrup or energy flowing down through your body as you acknowledge each and every part of your body.

To begin, take a few long, slow breaths. Starting from the top of your head, enter your body gently and slowly. First notice your scalp, then flow into your forehead, your eyes, your ears, your nose, your cheeks, your mouth, your tongue, your throat, your jaw, and your chin. Then flow slowly down through your neck.

Let your awareness slide into your shoulders, down your upper arms, through your elbows, into your hands, and down to the tip of each finger.

Then ooze slowly down through your chest, into your heart, your lungs, your ribs, your solar plexus, your stomach, and all those organs we never pay attention to, like your pancreas, your liver, your kidneys, and your gallbladder. Keep flowing down into your pelvis, your intestines, and your sexual organs. Down into your thighs, your knees, your calves, your ankles, and your feet. Let your breath go all the way to the tip of each toe.

When you can, return to your neck and go slowly down the back side of your body, one vertebra at a time all the way to your tailbone. Be there. Let your self stay there inside your tailbone.

Notice your breathing. Notice how your breath feeds each and every part of your body. Let your breath flow freely through your body.

Notice, too, what you cannot feel—your blood carrying oxygen to your brain, your liver separating out toxins, and your fingernails growing. Notice how all of your various body parts are nourishing you and working together without any effort on your part.

Sense how it feels to be fully in your body. Sense your whole body—its shape, the sensation of its weight on the floor, its position. Notice if you feel hot or cold, heavy or light. Notice any other physical sensations. Notice if it is difficult or scary to be fully in your body or in any particular part of your body. Give yourself credit for staying in your body as well as you do. Notice any judging thoughts that may arise and let them flow back on out to float away.

Notice if your body is talking to you. What is it saying? Listen very carefully. What do you hear?

Now take a moment to sense if anyone else seems to be in your body with you. If you happen to find others, ask them courteously to leave. If necessary, tell them to leave, urging them to go back where they belong, back to their own bodies. This body is yours. It is not available to others. Notice how it feels to be the only one in your precious body.

Now gently touch your body with your hands. See if you can meet that touch from the inside. This is you. This is your body. Notice it. Feel it. Experience it. It is yours. It is part of you. Thank it for being here for you and with you all these years. Say to your self, "I am in my body, fully experiencing my life."

When you are ready, open your eyes, if they have been closed. See if you can stay inside your body as you slowly sit up and look around the room. Notice your surroundings while also experiencing your body. See how long you can stay inside your body as you begin to move and go on with your life. Now you know how to return to your body whenever you want to.

REAWAKENING A NUMB BODY

But what if we have difficulty feeling our body? What if we discover that we don't have much awareness of the nuances in our body? What if our body seems dead, numbed perhaps by years of dissociation, addictions, and shutting down moments? Can we wake it up again? Can we resurrect our body from the depths of numbness? Yes, we can!

New experiences of all kinds reawaken our senses. With an attitude of curiosity, we stretch to explore new possibilities. With an internal point of reference, we experience our body with all its subtle nuances rather than merely look at it from the outside. We feel our body. We notice changes. We notice what we can do with our body—as well as what we can't or don't want to do.

So let's try some new experiences. Doing any one thing differently makes a difference.[25] Eat something unusual for breakfast to start your day differently. Wear brighter colors. Drive a different route to work. Park in a different place. Hike a different trail. Listen to different music. Buy new sheets. Look for a four-leaf clover. Go barefoot. Turn off the TV for a week just to see what happens. Play hopscotch with a child. Ask yourself, "What do ants eat?" and find the answer. Try to describe verbally what it feels like to smile. Or as Nora likes to do, hand a ten-dollar bill to a woman you don't know just to brighten her day.

New experiences wake us up. They catch our attention so that we more easily notice our responses. Staying inside our body can be a challenge, but life is certainly more interesting once our body is awake.

STAYING IN OUR BODY

Staying in our body is a skill that requires practice, preferably every day. Things like good self-care, gentle physical activities, and nonsexual touch invite us to stay in our body and thus serve as ways to practice. Self-care includes getting enough sleep and rest, drinking plenty of water, getting outdoors, eating foods that physically nourish our body, and doing anything that helps us feel safer. Gentle physical activities include going barefoot, taking deeper breaths than usual, meditating, participating in yoga or tai chi, improving our posture, stretching, walking, and laughing. Gentle non-sexual touch includes wrapping ourselves in soft blankets, feeling cool air on our face, taking a warm bath, massaging our scalp, and hugging our own shoulders.

Flowing is one of my favorite ways to practice staying in my body.

To flow, plant your feet solidly on the ground or floor, shoulder width apart (or sit if your balance is questionable). You are not performing for anyone else, so flowing works best when no one else is watching. With your eyes closed and perhaps some slow meditative music that doesn't have a strong beat, leave your feet where they are and let the rest of your body begin to move slowly in any way it wants to without any direction from your mind. Be aware of being inside your body. There is no need to keep time with the music as if you were dancing. Listen to your body and its own rhythm. Take your time. Let your arms and hands flow however they want to. Let your head move this way and that at its own initiative, and let your hips do whatever they want. Experience your body from the inside. There might be some very tiny movements. Notice those. There might be larger movements than you are used to. Notice those, too, without any judgment. Simply let your body flow, however it wants to as long as it wants to. Quit when your body is done and notice what you feel afterward.

Yella Werder, a singer in Colorado Springs, teaches something similar to flowing as a way to learn to sing. She suggests closing your eyes and then allowing your body to make whatever verbal sounds it wants to with no regard for volume, pitch, rhythm, or appropriateness. Play with your voice without any audience for twenty to thirty minutes, as she suggests, and see if that doesn't also help you stay with your body.

BUILDING A PARTNERSHIP
WITH OUR BODY

When we stay in our body, it sometimes hurts just as mine did when I broke my foot. Everyone's body hurts, at least at times. We tend to ignore pain, medicate it to make it go away, hate it, fight it as if it were an enemy—almost anything to avoid experiencing it fully. Yet pain is not the enemy. It is, after all, a clue that we are indeed in our body—and listening to its messages.

While pain is neither fun nor easy, let's consider the alternative for a moment. What if our body never hurt? What would happen then? We wouldn't know when our throat was getting sore, when we were developing a blister, when we had burned a finger, when something was too tight, or even if we were developing appendicitis. We wouldn't know these things until they were significantly more serious problems—or had possibly made us deathly ill.

Our body is fluid, flowing from one moment to the next, constantly adapting to the changes occurring both inside our body and in our environment. Sometimes these changes create physical pain. While some pain is unavoidable, we make pain and discomfort either better or worse by our *interpretation* of the physical sensations. There is a wise, old adage: "Pain is inevitable; suffering is an option."[26] In other words, when we interpret our physical pain as horrible, we make our experience of it worse. We can thus help our own pain situation by becoming aware of our beliefs and attitudes toward it. While we cannot control what physical sensations occur, we can choose how to interpret the meaning of the sensations and then respond to them in different ways as needed.

For example, we can go to the part of our body that hurts, surround it gently, hold it, and reassure it that we will take care of it as best we can. We can thank it for getting our attention and listen carefully to what it needs. We can cry, scream, moan, groan, or complain about it if we need to, making the sounds that express the pain to release it verbally. We can let our body move in ways that help to ease or express the pain. We can let our body hurt all it needs to rather than fight it. We can let it be okay for our body to hurt rather than judge it as bad. If we accept the reality of our pain, accommodate it, adapt to it, listen to it, and take good care of it, we will more likely stay in our body—and reconnect with our true self.

Jenny has fibromyalgia, a debilitating, chronic condition that unpredictably generates severe muscle pain, some days more than others. She is in the process of experimenting to see what helps her best tolerate the pain on her "bad" days. Trying to fight her pain to conquer it, trying to make the pain go away, and attempting to ignore the pain have not worked.

Jenny says she is learning to gently surrender to the needs of her body. She has learned that when she eats good food and manages her finances well, her general anxiety is lower and she can then more easily cope with the pain. She has learned that her pain is much worse when she is tired, so she rests and sleeps more on her "bad" days, sometimes simply lying completely still. She also allows her feelings during these painful times, thus permitting herself to complain about the pain and feel sad and compassionate for herself on those days. She has learned that the pain is less and her body more pleasurable in general when she takes really good care of herself and listens carefully to her physical sensations. She has developed a working partnership with her body.

My experience was somewhat similar as I eventually adapted to my broken foot. I gradually learned that pain and immobility were inviting me to listen more carefully to my body. As I became familiar with the various sensations in my body, I felt less afraid. As I learned to separate my bodily sensations from my interpretations of them, I could distinguish what I had no control over from what I had choices about. As I learned to distinguish discomfort from pain, I could rate my bodily sensations on a continuum from zero to ten, as doctors often do. Rather than viewing my body as an enemy attacking me and interfering with my life, I came to understand that we were working together as partners to heal *our* broken foot.

When we put pain on a continuum from zero to ten—zero being no physical sensation at all and ten being intolerable pain—early labor contractions, a mild headache, a cut on a finger, and a sore muscle might be a three. Perhaps a medium headache, the flu, or an overworked muscle would be a five. A sprained ankle, a broken foot, stronger labor contractions, a migraine, a toothache, or chronic lower back pain would likely be a seven or eight. Surgery, a serious car accident, the last few labor contractions, or intense nerve pain would certainly be a ten.

On a continuum, not every discomfort is a ten and not all uncomfortable body sensations are pain. Creating this continuum that distinguishes discomfort from pain helps us to tolerate more pain and all discomforts more easily. It teaches our brain to assess the severity of our discomfort by giving the bodily sensation a number that assesses its intensity rather than simply calling all uncomfortable bodily sensations pain.

Olivia found that she needed to reinterpret the data she was receiving from her body. She had been sick for days, utterly exhausted and worn out from working a high-pressure job that did not fit her personality at all. She had not been sleeping well. She was feeling anxious, overwhelmed, and depressed. Everything seemed hard, and her body was hurting all over. She dreaded going to work but needed the income. She had been pushing her body as hard as she could for months.

I spoke with Olivia as she was beginning to get well again, having missed work for a full week. She said, "Something's got to give, and

I don't want it to be my body." A little later, she said, "My body is screaming, and I've been interpreting it to mean there's something wrong with me or that I have failed somehow." There was her old belief that being sick meant she was a failure. When I asked if there might be a different way to look at this situation, she laughed, saying, "You mean maybe I need to reinterpret the data?"

The end result of that week away from work was that Olivia realized she hated her job and desperately needed to do something different with her life. When she reduced her work hours to part-time and made a choice to go back to school, she immediately began sleeping better and feeling less depressed. She explored various school possibilities and felt excited about feeling back on track in her life—all because she reinterpreted the data her body signals were giving her.

When we learn the language of physical sensations, we reinterpret the signals our body sends us. Rather than fight it as an enemy, we make peace with our body. Instead of judging our body, we listen. We see the Y in the road that offers us an opportunity to reconnect with our body as well as our true self. While pain especially challenges us to build a partnership with our body, pleasure provides unique challenges as well.

ALLOWING PLEASURE

Some of us have as much difficulty allowing pleasure as we do pain. Some of us cannot tolerate a lot of physical pleasure because we find any kind of physical sensations uncomfortable. Some of us believe that if we feel good, something bad will happen later. Some of us believe that we don't deserve pleasure. But we all experience pleasure at times, and the signals come from our body in the same manner that pain does. Can we learn to listen to pleasure, too? Can we learn to *allow* pleasure? Yes, we can.

Pleasure can be either physical pleasure or emotional—or a combination of both. If we put pleasure on a similar continuum from zero to ten, it is easier to allow and enjoy. On this continuum, zero would again be calm with little or no physical sensation. A three on our pleasure scale might be listening to the birds chirping on a spring morning or reading the funnies. Soaking in the tub, enjoying a good book, eating Mom's freshly baked bread pudding, or feeling relaxed after vigorous exercise might be a five. Taking a nap, laughing with a friend, and sex with a treasured partner might be a seven or eight. The relief when a child or spouse safely returns home from war would most certainly be a ten.

While the specific joys and accompanying rated numbers for pleasure vary immensely from one person to another, see if you can listen to your own pleasure messages from your body. What feels good? What warms you when you feel chilled? What cools you off when you are too hot? What kind of touch feels best? What do you feel when pain goes away, when you have had ample rest and alone time, when you are dancing, when you feel accepted as you are, and when you feel deeply loved?

RECONNECTING WITH
OUR TRUE SELF

Our body is a significant helper right here with us at all times. It is a reliable partner—solid, alert, and attentive. Our physical sensations guide us. They teach us how our body works, what needs attention, and what feels good.

When we listen to our body, life flows more smoothly. We are better able to respond effectively to various situations. We remain calmer, regardless of what might be happening around us. We feel safer. Our needs get met more easily because we are more aware of them. We feel better both physically and emotionally and deal with body issues of all kinds sooner. We experience considerably more pleasure and less pain.

When we hear our body, we honor our physical being. We realize that we cannot live this life without our physical being and make peace with this basic fact of our existence. We accept our body—as it is. Perhaps we even feel grateful for it.

When we practice staying in our body, staying longer and leaving less often and for less time, we are reconnecting with our true self.

Home at Last

I'm in here now.
Can you tell?
It's kinda fun.
There's room for me here—
All the room I need, in fact.
I can stretch and grow all I want to
Or curl up and rest
Or even hide when I need to.
Sometimes I still need to hide, you know.
Thanks.
Thanks for giving me a home,
A place I'm wanted
And needed and noticed and listened to.
I've needed that for a long time.
It's dark in here, though—
The dark before the dawn perhaps.
But just like the early dawn
When the sun promises to rise,
My own light begins to shine
And I begin to wiggle and giggle.

Chapter **6**

Engaging
Our Feelings

What Am I Feeling Right Now?

My right arm has been aching for a week. It's clearly talking to me but I have no idea what it is saying. I just know it's hurting. I'm not ignoring this body signal. It just seems silly and embarrassing.

I'm at a retreat in the gorgeous mountains of Colorado that I love so much. The women in this group have now spent several nights together, getting to know each other and sharing more than any of us usually do with friends. While my arm has been getting worse, my heart has softened. My shoulders have dropped in relief. My breathing is deeper and slower. I have even caught myself laughing and smiling more as I have come to feel safer. I am soaking up the unusual support I feel here.

But now it is 4:00 AM—way too early to get up. My shoulders are tight as a stretched rubber band. My jaw feels frozen shut. *Hmmm,* there's that strange frozen sensation again. The enormous energy rumbling around my abdomen is bringing me visions of a volcano about to erupt. My body is jiggling slightly all over with eager energy—or possibly terror. I can't tell which. I just know that I can't go back to sleep. I am aware that some intense, raw feeling is surfacing, and I don't recognize this particular sensation. It isn't sadness, my most comfortable feeling. It isn't joy—that's for sure! It doesn't seem to be fear, although I am more than a bit scared of it.

Oh, no, I think it's *anger*!

But wait a minute. I don't get angry! I *never* get angry! I'm a good girl! I may feel disappointed, hurt, frustrated, frightened, or sad. Those are okay feelings, but anger is despicable, unacceptable. Nice girls don't get angry. Certainly not me! No way. I don't get angry. I'm not going to. . . .

I'm obviously angry. I can no longer deny it. I suddenly remember that voice in the cave that once told me I needed to deal with my anger if I didn't want to develop rheumatoid arthritis. Well, ready or not, it's here! Now what am I supposed to *do* with it?

Several long, nervous hours later, we get together as a group. I manage to share what is going on with me—acutely aware that I need help. As difficult as it is for me to ask for help, I know I don't want to just quietly slink home alone with this scary monster!

The others pull together a few pillows for me to curl up on, inviting me to feel whatever is coming up. I start crying, definitely preferring tears to this mountain of rage I can no longer contain. Slowly, I surrender to what I hope is trustworthy guidance from my body. I listen through the fog of fear and yes, my body actually seems to know what to do. That overpowering, determined energy I had felt earlier begins to move through me. I squeak out some mouse-like, unintelligible noises and push those pillows around a bit, hoping it will be enough.

It's not. My body is still exploding inside. That energy continues to push, grinding me onward into new territory.

As I surrender more and more to the energy flowing through my body, my sounds grow bigger until I think I am actually screaming. No, I'm sure. I am screaming as I have never screamed before—ever! My aching arm begins to push and hit those pillows with a strength I have also never known before. I am big! I am strong! I am *angry*! I'm not angry about anything in particular, not at anyone in particular, just angry, angry, angry. . . .

Surprisingly, how I look or sound to others is not a concern in these surrendering moments. From deep inside my body, these forbidden feelings flow through me on out to the outside. I fully experience them as long and as loudly as my body needs to—and it feels glorious!

Oh, oh. All of a sudden, here I am once again, aware that there are other people around me. Oh, no! What have I done? What are they thinking about me? Have I broken the rules? Are they mad at me? Should I apologize? I'm not sure, but I notice how instantly my thinking has changed to once again focus on those others.

I refuse to look at them. I check inside, pulling my focus inward again. Physically I feel calm. My rage, amazingly, is gone. It's gone! My jaw is relaxed. My arm no longer hurts. My mind is still. I realize I'm no longer angry, and I am no longer afraid of what's inside me. I feel solid. I feel free!

So, inside I am perfectly okay, but now what about those other people? I wonder again about their reactions. What do they think about what I have just done with those forbidden angry feelings?

When I can finally work up enough courage, I cautiously open my eyes and peek at them. Oh, they are still here all right. They are looking right at me, but they aren't criticizing me. They aren't scowling at me. They don't appear to be scared of me or disgusted with me, and they aren't telling me what to do. No one is saying, "Go away; leave me alone." They haven't told me to shut up or get it together, and they haven't left—obviously my worst fears. I feel confused. Being left alone with my feelings is all I have ever known.

Curious, I sit up, slowly looking at each person, seeing their soft, kind eyes. I hear their gentle support and encouraging comments. "Thank you for sharing your deeper feelings." "I feel the same way sometimes." "I'm amazed that your arm doesn't hurt anymore." "No, I wasn't scared because you weren't aiming your anger at me." "Of course we didn't leave." "Thanks for doing your work."

I hear a sigh. My body melts with relief. I have stumbled into a world I have never known, and I *like* it. I can feel my feelings here—even anger.

I definitely want more of this. . . .

OUR FEELINGS—NOT THE ENEMY

Many of us were taught as children that feelings are generally bad. Like the old idiom, *children should be seen and not heard*, we were supposed to take care of our feelings unobtrusively, preferably alone in our room. We were to avoid inconveniencing or embarrassing others with our feelings. We were to smile and behave "appropriately," which usually meant pretending that we didn't have any feelings. In other words, behave and be good girls. Those were the rules of the Good-Girl Jail.

We can trust that if we shut down our feelings, we did so for a good reason, perhaps to be safe or at least to please others. Some of us may now be scared to reopen this door to feelings. After all, we are about to do something we were not allowed to do as children. Common fears about reconnecting with our feelings include becoming uncomfortable, getting embarrassed, feeling stupid, being silly, feeling crazy, being called crazy, getting hurt, making others angry, and the big one—losing control.

The interesting thing is that our fear of feelings tends to stop us from feeling anything *but* fear. Fear is a feeling, after all, and often it is the first feeling that we notice. While fears are not fun, we are not going to die because we are afraid. It is actually safer now to experience all of our feelings than it is to shut them down—much safer in fact. Feelings can be messy and inconvenient, but as we learn more accurate information about them, our fears begin to subside.

This chapter explores the vast, rich world of feelings. Once we reawaken our feelings and learn the truth about them, clearly distinguishing feelings from thoughts and behavior, we become better able to release them safely and purposefully. Engaging our feelings is the third essential self-skill that leads us directly toward reconnecting with our true self.

THE TRUTH ABOUT FEELINGS

Feelings are expressions of our sense of self that help us to know what's what. When we notice a feeling, it is as if our self taps us on the shoulder and says, "Hey, pal, I'm here trying to help you out. Will you listen to *me* for a moment?"

Feelings are a specific part of listening to our body, part of living in partnership with it, and part of living from an internal point of reference. They feel like proof there is a sense of self inside us and are a direct link toward reconnecting with it.

Feelings integrate our body with our mind and spirit. They are the gift that heals and a crucial part of healing past trauma. They tie our past together with the present. They connect all parts of us together and all parts of our life together. They give our life meaning.

As much as some of us may not want to admit it, feelings are natural and normal. We are built to feel, and every feeling has a purpose. Our senses make it possible to notice changes both within us and outside of us, and our feelings then tell us how we are responding to these changes. They help us to know what fits us and what doesn't, who and what we like and don't like. They help us make wise choices, change our environment to better meet our needs, and interact meaningfully with others. They tell us when we need to protect our self or get out of a situation. When we begin to interpret feelings as information and guidance to help us live our life, we find it easier to accept the existence of feelings.

There must be several hundred words in the English language for feelings, illustrating that we are capable of experiencing many varied feelings with many specific nuances. A list of common feelings includes the following:

sad	betrayed	disappointed
angry	calm	frustrated
happy	desperate	confused
scared	excited	curious
loving	playful	inadequate
grateful	vulnerable	powerful
empty	overwhelmed	powerless
alone	hurt	devastated

Feelings are neither good nor bad. They simply are. We tend to think of feelings like joy, love, and happiness as *good* because they feel pleasant and we want them to last. In contrast, we often think of rage, hate, and powerlessness as *bad* feelings because we have had *bad* experiences with them, are uncomfortable feeling them, or simply do not know what to do with them. But feelings are neither good nor bad, and it is not possible to eliminate undesirable feelings to choose only the feelings we want. We need all our feelings to fully experience the wide range of aliveness. All feelings help us reconnect with our true self.

Unfortunate as it may be, we cannot make any particular feeling happen whenever we want to. Something triggers a specific feeling, whether we notice the change that initiates the feeling response or not. When we watch a sad movie, we cry. When someone shares our secret, we feel betrayed. When plans fall through, we feel disappointed—or perhaps elated. So no, we cannot feel happy all the time just because we want to.

Neither can we completely stop all feelings from flowing through us. Some of us may do our best to shut down feelings—at least those that we dread. Addictions, for example, can powerfully numb our awareness of feelings. Other activities may also lessen the intensity, such as keeping too busy or sleeping a lot. Some of us may wish we could shut all our feelings down forever, but we humans simply do not work that way.

STORING FEELINGS FOR LATER

On the other hand, we have an amazing ability as humans to store our feelings to feel them later, if we choose to. Remember my story about the coyote that attacked my dog? The fear came through me *later* when I was home again and safe from the threat. This mechanism allows us to get away from a situation that triggers feelings—perhaps to be safer or more socially acceptable—and then release our feelings later.

When we repeatedly attempt to shut down feelings with no later time to release them, though, what happens is similar to overloading a garbage can. We can stuff and stuff, trying to get more in, but eventually the trash spills over and falls out because it can no longer be contained. Similarly, when our emotional garbage can becomes overloaded, feelings just spill out whenever they can, whether appropriately or not. When someone's emotional garbage can is full and in danger of overflowing, we might hear, "If I let myself start crying,

I'll never stop!" or "You don't even want to know how much anger is inside of me!"

Nora was cautious around her husband, Les. He occasionally snapped at her with fierce anger and criticism. She resented these times so much that she was considering divorce. One day she invited Les to therapy with her and brought up an example of this difficult issue to discuss. He exploded in anger: "Are you still thinking about that? That happened three weeks ago! It's over and done with. Why are you still thinking about it? Can't you see I'm a nice guy?" Les "dumped" a few feelings from his emotional garbage can occasionally so that he could get the lid back on. Doing so helped him continue to believe that he was a nice guy.

Nora's experience was very different from her husband's, however. She got the brunt of his anger when it inappropriately spilled out and she got "trashed." Sharing their experiences with each other turned out to be a good beginning to learning more about releasing feelings appropriately. The truth about feelings is that we all have them. They are natural and normal. Our body already knows how to release them from the inside to the outside, and we are built to do so. But, like Les, some of us need a little help learning what to do with feelings. Distinguishing feelings from both thoughts and behavior is a necessary first step.

DISTINGUISHING FEELINGS FROM THOUGHTS

Feelings are simpler when we separate them from thoughts. Feelings often stimulate thoughts, and thoughts may create feelings. We may not know which comes first, but they are distinctly different activities serving different purposes.

Thinking is a mental activity. The thoughts that develop include ideas, opinions, observations, judgments, beliefs, and conclusions. We experience thoughts privately in our head. They are not known by others unless we communicate them somehow, as with words or facial expressions. Examples of thoughts include the following statements:

"My back hurts."   "My favorite flavor is strawberry."

"I can learn this."   "I can't seem to do anything right today."

"You are pretty."   "I am good at my job."

"I like your T-shirt."   "This chili is too spicy for me."

"I don't like your T-shirt." "I am right; you are wrong."

"She's a good kid."   "That's a good idea."

Sometimes we are surprised by our thoughts. They simply come, all kinds of them, one after another. Sometimes we enjoy our thoughts; sometimes we don't. Often, they are judgmental.

While we cannot stop our thoughts, we have choices about what to do with them. We can ignore thoughts, observe them, react to them, let go of them, or be amused by them. We can also follow them, focusing our thoughts as a way of sorting something through. We can even change the meaning we give to specific thoughts as we gather new information.

Thoughts are real. They are just not always particularly helpful. It can be challenging to know which thoughts are trustworthy and which are irrelevant. We tend to trust the ones that seem logical and make sense. We also tend to trust the thoughts that keep coming back, whether or not they seem rational and true.

Thoughts become less trustworthy when they get mixed up with feelings or are driven by feelings. At these confusing times, we can choose to either stay with our feelings or observe and follow our thoughts. Either choice will bring us more information and clarity.

At one point, I realized I was becoming frightened that my husband would die on one of his many business trips. This particular time I chose to follow my thoughts to see what I could learn.

My thoughts went like this: *He will have a heart attack and suddenly die. I will get the terrible phone call and have to fly there to bring his body home. It will be awful! I won't be able to handle it. I will get overwhelmed and completely fall apart.*

My thoughts ran on and on: *But what if he has his heart attack here? I won't be able to stop a heart attack! What will I do if he dies suddenly right in front of me? What if I wake up next to his dead body?* I began to feel a bit panicky. By this time, I could tell that my thoughts and feelings were completely mixed together. I didn't know what to trust.

Then my thoughts got to the really interesting part: *I can't handle this! I just don't want to go through his death. I need to get out of here immediately. I need to divorce him right now so that I won't have to deal with his death!*

"That seems a little extreme," I said to my thoughts, and they quickly answered back. *Well then, how about this: When he has his heart attack, give him an aspirin, and call 911. Then drive to the airport and get on the next plane out of town!*

Ha! At this point, I actually laughed out loud. I knew I would not leave town if my husband had a heart attack. Fortunately, I also knew that I didn't need to do everything my thoughts told me to do.

When my thoughts got ridiculous, I recognized that feelings were likely the real issue. Thoughts sometimes serve to protect us from feelings. They can easily get mixed up together. Demanding any sudden action when there is no current danger is nearly always a good clue that the deeper issue involves feelings. So, when I heard my thoughts say that I needed to divorce my husband right now to avoid dealing with his death, I was reminded that I could choose to follow either my thoughts or my feelings.

When I then "slid under" the thoughts to follow my feelings instead, I quickly began to cry. I clearly didn't want my husband to die. As I moved through my fear of him dying, the thoughts calmed down. I remembered that I couldn't know what would happen in the future, but I didn't have to divorce my husband to avoid dealing with his death. I could choose to stay with him . . . even if he died. And while his sudden death, if it happened, would indeed be a challenging situation, I would ultimately be okay. I chose to stay, and the bothersome thoughts melted away after doing this work. Sorting feelings from thoughts is not always easy and can be confusing. Journaling is an excellent tool for this purpose. There is no need to monitor sentence structure or penmanship when we journal, as it is not for anyone else to read. In fact, it is imperative to protect journaling from others in order to write freely and honestly.

To begin journaling for this purpose, sit alone in a quiet place that feels safe to you and draw a vertical line down the middle of a piece of paper. Label the two sides "Thoughts" and "Feelings." Ask yourself, "What am I thinking right now?" and write whatever answer comes to you on that side of the paper, whether or not it seems rational or true. When you are ready to shift, ask yourself, "What am I feeling right now?" and write whatever comes to you on the other side of the paper, whether or not it initially seems to make sense. Journaling in this way can help you to distinguish your thoughts from your feelings.

DISTINGUISHING FEELINGS
FROM BEHAVIOR

We also confuse feelings with behavior. Behaviors are body movements, most of which can be readily seen by others when they are looking at us. They are our actions, our conduct, what we do.

We experience behaviors in various parts of our body, depending upon which muscles and joints are moving. They can be large movements, like jumping, or nearly imperceptible movements, like swallowing. They can be important movements, like signing our name, or nearly meaningless, like wiggling our toes. They can be valued behaviors, like feeding a child, or repulsive behaviors, like vomiting—depending on how we judge the specific behaviors.

Other examples of behaviors include the following:

Texting	Fixing a bicycle
Running	Making eye contact
Journaling	Telling a story
Arguing	Driving a car
Walking	Hugging
Crying	Singing

Feelings and thoughts are internal sensations that spontaneously happen and cannot be seen by others unless we choose to share them. Behavior, in contrast, can be observed by others and may affect them. We are not responsible for our thoughts and feelings, but we *are* responsible for our behavior. Behavior is presumed to be chosen. Comparing the three lists of examples for behaviors, thoughts, and feelings can further clarify the differences.

Sometimes both feelings and thoughts get mixed up with behavior. As a child, Olivia was told to protect her little brother. When she couldn't stop an older boy from beating up her brother one day, she felt powerless. Her mother then punished her and told her she didn't deserve to play if she didn't protect her brother. Olivia concluded from that experience that when she feels powerless, she is bad and doesn't deserve good things. By the time I met her, she had deprived herself of pleasure for many years.

The feeling in this example is *powerlessness*. The thought represented here is *I am bad*. The behavior is refusing to allow goodness and pleasure. While obviously intertwined, the three can be distinguished.

When Olivia learned to distinguish feelings from thoughts and behavior, she could see that feeling powerless didn't make her a bad person—or a good person for that matter. Instead of being a dreadful truth about her as a person, powerless became simply another feeling. Then she could feel powerless at times and still allow herself to have fun.

Feelings tend to be simpler than we think they are. When we separate feelings from thoughts and behavior, they become easier to listen to.

LISTENING TO FEELINGS

A feeling arises as a wave of energy that appears to come out of nowhere without any conscious choice. Like an ocean wave, it washes over and through us, uncomfortably increasing in intensity, temporarily throwing our emotional equilibrium off balance, and then decreasing until our emotional equilibrium is fully regained.

Like other bodily processes, feelings get our attention and if we don't shut them down, our body naturally releases whatever needs to be released. Then we feel comfortable again. It is not our choice whether or not to have feelings any more than it's our choice to sneeze.

Eighteen-month-old children remind us what comes naturally to us all when there is no build-up inside of stored feelings. They are at the height of freely and fully experiencing many feelings without yet shutting them down. When a toddler feels angry, she shows it with her entire body. She plops her little bottom on the floor, throws her arms around, and makes loud noises. The *tantrum*, as we call it, may last only a few minutes but is often very intense. When finished, the toddler quickly gets up and finds something else to do, having completely released her feeling response to whatever had happened in her environment. Hence, there are no feelings leftover to hang on to or shut down. Sadness, fear, and joy are also short-lived but very intense at this age. This is how we are built to process feelings.

To relearn to move through a feeling as an adult means to notice the feeling coming up inside us, claim it as ours, and then release it, letting the energy flow safely from our body both physically and emotionally. To notice, claim, and release means to listen to our feelings and work in partnership with our body to flow into the feelings and through them.

When a feeling begins, we feel a physical shift, a change in our body that gets our attention. We become aware of the surge of energy coming from within us that is the language of feelings. We may start to feel uncomfortable and tense. Our mood changes. Our thoughts change. Our behavior changes. We might feel irritated and inconvenienced. We might get teary. Our pulse increases. Our breathing may get faster—or more shallow. We likely feel some physical sensations, perhaps in our neck, back, stomach, or jaw. We probably stop doing whatever we were doing before the feeling started. We may not even know what the feeling is, yet we can tell that *something* is coming. This is how I knew something was coming when I was at that retreat, even before I knew it was anger.

Gradually, as the wave of feeling increases in intensity, we get more and more uncomfortable. By this time, we may know what the feeling is and our thoughts may be getting quite busy, perhaps trying to distract us from the feeling. This is the point at which some of us shut down and follow our thoughts instead, as I first did when I was afraid my husband would die. Instead of shutting down at this Y in the road, we can choose to go toward the feeling, stay with it, and invite it to stay with us. This might take five seconds. It might take twenty minutes or even an hour. The amount of time doesn't matter, but learning to listen to our feelings at the Y in the road matters a great deal—if we want to reconnect with and experience our true self.

When we listen to our feelings more frequently, we increase our tolerance for feelings. Our entire inner system seems to learn that it is again safe and acceptable to feel our feelings.

We also learn to move through both a wider variety of feelings and more intense feelings. We come to know from experience what our feelings are all about and how our particular body needs to release different feelings. Our body guides us to what needs to be done to fully release the energy of each feeling. Our body thus shows us how to release our feelings. All we need to do is listen.

Different people release feelings in different ways, even though the general process is the same. Some people need to make sounds or express their feelings verbally (saying specific things to somebody who is not present, swearing, screaming, grunting, growling, or sighing). Others need to physically move (make faces, kick, hit, tremble, throw something, curl up, or hide under the covers). Some of us need to both move and make sounds to release feelings.

At some point, the wave of feeling crests on its own and begins to subside until it naturally melts away. We can tell we have completed a wave of feeling when our thoughts calm and our body relaxes. Sometimes we feel so relaxed that we describe the sensation as being tired or crying ourselves to sleep. It is this *completion* of the wave of feeling that brings the full release that comes so naturally for toddlers who have not yet shut down.

Completion is the part that rewards our hard work and encourages us to want more release. That is what I experienced for the first time when I processed through that wave of long-buried anger. That is what felt so incredibly glorious.

Notice, claim, release: this process, repeated over and over as different feelings arise, can clear the garbage can of old stuffed feelings leftover from previous experiences. It doesn't matter which feelings we process through, but it matters that we learn to release them effectively—and safely.

RELEASING FEELINGS SAFELY

The one necessary rule as we learn to move through feelings is to do it safely—safely for us as well as for all others. This means not hurting our own body in any way, not hurting the body of anyone else, and not intentionally hurting others either verbally or emotionally. All feelings, regardless of how intense they may be, can be fully processed through in ways that are safe for everyone. Hurting our self or others is never a necessary part of releasing feelings.

We can thus yell and scream all we want to—as long as we are not aiming our anger directly at other people. We can throw things—as long as we are not throwing them at other people or destroying property. We can say nasty things about others—as long as we are away from the person we have the feelings about. If we release our feelings away from the person who may have triggered them, we are much less likely to verbally trash someone else the way Les did when he aimed his overflowing anger at Nora.

When we invite our current feelings, old feelings often surface, too, and we may find it difficult to distinguish the two. We may believe we are grieving about a current loss when we are also grieving past losses. We may feel sad about a child's situation when we are also crying about something that happened to us. We may feel certain that our intense anger toward someone is completely justified, when, in reality, we are experiencing a flashback to the same feeling we experienced years ago in response to a different person.

Eventually, we learn that our feelings have very little to do with other people. They are *our* feelings. They come to clarify how we are responding to what has happened or changed. They may come to help us know what we need to do. They definitely come to help us feel alive and to reconnect with our true self. Yes, they are about *me* and for *me*—not about others.

Below is a list of specific skills helpful for safely noticing, claiming, and releasing our feelings. This list will help you assess your current strengths as well as the specific areas in which you may need assistance:

- ✦ I know the difference between feelings, thoughts, and behaviors.
- ✦ I can temporarily calm my feelings when necessary and appropriate.
- ✦ I can identify when feelings are coming up inside me.
- ✦ I can tolerate the discomfort of feelings.
- ✦ I accept feelings in general as purposeful and helpful.
- ✦ I can experience a wide range of feelings (sad, mad, glad, scared, etc.).
- ✦ I know that feelings do not make me a bad person.
- ✦ I no longer blame others for my feelings.
- ✦ I remain aware of my present surroundings when I am dealing with feelings.
- ✦ I am confident I will not hurt anyone when I feel my feelings alone.
- ✦ I have at least one person I can call if I need help with my feelings.

This chapter, other books, friends, and support groups may offer all the help you need, but if you are in any danger whatsoever of hurting yourself or others when you invite your feelings to surface, then I suggest you seek the assistance of a trained professional psychotherapist.

A major part of being in psychotherapy is learning to safely and effectively release feelings. This includes learning both sets of skills—the skills to temporarily shut down feelings when necessary and appropriate, and the skills to notice, claim, and release feelings as described in this chapter. Once we have developed both sets of skills, we can choose what best fits us with any particular feeling in any particular situation. We can choose to either process it through when the feeling arises or temporarily shut it down to move through it later in a more appropriate situation. When we develop both sets of skills and the confidence to use them both safely and effectively at a Y in the road, we know we can trust our self to listen to our feelings.

RECONNECTING WITH OUR TRUE SELF

Feelings can certainly be inconvenient and uncomfortable—perhaps even painful at times. They are not always fun, and sometimes they appear to complicate our life and interfere with getting things done. So why do we even bother listening to them? As one of my clients once said, "Why bother? Feelings don't change anything."

What she said is partially true. Experiencing feelings—to notice, claim, and release feelings—will not change the external reality of any current situation. However, doing so changes everything inside us so that we can think clearly, make better decisions, take more effective action, better cope with adversity, and reconnect with our true self.

Releasing feelings clears us out internally, creating room for new things to come in. When we empty the barrel of sadness, we create room for joy. When we move through the fog of fear, we create room for curiosity and become open to new experiences. When we release the mountain of rage, we create room for loving relationships. We relax our physical body and clear our mind of unneeded worries. In other words, we empty our emotional garbage can.

When we listen to our feelings, a door opens wide to bring us more completely into the present. Then we can more fully experience holding a newborn baby or walking with a friend, watch in awe when the full moon rises or we see a mountain lion in the wild, and feel our sadness when a friend moves away or a child gets hurt. And we can laugh when something tickles our funny bone.

When we engage our feelings, we accept the emotional part of our being at a fundamental level, realizing that feelings are an essential part of being fully alive. We acknowledge a partnership with our feelings and accept the gifts that come with being an emotional creature. And yes, we reconnect with our true self.

The Promise of Tears

Earthquakes all around,
Fears splashing like tidal waves
Fast encroaching on my personal garden.
Tears come, then some more,
And more and more,
Pulling me down into my protective cocoon.
Shaking, hiding,
Downtrodden, alone again.
Will this last forever?
Hope evaporated.
Oh, where did it go?
Can't find my garden,
My anchor, my safety,
My me.
But look! There through the blur of tears
And the fog of sniffles,
The sun returns,
Rising again all peachy and orange,
Bringing light again to my darkness,
Life again to dawn,
Peace to my soul.
And bringing me back home.

PART III
REBUILDING OUR TRUE SELF

REBUILD:
strengthen
gain energy or vigor
increase one's capacity to act

As we repeatedly choose to reconnect with our true self, the differences between being connected and losing that connection become more obvious. Emphasizing the choices we make, effectively utilizing our time alone, and updating our core beliefs are three powerful ways to purposefully rebuild our sense of self to more consistently maintain that precious connection.

*"To be yourself in a world that
is constantly trying to make you
something else is the greatest
accomplishment."*

—Ralph Waldo Emerson

Emphasizing Choices

How Many Possibilities Can I See?

I finally ended my relationship with Miles. It happened when my mother came to visit six months after my black eye. I had spent that time in between listening internally, discovering the surprising strength of a deeper truth I had never before known. I realized for perhaps the first time in my life that I truly had a right to be safe in this world, a right to take whatever action I deemed necessary to keep myself safe.

We were in the basement arguing. Actually Miles was pulling my hair and we were both screaming. I don't even remember the particular issue that started it all, but this time felt different. All of a sudden I couldn't do it anymore—the arguing, the violence, the ups and downs—not even for those occasional loving crumbs that were so wonderful when they came my way. I couldn't live this way anymore.

I couldn't violate my own integrity anymore. I couldn't do it to my kids, I couldn't do it to my mother, and now I finally couldn't do it to *me*. It just wasn't right. Nothing about the violence felt right. After three long years, it suddenly wasn't worth it anymore. I was done.

My body sank into doneness. My mind wouldn't argue anymore. I just quit participating. Something inside me screamed "NO MORE!" Something in my body shifted. Something clicked into place. I didn't think about how I was going to end our relationship. I just knew all the way to my toenails that I had to do it. The time had finally come.

That awakening moment wasn't big and it wasn't dramatic. I didn't scream in rage. I simply and calmly said something direct like, "It's over, Miles. I want you to move out." And he was gone.

Well, it wasn't quite that simple, of course, but he is gone now and I've declared a five-year moratorium on relationships. Five years? Yes, five years. Something inside keeps telling me it's what I need to do, so I'm doing it. While I don't completely understand where this idea is coming from, I trust it. I'm listening. Even I have laughed about it at times and my friends don't really believe me, but I am serious. I need some time alone. I need a lot of time alone.

It scares me how much I surrendered to Miles. It scares me how much I began to lose my connection with my sense of self again. I didn't even think that was possible. I can't forget that NO ME LEFT moment that became such a turning point when Susan asked me that magical question. I don't *ever* want to feel that empty again!

Five years seems extreme, I know, but after a divorce and now a battering relationship, I comprehend that I need to change something significant about how I am living my life. I certainly need to quit looking for a man to attach to! That's all I really know. I need to take long enough to reorganize my life around something different— but *what*? I'm not yet sure. I don't see many alternatives. I obviously don't know what else is possible. I just know for now that I don't want my old way. Something needs to give, and I certainly don't want it to be my precious connection with my true self.

I can already see that living without a primary partner—without even the intention of finding someone else—is giving me a long-overdue, badly needed opportunity to rebuild and strengthen this true self I now finally know. Little by little, I am discovering what I like, who I like, how I want the furniture arranged, what kind of blankets I like on my bed, how I like my eggs, and what music I enjoy. With no man to defer to, I am slowly building my own friendships, my own career, and my own parenting style. I am sometimes lonely and uncomfortable, but that's not so bad anymore either.

I am finding my truth. Is it possible to center my life on that? I'm not sure yet, but I can tell I am learning to think for myself. And most importantly, I am learning to make my own choices.

WHAT WE HAVE LEARNED ABOUT CHOICES

We have a basic right to make our own choices. Of course we do. Because our brain is capable of becoming aware of what we want, what we need, and what we like, we are able to learn to make the choices that best meet our individual needs. Yet, many of us make choices we later regret, choices that are self-destructive, or choices that consistently meet the needs of others at the expense of our own needs.

Why do we do that? We have all learned from our childhood experiences what happens when we make various choices. Maybe we got hugged when we cleaned our room. Maybe we won ribbons when we ran really fast. Maybe we were praised when we finished a big school project. But maybe we got scolded when we played too much or made too much noise. Maybe we were told to do it alone when we asked for help. Maybe we got slapped for being angry. Children are astute observers and notice what happens when they make different kinds of choices.

Some of us learned and may now still believe as adults that we are incapable of making choices—at least *good* choices, the *right* choices that follow the rules and please other people. Some of us may not try anymore to make our own choices, believing that we should simply give in and do what others want. Some of us are too scared to choose what we really want. Some of us are really scared. We may no longer even see the multitude of choices we genuinely have available to us and feel trapped into doing only the few options we see in front of us. It is part of the Good-Girl Jail.

If we don't honor our own choices now as adults, our reference point continues to be external. Our choices get made on the basis of whatever rules we think apply to the current situation, what others will think of us, who might get mad, or what danger threatens us—external factors. Making choices this way makes us vulnerable to the whims of others—the neighbors, our employers, friends, advertising—and battering relationships.

Making our own active choices, in contrast, rebuilds our precious core, our sense of self. Just as we have learned to take action to feel safer in the world, to stay in our body, and to notice, claim, and release our feelings to reconnect with our sense of self, we can now learn to make our own active choices to rebuild and strengthen our self. It is our choice at the Y in the road.

This chapter defines active choices, distinguishing them from the automatic passive choices we frequently make from an external reference point. It describes the powerful tool of brainstorming and the overall process of becoming clear to know what choices best fit us. It suggests simple ways to begin building our skills to make active choices and shows us how doing so rebuilds our true self.

DEFINING ACTIVE CHOICES

Active choices are intentional and conscious. We are alert to what we are doing and we do it on purpose. No one else is making the choices, and we are not making them primarily to please others. Active choices are the ones that fit us best and most effectively meet our own genuine needs.

When our choices are active, it doesn't mean that they are anti-others. Our brain tends to be quite dualistic about this issue, often seeing only the two options of either meeting our own needs *or* meeting the needs of others. Active choices rarely have much to do with others. They are what we *just know* we must do—as I *just knew* I needed to end my relationship with Miles.

Passive choices, in contrast, are best illustrated by those times we simply let things happen as they usually do or we just go along with others. It is easy to be unaware of the many passive choices we make. When we are driving, for example, we sometimes make a passive choice to drive on autopilot, going directly home as we usually do when we had intended to first stop at the grocery store. While laughable at times, this phenomenon can be inconvenient or even embarrassing.

Many of us passively eat the same thing for breakfast every morning, brush our teeth in the same way each time, or drive the same way to work. We call these repeated patterns routines that simplify our life. They are also passive choices.

Another interesting place to observe passive choices is when making decisions with siblings and parents. As children, we likely went along with whatever our parents decided to do. Now as adults, are we still doing the same thing, perhaps in the name of being respectful? Are we really making active choices or are we just passively going along to keep the peace?

Our challenge is to make the choices that best fit us, and active choices are more likely to fit us than passive choices.

Let's look more closely at how we make our choices.

NO MORE

I have observed a turning point for many of us that I have come to call NO MORE. It is a point of no return, a point when we have reached our absolute limit about something that we can no longer tolerate. Prior to this point, we couldn't yet do whatever seemed essential to do and after this point we know we must take the risk. We might not yet know how we are going to do it, but we know deep down that we will. The internal gears seem to shift on their own, and we are not likely to go backward. This is the point I reached that moment in the basement when I knew I was ending my relationship with Miles—no matter what it took and no matter what happened next.

This NO MORE point is not merely an intellectual decision to do something we believe we should do. It does not always feel rational. It cannot be reached on purpose or to please anyone else. We get there when we get there, and it takes whatever it takes to get there. Some call it "hitting bottom" or "hitting the wall." Jenny, the woman who adapted so well to fibromyalgia, affectionately calls it "going bonkers." It is our absolute personal limit. We can no longer continue living our life the way in which we have up to this point. While sometimes terrifying, NO MORE is also a precious opportunity to make the choices that deep down we may have already wanted to make. From this point, we can only move forward in our life.

NO MORE is one way we make the choices we need to make. It works, but it is sometimes harsh and sudden. There is a more gentle way to make active choices.

The Need to Become Clear

Many clients come into their first session confused about what to do, saying something like, "I don't know whether to stay with my husband (job, girlfriend, parents) or leave." They feel the need to become clear about some kind of decision but have been unable to do so. Often they can see only two options—to stay or to leave—and neither option feels comfortable. Or perhaps they know they need to leave but can't for some reason or don't yet feel ready. This kind of confusion is a good reason to seek professional help. The actual decision made, however, may turn out to be less important than developing the skills to become clear about the choices we make.

Common clues that we may be stuck in our external reference point when we want to become clear to make a more active choice include the following:

♦ Not knowing what we want to do
♦ Being scared to make a mistake, do something wrong, or hurt others
♦ Trying to be a good girl/wife/person/mother/employee/patient/grandma
♦ Deferring decisions to others viewed as more important
♦ Saying, "I don't care" or "It doesn't matter"
♦ Feeling stuck, trapped, or crazy
♦ Making the same decision over and over but not following through
♦ Seeing only one or two options that we don't like
♦ Knowing what we *should* do but not wanting to do it
♦ Being unable to stop thinking about a particular issue

Once we become aware that we want to make an active choice, brainstorming becomes critical.

The Power of Brainstorming

There are millions of possibilities—well, at least many more than we can possibly imagine. Brainstorming reminds us that this is true. Knowing that there are many possibilities is what makes our choice a genuine active choice.

I find a lot of downy bird feathers. I find them out on hiking trails and on city streets. I sometimes even find them inside buildings—everywhere, it seems. One day I asked a couple of friends if they also found downy bird feathers. When both said no, they didn't, I wondered why I was finding them.

I went for a long sunrise walk alone in the foothills. Completely open to all possibilities, I finally asked the question I wanted the answer to: "Why am I finding all these downy bird feathers?" What came to me in that openness was that a downy feather was the logo for my private practice as a psychotherapist.

Then the rest of my deeper truth also came to me. My image of the Y in the road at the time was standing on the edge of a cliff. I had always been afraid to jump off that cliff. I was afraid I wouldn't be able to fly, which was what I believed I had to be able to do. The only alternative I could see was the other extreme of crashing and burning at the bottom of the cliff like in the old cartoons—*splat!* Both options were terrifying to me, as I was quite certain I could not fly. I would then cling to the edge of that imaginary cliff, unable to move. This frightening image had stopped me from taking risks and making my own active choices many, many times.

On that walk, I began to understand that those downy bird feathers were showing me a third option. I could take the risk of symbolically stepping off that cliff to see what would happen if I floated, the way a downy bird feather does, riding the air currents for support and guidance. I realized that day that there are always more options than

I can see and that I can choose whatever best fits *me*. The support and guidance I need will be there to trust, just like the air currents for a downy feather.

If our brain can only see one option, we tend to feel trapped into doing something we may not want to do. Maybe that one option doesn't fit, but it is the only path we can see. We may push ahead to do it, but we often get immobilized and just feel stupid or crazy.

If our brain can see two options, we may jump back and forth between the two, still unable to make a choice. We may even list the advantages and disadvantages of each option but then crumple up the paper and throw it away, vaguely aware that some choices cannot be made in that logical manner.

Some choices are, in fact, too big or too important to only make rationally. They need to be made from our true self. To make this shift, we need to know there are many possible options—at least more than two. Brainstorming with a friend can help and it can be fun, as others nearly always see more possibilities than we do. Playful options can help to expand the list and can lighten the intensity of a difficult decision. After all, we could always stand in the corner all day, clean the house from top to bottom, make chicken soup, dance like a fool, or wax the car.

Generating many options, including ridiculous ones, often leads to the clarity we need about what choice feels right. I used to be amazed when my son and daughter wondered what to do about some worry they had. We would have fun generating possibilities, including ridiculous ones. Then they would suddenly run off knowing what they needed to do but not even bothering to announce their decision.

We don't need others to tell us how to live our life. We have had plenty of that. We need others to help us open the door to our own life, to open our minds to the millions of choices available when we are ready to choose to live our own life.

When We Still Can't See Options

If we still cannot see multiple options in a situation, we might be caught in the old vortex of rules and roles beginning to experience its downward spiral. We may feel considerable pressure to do something we don't want to do. Perhaps we don't want to do what we believe is expected of us. We may feel angry, trapped, powerless, or afraid to make the choices we want to make. We may feel victimized by life not being fair, by others cruelly hurting us, or by believing that God is punishing us. Maybe we desperately want to blame someone else for our misery. We might begin to use our addictions to numb our resentments. We might sit in despair—that endless pit that appears to have no way out—completely immobilized and unable to take any action, unable to make any choices. Maybe we refuse to go on, seemingly frozen in time. Maybe we feel stuck in misery. Suicide may begin to play its seductive game with us, promising peace forever. We might feel stuck in the same old patterns we don't like, the same old outcomes we keep trying to avoid, the same old . . .

As we spiral down at these times, our negative thoughts and beliefs seem to devour our spirit—"emotional cannibalism" as John Powers humorously describes in his book *Odditude*.[27] Sonia, the woman who chose to nurse her baby when he was hungry, calls it "drowning in negativity." I call it landing back in the Good-Girl Jail.

What is often going on during these dark times is that we are unable to see the many options available to us, because we are remembering ever-so-clearly the expectations of what significant others have told us we *should* do. What if we learned to interpret these stifling negative times differently? What if we see these awkward times as signs in the maze of life that simply say "dead end; find an alternative." Perhaps they are the kick in the pants we need sometimes to generate more possibilities. Without judging these times as bad, we can then move on to try something different that might work better. We can shift the "shoulds" to "coulds," understanding that we are simply having a moment of difficulty seeing options. We could say, "*Hmmm* . . . that didn't work very well. I need to try something different." In doing so, we learn to trust our own learning curve. We learn that there are always more possibilities than we can see. We learn to grow beyond the Good-Girl Jail.

❖   ❖   ❖

Jade came to therapy following a serious attempt to kill herself. Some days were more difficult than others for her to get through, but we soon learned that she was experiencing flashbacks. When she felt suicidal, intense feelings about the traumatic events earlier in her life were coming through—mostly rage, powerlessness, and terror. Something was telling her to kill herself *right now*. She experienced no other option at these times, which made them especially frightening.

With determination to get well, Jade learned to call me at these times and we would explore what was coming up for her emotionally. Every time she could notice, claim, and release these feelings from the past, her suicidal impulses melted away. When she learned to see this pattern as her thoughts attempting to protect her from the traumatic memories and their accompanying leftover feelings, she learned that she didn't have to act on the thoughts and impulses to kill herself *right now*. No, she didn't need to kill herself at all. That wasn't the issue. Suicide was never her only option. She just couldn't see other options in the middle of the flashbacks.

Jade thus learned that when she noticed, claimed, and released the feelings from her past, she could once again see more options for herself in the present. She learned to make the active choices that best fit her whenever she came to that Y in the road.

There are always more options—always.

THE CHOICE POINT

Once we know that many options are truly possible, our world begins to open up. We no longer feel so pressured to do things we do not want to do. We reach that *choice point*, that glorious specific moment in which we experience a genuinely free choice at the Y in the road.

We may then need some time alone to become clear which choice fits us best for the particular issue or situation in front of us. Sometimes we need a great deal of time alone. We can journal, take a long walk, pull weeds, pray, breathe, meditate, do yoga, sleep on it, or whatever else helps us to shut out external distractions long enough to turn inward to listen to our self. Usually we need more time than we think we should need, as this part of the process cannot be rushed. Active choices do not go by the clock and definitely do not respond well to deadlines.

Sometimes we ask others what to do in a particularly confusing situation. While sometimes a good idea, asking for help can be tricky. If we ask others for their opinions regarding what we *should* do, they will likely tell us what they think we should do—and then expect us to do it. We might then stop thinking for our self, especially if we feel judged or intimidated by that particular person.

It works better to ask others for help with ideas and possible options regarding what we *could* do. We are then asking for help with the brainstorming portion of the process rather than help with the becoming clear portion—two very different and distinct steps in the choice-making process. We need to keep thinking for our self in order to make active choices.

I remember when we named our dog. My son Eric, my daughter Sarah, a friend, and I sat around one afternoon brainstorming all kinds of names, none of which seemed quite right. We even came up with some ridiculous options like Hortense and Neptune. Then when I awoke the next morning, I *just knew* her name was Elliott. I couldn't explain how I had come up with that name, especially since she was a female, but I *just knew* that it fit. We had brainstormed possibilities, and then I had literally slept on it to shift to that deeper level of clarity that comes when we reconnect with our sense of self. And yes, the name fit her well.

Humor can also help us to get clear. Celeste and Seth came to see me for marital issues. Seth couldn't handle any confrontation or anger whatsoever. Anytime Celeste wanted to discuss something about their relationship, Seth would start talking about ending their relationship and moving to Mexico. They were getting nowhere on their own. Moving to Mexico had become a serious issue to both of them. When I asked Seth about it, he hesitated but acknowledged that he would never actually do it. It was his way of saying that he felt like running away from conflict. As he developed his skills to take smaller breaks when he felt like running away, he walked around the block. Moving to Mexico then became a ridiculous option that brought them both some much-needed laughter—but only once it had become truly a ridiculous option for both of them.

Our clarity will come sooner or later and we can tell when it does. We might wake up one morning and *just know*, or someone else might say or do just the right thing and then we *just know*. When we finally become clear and find the choice that best fits *me*, we feel settled inside. We feel relief. Our brain quits thinking about the issue and our body relaxes. We feel free. We smile. Everything inside says YES! Nothing else feels more trustworthy in that moment, and we become able to follow through with our choice.

Even if we feel hesitant about following through, we know that we can and that we will. We may not understand why we need to do this certain thing or what the ultimate meaning or outcome might be, but we know we need to do it. We may not even know how to do it, but we know we need to do it. While it can feel lonely and risky, our clarity always feels right deep down inside of us. It fits our true self. This internal peaceful feeling makes becoming clear worth the time and effort the process takes.

When I reached NO MORE that day in the basement with Miles, I felt all these signs of clarity. It was indeed a lonely and risky moment, but that peaceful "this is right" feeling in my gut that no one could have talked me out of stayed solid. I needed to end our relationship—no matter what followed.

PRACTICING ACTIVE CHOICES

Rather than wait for that dramatic NO MORE moment to become clear, it is easier to practice making active choices about things we believe will not affect other people or even show to other people. Maybe we make the same choices we have made passively, but we make them more consciously and intentionally. For example:

+ I choose to eat oatmeal for breakfast this morning.
+ I choose to drive to work a different way today.
+ I choose to wear this grubby, old T-shirt.
+ I choose to read this book.
+ I choose to listen to bluegrass music.
+ I choose to go to sleep now.
+ I choose to take some time to pet my cat.

If the language "I choose" is too strong for you at this point, you can begin with "I am petting my cat right now" or "I like to pet my cat."

It is difficult to describe how powerful it felt for me to say "I choose to throw away this piece of junk mail" when I went through my mail each day after I had ended my relationship with Miles. While it seemed silly to speak these words out loud, I could feel the strength that was rebuilding internally when I did it privately every day for several months—until I could go on to active choices that showed more to others.

As we keep practicing simple choices, our skills build so that we keep thinking for our self more and more of the time. We discover that it is safer now to make our own choices than to allow others to make choices for us—no matter how significant those others may be. And when we become ready and get more courageous, taking bigger and riskier steps, our active choices quite naturally begin to be noticed by others.

WHEN WE ARE READY

Readiness is a developmental term referring to a level of required maturation necessary to learn a new skill.[28] We can't learn to walk until we are ready. We can't become toilet trained until we are ready. We can't learn to read until we are ready. It's difficult to leave home when we are not yet ready. Until we are ready, we ignore, fight, and reject learning any new skills or information and often are not yet even interested in doing so, as the new task seems to hold no meaning for us. Then later, one day when we are genuinely ready, we are not only open and eager to learn that new skill or piece of information but we are interested in it, seek it out, and put forth the effort needed to engage in it.

In adults, we see a readiness to be promoted at work, to get married, to have children, to have our grown children leave home, to retire, to quit smoking, to start exercising—and to make active choices that show to others. We can feel this readiness in our body when it comes—an unusual, new energy flowing or perhaps a slight eagerness for something new that hasn't been there before. Life-changing experiences like divorce, working for an overly controlling employer, hitting bottom with an addiction, and giving so much to others that there is NO ME LEFT tend to facilitate our readiness to make active choices.

Connie came to see me saying that she needed to leave her husband but was having extreme difficulty doing so. Four years later she filed for divorce, but those long four years were remarkably full of growth until she was genuinely *ready* to leave her marriage.

Connie's husband was cruel to their children, in her opinion, holding the younger one too close, completely ignoring the middle one, and critically pushing the older one away. Connie gradually became clear that she couldn't divorce her husband until all three were old enough and safe enough to make their own choices. In the meantime, she moved to a house nearby so that the children could walk back and forth between their parents' two homes as they needed to. In this way, she intentionally gave her children a second home option that included consistency, respect for their needs, room to practice making their own active choices, emotional safety, and encouragement for expressing their own feelings and meeting their own needs.

When all three became strong enough to think for themselves and make their own active choices around their dad, Connie filed for divorce, continuing to provide the consistent anchor her children needed. All the way through the transition, she took one step at a time when she was ready and the timing felt right. She emphasized each active choice along the way. Recognizing her own readiness and seeing options at every step of the way were powerful parts of divorcing her husband in this manner that best fit her integrity. When we honor our natural need for readiness, active choices become much easier.

REBUILDING OUR TRUE SELF

We have grown up in families where parents set the rules. We went to schools where teachers set the rules. We work where bosses set the rules and live in communities where laws set the rules. There have always been rules, and many of us have been well trained to defer to them. Of course, it is scary to step forward and say that our true self matters. We don't automatically have confidence that we can make active choices. It is a learning process.

The critical aspect of making active choices is not about making the *right* decisions according to others, and it certainly is not about getting our own way all the time. The critical part is the *process* of generating options, becoming clear, and taking action toward the choices that best fit our sense of self. As we choose what to do, how to do it, and when to do it, we are choosing to grow beyond the Good-Girl Jail. We are rebuilding the strength of our true self.

Every time we make an active choice, no matter how small and irrelevant to others that choice may be, it feels as if the universe issues us one of those tiny children's Lego blocks as a reward. It goes into that giant emptiness in our gut. Eventually, these little blocks fill our emptiness so that we feel much more solid inside. That is our internal, true self rebuilding—and it is indeed precious.

Possibilities

Sometimes suicide taps me on the shoulder
And seduces me with promises of instant freedom:
"No pain over here,
Nothing to worry about,
Nothing you have to do."
Sounds like, "C'mon in, the water's fine."
Is it a trick? What is suicide really like?
I wonder. I think about it.
I consider the possibility.
Then I remember the effort it took
To get born into this life,
To graduate from school,
To give birth to my precious children,
To grow through relationships ending,
To move, to change jobs—
Even to make my daughter's wedding dress.
I remember that effort does have rewards.
I remember that pain is never permanent—
And that life actually does go on.
There are other possibilities inviting me, too,
Like hiking in the woods,
Writing books, taking a nap,
And playing in my garden.
Why choose just one?
If life is a smorgasbord of possibilities,
Why would I eat only liver and onions?

Chapter **8**

Cherishing Time Alone

What Would Nourish Me Today?

I am spending my first Christmas alone. Growing up and when I was in college I was always home for Christmas, meaning at my parents' house. When I was married to Tom, I spent Christmas with my husband and our kids, even when we went to our childhood homes. After my marriage dissolved, I still spent Christmas with my kids—until this year. This year, they are spending their entire winter break with their dad, and I am alone for Christmas.

I am in the middle of my five-year moratorium on relationships. I have struggled at times, I'll admit. Sometimes I feel relieved to simply have more time to myself to catch up on sleep or other things that need doing like shopping, cleaning, and paying bills. But sometimes I don't know what to do with myself. There are times when I feel so scared that even a baby sleeping in the next room would help me feel safer. Cooking for one has always felt weird and sometimes unnecessary when popcorn would do. The first time I went to the movies by myself was a major accomplishment, and driving six hundred miles by myself to visit my mother has been my biggest alone accomplishment of all.

Sometimes I want to do things but can't find anyone to do them with me, so I stay home, pouting and resentful. One empty weekend I really wanted to go skiing. I called everyone I knew who skied, but no one could go. Then I called everyone else I knew to take a walk or go to the movies or come over for dinner or go shopping or read books together. Well not really, but you get the sense of desperation I felt that particular weekend. Nobody was available to do anything with me. Yes, I pouted. Yes, I felt sorry for myself. Yes, I felt lonely, abandoned, and angry. Didn't anybody love me anymore? Where were people when I really needed them? Well, they weren't there. I cried. It was a rough weekend.

Now I'm facing the challenge of my first Christmas alone and more than a bit of panic is oozing up inside. Does it say something bad about me if I am alone for Christmas? What will people think? *Oh, poor Sandy; nobody loves her.* . . . I am flooded with memories of many other Christmases spent with various loved ones—good memories that also make my aloneness now acutely more vivid.

As Christmas day draws closer, my apprehension grows and I scramble to get my plans in place. I brainstorm possibilities with a friend. I get my focus back from feeling desperate and sorry for myself to taking care of myself. I buy myself a nice sweater to open on Christmas morning and have it gift-wrapped at the store. I think I will feel loved if I have at least one nice present to open. I go to the tuba concert in the park and sing carols. The tuba carols tickle my funny bone a bit.

I consider taking a last-minute trip to visit somebody—anybody would serve the purpose. I consider asking to be included in someone else's family gathering. I consider creating an "orphans" gathering at my house for those who find themselves alone on Christmas. I consider going to church or the movies. Anything will be better than being alone for Christmas, won't it? Well, none of these ideas feel quite right. I keep brainstorming ideas until I finally get clear how I want to spend this Christmas. Then I go to the store to get the needed supplies.

On Christmas Eve, I go to the early service at my old church where I haven't been for a while. It is as beautiful and touching as ever. I remember what Christmas is all about. I again remember many other wonderful Christmas Eves and have another good cry. It all feels good.

Then on Christmas morning, I go for my usual glorious early morning hike in the hills and open my special present. It comes from someone who loves me. I feel loved. I put on some Christmas music and sing and dance around the house. I flow until I feel great. I get out my sewing machine and begin to make a new tablecloth—the project I had planned that takes most of the day. I watch a couple of good movies and fix myself a really nice dinner with plenty of leftovers for the next few days. I don't cook a whole turkey, but I bake a chicken and sweet potatoes and add salad, cranberries, and pumpkin pie—some of my favorite holiday treats.

Nobody calls me all day. No, the phone is quiet and nobody comes to the door. In fact, I don't see anyone all day long, but that part feels okay.

Now as I crawl into bed, I check inside with myself. I feel warm and loving. I have enjoyed this day. I even feel rather proud of myself. It has been a good day—a great first Christmas alone, actually. It has been simple, not bad in any way. This Christmas there is much peace in my heart and much to be grateful for. I have discovered that being alone, even on a holiday, can be very pleasant. And I will never again have to be afraid to spend Christmas alone.

AVOIDING TIME ALONE

In our always-busy, get-it-done society, most of us don't spend much time alone. Some of us quickly ask "and why would we want to?" Isn't happiness all about having loved ones to be with on weekends and holidays, someone to live with, someone to sleep with, and someone to do things with? Isn't *happily ever after* all about having a special someone? Isn't it pathetic to spend Christmas, New Year's Eve, and our birthday alone?

Well no, not necessarily. Not when time alone feels peaceful and safe. Not when time alone is a relief from too much stimulation and too many complicated expectations. Not when time alone leads toward feeling more secure in the world. Not when time alone rebuilds our true self.

This chapter takes a look at how temporarily eliminating expectations from others affects us. We have learned to recognize and reconnect with our sense of self. We are beginning to make active choices that fit us. Now, we discover that time alone creates golden opportunities to further rebuild our self, especially when we emphasize the *process* of whatever activities we choose to participate in.

Some of us crave alone time and enjoy it immensely. My friend Barbara spent a great deal of time alone after she quit an intense job that required numerous business trips away from home. She said it took her eighteen months to feel rested again, and time alone was essential to make that recuperation possible.

Kathy realized after her fourth surgery that she truly appreciated the alone time that came with staying home from work to recover physically. After that awareness, she allowed herself more alone time—without needing another surgery to get it.

When I ask others what it is like for them to be alone, however, I often hear a lot of fear.

Anna, for example, says that anything is better than being alone with her thoughts. Since her husband works long hours and her children are in school all day, I ask for more information. She volunteers several mornings a week. She shops. She reads. She keeps their home spotless and their refrigerator full. She keeps extremely busy during the day when she is alone and then drinks a bit in the evening before going to bed. She manages to rarely be alone with her thoughts and feelings.

Olivia says she just daydreams when she is alone. To her, being alone is just "wasted time."

June says that her thoughts get too negative when she is alone. "I shouldn't have done that" comes up often, creating a lot of worry about all that she believes she has done wrong. Alone time thus leaves her feeling terrible about herself.

Gillian quickly retorts that she is never alone. I happen to already know that she lives alone in a house she owns and is not currently in a relationship. I ask how that can be, and she tells me that she cannot tolerate even a single evening home alone. It absolutely terrifies her. She panics, but she doesn't know what frightens her. She just keeps an extremely busy social life with friends and activities to avoid feeling that uncomfortable panic.

Others describe feeling bored, lonely, abandoned, unloved, or vulnerable when alone. Some of us wonder when we are alone if we truly even exist.

Clearly, time alone is uncomfortable for many of us, especially if our sense of self is underdeveloped. It may not be as scary as expected, though, once the meaning of time alone is better understood.

THE MEANING OF TIME ALONE

Time alone is not bad. Having time alone does not mean that we are bad. It does not mean we have failed somehow or that nobody wants to spend time with us. It does not mean others hate us or no longer love us. It does not mean we have been abandoned, left behind, or rejected. It does not mean we are in danger, the way a young child might be when left alone. It doesn't automatically even mean that we feel lonely or bored.

Time alone is simply the portion of our day that we spend away from other people. It can be time away from the expectations and judgments of others, a break from distractions and unwanted influences that reinforce that old external reference point.

We are social creatures. There is no doubt about that. Many of us choose to live together in communities. We share housing. We share activities. We celebrate together. We often work and play together in groups. Some of us partner up with a special someone. We live with our children for many years and tend to care for elderly parents. All of these activities involve being with other people, but being with others has never automatically guaranteed that we feel happy, loved, successful, or fully alive. And being with others rarely facilitates listening to our self.

The truth is that we need both alone time and time with others. One is not better than the other. The two activities meet different needs, and it is a challenge for all of us to balance time alone and time with others to adequately meet both sets of needs. Maintaining the balance we each need requires listening inside. When we listen inside, we can tell when we need more of one or the other.

We can tell we need more time with others when we want to talk with a friend, when we need comforting, when we want company for a particular activity, when we miss a special loved one, or when we feel lonely. Most of us know these clues well.

But how do we know when we need more alone time? Here are some of the clues:

+ Feeling exhausted, overwhelmed, grumpy, or confused
+ Having difficulty making active choices
+ Forgetting important things
+ Blaming others for more than their fair share
+ Shutting down emotionally, creatively, or spiritually
+ Trying harder than usual to please others
+ Saying we "can't think straight"

When we experience any of these clues, time alone can be reparative, healing, and nourishing.

HOW WE SPEND OUR TIME ALONE

Let's take a look at what we do when we are alone. Perhaps we can transform our discomfort about alone time into something cherished.

Shutting Down

Shutting down is the common term that means to escape or detach from our present experience to avoid the intensity of our feelings, the discomfort of our body, or the pressures of our environment. Shutting down is a numbing path away from our true self. We tend to take this path when we choose to avoid what is happening in our life.

Shutting down, remember, is one option always available at the Y in the road. We can tell we are shutting down when we numb our feelings, don't notice what our body needs, use any addiction, or seek excessive stimulation to distract our attention. Maybe we would rather do anything other than what is expected of us. Maybe we feel so exhausted that we don't care what happens.

Developing awareness of what we do during times we are alone gives us more flexibility to choose activities that give us a needed break while not also causing other problems. Often it is not what we do that shuts us down as much as how we use the activity.

Gillian cannot stand to have any unfinished projects. Once she starts something, it is done, she says. Her entire focus becomes getting the job done. For her, there is no intervening process, no pleasure in the activity itself. It must get done and it must get done now. She says she only feels good about herself when things are done. She is also aware that she doesn't want to feel her feelings and that she can't slow down or tolerate the messiness of anything halfway done. The speed with which she works and her determination to finish the task at hand serve to numb her emotionally, allowing her to check out—perhaps even more often than she wants.

At one point, I started knitting. It appeared to be a relaxing activity, and I thought it would be pleasant for me. I enjoyed it a lot for a few months, but then one day I realized that I was using knitting to numb out. My shoulders were hunched over and tense. I was knitting fast—as fast as I could. I was so focused on knitting that I was immersed in it, unaware of anything else, including the conversation around me and what I was feeling. Knitting had become a way to shut down rather than a relaxing activity.

We are not meant to shut down, at least not all the time. We are meant to see both paths at the Y in the road so we can make the active choices that fit us best.

Getting Off the Merry-Go-Round

As I write this chapter, it is early in the morning on a day my current husband Dan is about to leave on another business trip. I will have the house and considerable time to myself. No longer worried that he will die on a business trip, I have taken this week off from work to write and have been eagerly looking forward to once again sinking into writing after several busy weeks of other demands. I already feel myself gratefully settling into this week, aware that I definitely need some time alone.

But then last night I suddenly started crying about my friend and neighbor who had died several months earlier. What was that? Where did it come from? We don't always understand and welcome what happens inside us when we begin to slow down our activity level to get off the merry-go-round.

When we keep busy and overstimulated, our focus tends to be external and toward the future. What is going to happen next? What do I need to do next? What is the next priority on my to-do list? Who needs what from me next? We focus on whatever is next.

Meanwhile our sense of self seems to sit quietly, patiently waiting for a crack in the wall to bring up whatever internal issues may be present. When we finally step off the merry-go-round and begin to slow down, these internal issues begin to surface—perhaps unwanted fears, unprocessed feelings, unmet needs, or even unacknowledged dreams for our life. The internal issues come through when the external world quiets and calms and we give them enough time and space to surface—as when we are quietly alone.

That is why my tears surfaced when I slowed down to write. I hadn't completed my grieving about my neighbor dying. I liked him a lot and felt truly grateful he had been in my life. I sat down to write a letter to his family about how much he had meant to me and what I remembered about him. After my good cry and completing the letter, I could settle into writing.

We may think that such emotional moments are irrelevant distractions. Yet when we take a moment or two to honor whatever surfaces when we get off life's busy merry-go-round, doing so often helps us settle into our time alone. In other words, we can trust the way in which our time alone evolves.

Choosing Our Own Influences

To utilize our alone time to rebuild our true self, it helps to create a nourishing environment that invites us to listen internally. In this way, we choose our own influences to create the effect we want for our self.

We need to feel safe when we are alone, so this is a time to remember and honor the teddy-bear phenomenon. What helps you feel safe when you are alone? Do you feel safer at home, out in nature, or in your car with the doors locked? Do you feel safer with your puppy nearby, with a teddy bear, or with your children asleep in their rooms? And what time of day feels safest to be alone?

Many of us also need silence. While some of us may prefer to listen to music or find traffic noise comforting, others of us find background noises distracting. In general, silence helps us settle into our body. It makes it easier to listen internally. When do you experience the most silence? Where?

Most of us will sooner or later notice all the tasks that are not yet done. Our mind often comes up with what we *should* be doing now that we have a few minutes to choose what to do. Perhaps the kitchen is a mess. Perhaps there are errands to run or that big project to finish for work. Of course, everything is not done. It never is, really, and those things can also be done later. Taking time alone now might actually make it easier to do those other tasks later. If this is your precious time alone, can you simply accept *what is* without any judgment—at least for a while? Can you let time alone be at the top of your list of priorities—at least for a while? Can you give yourself permission to respect your own need to be alone?

When I have a lot of unstructured time to myself, I sometimes begin to think that I am just wasting time, I am being lazy, and that being lazy is bad. It makes *me* bad. It makes *me* worthless. This line of thinking is one of the whips to be a good girl that still occasionally creeps in on me. "Oh, it's you again," I acknowledge. I let it be and just sit with it a moment. It doesn't have much to say to me anymore. I know now that quiet solitude is not worthless. Rather than pulling me into it now, hearing these old familiar words simply reminds me that I can choose which path to follow at the Y in the road and that I can choose my own input when I am alone.

Being Alone with Me

Time alone suspends the need to please other people, at least temporarily. Once alone, we are more likely to feel a genuine choice about what to do. So, what do we do when we are alone?

There are activities we can choose when we are alone that help us return to our body, that bring our reference point back inside, that nourish, strengthen, and genuinely rebuild our sense of self. I refer to these activities as *mindless* because they seem to require so little concentration to do, but perhaps they are actually mindful activities because we are present in the activity of the moment and completely honoring our own natural pace. Sue Monk Kidd similarly refers to "sacred dawdling."[29] Whatever we call these particular activities, we putz at them, rather than hurry in a goal-oriented manner toward task completion. In other words, we fully experience the *process* of doing the activity.

Mindless activities come in many forms, and the specifics vary from one individual to another, but they are often simple, effortless activities—ones we already know how to do without much thinking effort. Perhaps they utilize a different part of our brain, as they actually calm both our thinking mind and our busy body. They are often what we really want to be doing, yet they are rarely productive in terms of achievement that is noticed by others. Creative activities and hobbies often meet this need. In fact, the reason we adopt a particular hobby or mild physical activity we enjoy is often because the activity meets this particular need to be alone with *me*.

Walking, swimming, gardening, washing dishes, journaling, and easy cleaning serve this purpose for me. Sometimes I still sew, as I did that Christmas day I was alone. Others might dance, play music, whittle a piece of wood, cook, stretch, play basketball alone, read, or meditate.

My friend Barbara meanders through the hills on her bicycle at a moderate pace. Marsha loves to swing in the park. Alice paints whatever seems to need to be painted. Celeste enjoys her morning yoga. Jade journals and occasionally writes poetry. Sonia creates jewelry. They have all found nourishing ways to spend their alone time.

One Saturday morning when I had no other plans, I woke up wondering what to do. Cleaning the garage immediately came to mind. I spent the next hour, as I ate breakfast and read the paper, not quite trusting this suspicious idea. Sure enough, though, it stuck with me, so I spent the entire day cleaning my garage—and enjoying it! I wasn't rushed. I didn't feel pressure to get it done or to do it perfectly. I just putzed, taking breaks when I needed them, until pretty soon my garage was clean. I was ready to do it, I actively chose to do it when I wanted to, and I did it in my own way at my own pace. It became a pleasant mindless activity for my alone time that weekend rather than a dreaded chore needing to be completed.

It is this shift to fully experiencing the *process* of an activity that rebuilds our true self.

TUNING IN

So we practice being alone. We practice feeling safe in the stillness. We practice choosing the influences we want on our alone time. We notice what we want to do when we are alone—and how what we do affects us. We notice our own ways of doing things—how we cook and wash dishes, how we do the laundry and wash the car, how we take our walks, how we do our hobbies, how we approach a work task, and how we plan what to do for our birthday—and Christmas.

We settle into the silence and listen deeply, noticing what is happening inside us—not with judgment or shame and not to criticize or berate our self. We simply notice, experience, stay with it, and let it all be. In other words, we listen.

Try it and see what you notice. What are you feeling? How is your body? Are you hungry or tired? Does anything hurt? Are you worried? Are you doing what you need to be doing today? What is creeping in around the corners? What is trying to get your attention? What are you aware of? What do you notice? What do you hear when you listen?

REBUILDING OUR TRUE SELF

Time alone gives us a valuable opportunity to tune in and listen to whatever is coming up from inside us. It gives *me* room to breathe and be real. It reconnects us with our sense of self, aside from whatever we have been doing and whatever is happening in our external world—all the usual pressures and expectations. It tells us what is going on inside us right now at this moment and what is right for us at this time. Time alone takes us straight to our internal reference point, our true self.

It's not that we need to become hermits, spending all of our time alone. That would be going to the other extreme. Becoming able to enjoy our time alone, however, releases us from the constant pressure of responding to the needs and expectations of others. And it rebuilds our true self.

While we can't know what the outcome of this growing path will be, we can trust that this journey will take us toward feeling alive and fully living our life. The more consistently we experience and listen to our self, especially when we are alone, the more it grows and flourishes. You might even begin to feel your true self wiggling and giggling inside, wondering what is next.

Unjiggled

Yesterday was too much—
The grocery store noisy,
The traffic too fast,
People demanding,
Expectations everywhere.
My ears fought the incoming booms
Like tiny fearless soldiers
With spears and shields.
My jaw clenched firmly, familiarly,
Locking me awkwardly away
From the flooding overwhelm.
No room for me;
No flowing rhythm to trust.
I couldn't breathe,
Couldn't feel,
Couldn't dance—
Just had to shut down.
Yesterday was too much.
Today is already better—
My quiet walk at dawn,
The birds chirping,
And room to relish the still calm air.
Now, can I stay unjiggled
By today's busyness and fireworks?

Updating Core Beliefs

What Do I Really Believe About Myself?

Things don't change very fast here. I grew up in a tiny rural town surrounded by cattle and cornfields. There were thirty-two students in my graduating class and twelve of us had started first grade together. The drug store, gas station, and funeral home have all passed from father to son. Many of those who left for college or the military have not moved back. Others stayed, often living on farms nearby. The river is still full of bullheads, and teenagers probably still dance at the American Legion Hall on Fridays after the football games.

I am here for my twenty-fifth high school reunion and am flooded with memories. Driving into town over the railroad tracks stirs up memories of the adjacent grain elevators, which were newly built and rather busy several decades earlier. Stopping at the stop sign downtown reminds me of the many carnivals that once blocked that main street during hot summers. The one grocery store has apparently changed owners again, as it has a new name. The abandoned theater, where movies were once only fifty cents, reminds me of invading aliens and the film *The Wizard of Oz*. The vacant lot where the volunteer firefighters once created an ice skating rink has now been filled in with an apartment building.

Our old house still stands at the corner, though. I remember a soft yellow color, but it has been repainted white. Built around 1900, it cost my parents only $1,500 when they moved to town years ago, hoping for a better life. My three siblings and I spent our early years living here before we left for college. I remember thinking it was funny how my mom sat on the porch swing just watching the cars drive by. We all love that big swing now, even though we no longer bounce it up and down loaded with kids the way we used to.

Walking through the front door now to visit my mom reminds me of how we played house with our dolls under the dining room table that is still there, of how we ate thousands of meals at the same yellow kitchen table, and how the old coal furnace kept us warm for breakfast before we walked to school three blocks away.

Walking around the yard reminds me of how we created a neighborhood zoo with our old chow, Tubby, as the lion, slept outdoors in the playhouse on hot summer nights, made mud pies, dug a hole to China, and swung on the bag swing tied securely to a sturdy tree limb.

So many wonderful memories ripple through me, some nearly forgotten until this vivid moment of reentering, and even though the town hasn't changed much, I have changed a lot in these intervening twenty-five years. I have attended college and graduate school, married and divorced, reared two children who are now teenagers, moved numerous times, and worked several different jobs. I have grown up—or so I think.

But here, surrounded by these old memories as I attend my high school reunion, it seems impossible to remain the adult I believe I have become. I start walking more stiffly and become generally more cautious and self-conscious. My jaw clenches into an old familiar pattern. I start comparing myself to others and end up feeling inferior. I withdraw and shut down—just as I did in high school. Why do I feel so different coming back here when I remember so many good things?

The memories keep coming—senior prom, boyfriends, English class, band, wanting certain classmates to like me. My poor body remembers wearing straight skirts, girdles, and four-inch high heels—and it starts twisting to accommodate them. I remember being trained to walk without moving my hips, to play the piano, and to sew—all kinds of things to be a good girl.

While the memories are amusing for a while, I watch myself gradually transform into that quiet, scared perfectionist I was in high school. I quit talking. My smile disappears. I crunch up inside. I feel ugly and worthless all over again. I become afraid I'll do something wrong. A few tears begin to trickle down my cheeks. I can't remember who I am now. . . .

No, no, I don't want to do that! I don't want to be that way again! Why is this happening to me? Why can't I stop it? I have worked hard over the years to break free of these embarrassing and ineffective ways of being in the world. I don't want to lie low to stay out of trouble! I don't want to be too serious to play! I don't want to shut down my feelings and keep my mouth shut!

I have broken some of the old rules that seemed so important back then and discovered that I am actually quite lovable and capable without obeying them. I have found that there is life beyond the restriction of a girdle—and I truly do not want to go back!

THE VORTEX OF RULES AND ROLES

High school reunions and family gatherings for holidays, birthdays, weddings, and funerals remind us of particularly significant aspects of our own history. These moments of remembering create windows into our past, moments of direct connection between the past and the present. Some of us seem to walk by these windows without even noticing them. Some of us eagerly accept these seductive invitations into the past, perhaps even staying as long as possible, enjoying the temporary nostalgic ride through warm, playful, loving memories. Others dread these sneak attacks, as I did at my high school reunion.

I call this unavoidable, deep black hole we sometimes feel sucked into the *vortex of rules and roles*. It is there for many of us, and it is real. The vortex reminds us of the rules we once had to follow to please others to keep safe or belong. It reminds us of the roles others may have assigned us, perhaps to meet their needs more than our own. While not always negative, flashbacks often take us to this vortex, to those familiar shutting down moments when we chose to hide our precious self and adopt an external reference point instead.

Sonia gets hooked back into the vortex whenever her parents come to visit and her mother invasively goes through all of her drawers without asking. She feels violated but helpless, unable to stop her mother, even though she feels strongly that she wants her mother to stop checking her drawers. She says she still can't do anything about it. The flashbacks remind her of losing the privacy power struggle many years ago.

Olivia hears the old expectations in her father's voice whenever he asks to borrow money, which he never returns. She has always given in to loaning him money at these times, even when she cannot afford it and doesn't want to. She still feels powerless to resist his demands. She still believes she has to do whatever her father wants her to do—no matter what it is. She came to that conclusion many years ago. The flashbacks remind her.

Jenny has flashbacks into the vortex whenever it's her birthday and her mother tells her annually repeated story about how she had to drop out of school when she got pregnant with Jenny. Jenny has always known this story, yet every time she hears it, she feels deep shame and withdraws, believing that she can never make up for this original crime of being an unwanted pregnancy—as if it had been her fault.

Unable to remain our adult self in specific situations is a major clue that we are experiencing flashbacks into the vortex of rules and roles. This chapter helps us understand the dynamics and power of flashbacks and how they help us become aware of what we learned earlier in life. When we listen to the memories brought to us via flashbacks, we can reconnect with who we used to be and choose to reinterpret the data to more accurately fit us now. Updating core beliefs is the third way to rebuild our true self.

The Gift of Flashbacks

Flashbacks are sudden, usually brief, vivid shifts back in time through any of the senses to significant events earlier in our life. They are natural, normal, and real. We can try to shut them down if we want to or we can choose—with professional help, if needed—to accept the invitation at the Y in the road to listen to these portals to a deeper truth. Flashbacks are not the enemy we may have come to believe they are. They come bearing gifts and asking, "Are you ready to listen?"

Flashbacks typically begin suddenly. It is this suddenness of the change within us that is our best clue that we may be experiencing a flashback. Typical sudden changes include the following:

- Suddenly feeling transported to an earlier time or place
- Suddenly feeling little, unsafe, or vulnerable
- Suddenly feeling like an earlier, younger version of your self
- Suddenly dropping into an old, protective safety pattern
- Suddenly having surprising body sensations
- Suddenly changing a behavior, perhaps overreacting
- Suddenly feeling crazy or saying, "There is something wrong with me"
- Suddenly considering suicide, homicide, or some other extreme option

Something triggers a flashback. That trigger can be almost anything that reminds us of a similar situation from our past—a word, a look, a particular person, or perhaps a familiar reaction from someone. When we get triggered, everything seems to suddenly change—our mood, our feelings, our thoughts, and our body sensations. We feel as if we are really in that past moment again, and we often react in old, familiar ways, whether or not they are appropriate to the current situation.

Needless to say, flashbacks can interfere with our day-to-day life and relationships in ways we don't like. When Sonia heard that a good friend had decided to move out of town, for example, she came home sobbing and feeling unusually vulnerable. Her husband tenderly tried to reassure her that she would be okay, but Sonia thought he wasn't taking her seriously. She snapped, turned away from him, and ran to her room with no explanation. Her anger with him had *suddenly* become a bigger issue than her friend leaving. She gradually realized that she was experiencing a flashback to a time much earlier when she had told her mom something important and was told to go to her room. Once she noticed, claimed, and released her anger about her mother not taking her seriously, she became able to separate the past from the present enough to quit blaming her husband and return to feeling her sadness about her friend moving away.

Flashbacks provide us with a gift, in that they bring us present-day opportunities to finish healing significant past events and help us to rebuild our true self in the process.

SIX TYPES OF FLASHBACKS

Trauma is more than an unpleasant experience. Trauma is a threatening experience too overwhelming to fully deal with emotionally at the time of its occurrence. While not always literally life-threatening, traumatic experiences are definitely perceived as threatening. We then shift to focus on the expectations of others. We shift to live from an external point of reference. We shift in whatever ways we need to in order to survive the threatening experience.

Identifying the various kinds of flashbacks as they relate to the different steps in a traumatic experience helps us better understand what is happening inside us when we can't keep being the adult we believe we have become. I distinguish six distinct stages for a traumatic experience, each of which creates its own style of flashbacks:

1) **The anticipation.** From the moment we first become aware of a threat of danger, we scramble desperately to avoid whatever we believe is about to happen to us. All emotions and our precious sense of self are set aside to better handle whatever is coming. Flashbacks to this part of trauma take us to expecting the worst and feeling intense fear.

2) **The moment of 100 percent powerlessness.** When we realize that nothing is going to stop what is about to happen to us, we feel 100 percent powerless. Flashbacks to this part of a traumatic experience take us to feeling powerlessness.

3) **The injury.** This is "the newspaper account"—the facts regarding what happens to us and how we get injured. Flashbacks to this part of our trauma take us to the memories of who did what to us.

4) **The aftermath.** What happens immediately after an injury also affects us tremendously. Perhaps we told others— or not. Perhaps we were believed—or not. Perhaps we were supported and comforted—or left alone with the overwhelming situation and feelings. These flashbacks take us to how others responded to us and how we felt after the injury was over. We may even remember whether we made the shift to an external reference point or managed to return home to our internal anchor, our sense of self.

5) **The feelings.** Our feelings, set aside when we first anticipate danger, don't just go away forever. They tend to return later, perhaps when we finally feel safe enough to notice, claim, and release them or when they are triggered later by other events. Flashbacks to these leftover feelings can feel like current feelings even though they are about the past.

6) **The conclusions.** Most of us vow never to let the traumatic experience happen to us again. We do our best to figure out both what caused us to get hurt and what will keep it from happening again. The conclusions we come to are so important that they tend to feel like the truth about how to live life. Flashbacks to these conclusions serve as reminders of the core beliefs we adopted as truth long ago and give us an opportunity to update our beliefs to fit us better now. These flashbacks can be difficult to identify and are the focus of the remainder of this chapter.

CLUES TO CORE BELIEFS

Our core beliefs are what we believe is *the truth* when they are simply the conclusions we came to earlier in life about how the world is, how things work, how people are, and what is important. They tell us what we believe about our self, our body, and others. They tell us who we believe is in control and what it takes to be safe. They tell us what we believe is right and wrong and what we need to do.

Core beliefs color our life in much the same way that color filters on a camera make everything appear pink or green or yellow when it truly is not. Core beliefs reveal our interpretation of the data we have absorbed through our many senses and are the guidelines we utilize to determine our responses to life events. Core beliefs seem so basic to us that we rarely question them. We are seldom even aware of them.

Perhaps the most specific clue that we are running into old core beliefs is complete exhaustion with no apparent physical cause. Core beliefs are the impossible rules that we must follow to make up for something that isn't even true. They drive us like a whip. We can't do or achieve enough to get beyond them. We can't be good enough. We do the same things over and over, yet never seem to get anywhere and end up tired of the same old things happening. We can't seem to get past this wall that is in our way.

Gentry defined herself as a failure. She had come from a family of very hard workers who became tremendously successful in the business world. She learned early that money was essential and defined success. She pushed hard to graduate from college and became a top employee for a major corporation. She worked extremely long hours for years—until she was so seriously injured that she became too disabled to work. Inside of her it was perfectly clear what she believed: "If I don't make lots of money, I'm just not good enough." To her, being disabled meant she was a failure by definition. She saw no way out until she began to see this core belief as a conclusion she had adopted years ago based on her experiences, a conclusion she had re-experienced many times since through flashbacks. Once aware of the core belief driving her and when she was ready, she updated her belief to "Taking good care of myself physically really is being good enough."

It is important to realize that what we learned about our self years ago may be true, but it may also not be true or only partially true. Or could it possibly be both true and not true? An old example of several blind men walking up to an elephant for the first time illustrates this concept. One man describes the elephant as a big, flat, rough wall. One describes it as a long, skinny thing that wiggles like a snake. The third man describes it as a big upright pillar. Who is right? What is the truth about what an elephant is like? Actually, they are all right, but each has experienced a different part of the truth, a different perspective.

What we have learned about our self can be selective like the blind men defining that elephant. Perhaps we had one significant experience and came to a conclusion. Maybe we failed miserably at playing tennis in gym class and concluded from that humiliating experience that we were lousy at sports. From that point forward, we had a failure lens through which we looked at all our athletic experiences. We expected to fail and every little mistake or setback proved to us that yes, we truly were a failure. Perhaps, over the years, we even generalized "I'm a failure at sports" to "I'm not good at anything I do."

But what if this same hypothetical person loved playing tennis, even though she was not very good at it? What if she took private lessons that were less humiliating? What if she played frequently with a good friend who didn't judge her? What if tennis became fun and she was determined to get better at it? The resulting core belief might instead have become something like this: "I can learn things even when they are difficult."

Core beliefs can be positive or negative. They can be helpful or get in our way. They can be true about us—or not. It is the old, outdated, negative core beliefs that feed our safety patterns and keep us in the Good-Girl Jail that prevent us from rebuilding our true self. These are the ones we want to become aware of and update—the ones that may still feel true but are not.

What We Have Learned

The question to ask is this: what have you learned about your self? If we have lived with smiling faces, we probably learned that people enjoy us. If others helped to meet our needs, we likely learned that we are valued. If we have lived with encouragement, we probably learned to be persistent when something is difficult. If we have lived with kindness, we hopefully learned that we are lovable.

On the other hand, if we have lived with criticism, we may have learned that we did things wrong and made mistakes. If we have lived with humiliation, we likely learned that we were bad. If we have lived with neglect, perhaps we learned we were not very important. If we have lived with rejection, we may have learned that we didn't belong. If we have lived with people who didn't respond to us, we probably learned to quit asking for what we needed. And if we have lived with violence, we most certainly learned that other people might hurt us.

Whatever our particular experiences have been, we have learned from them. We figured out from our point of view and with whatever limited information we had at the time what made good things happen, so that we could hopefully make them happen more often. Likewise, we tried hard to comprehend why bad things happened in order to make sense of our experiences—and because we desperately didn't want that negative experience to happen again. The challenge is that we usually were vulnerable young children when we came to these conclusions.

Jean Piaget, a Swiss child development theorist, has taught us that children perceive cause and effect differently from adults.[30] As preschoolers, our limited way of understanding cause and effect was that whatever happened first caused whatever happened next. We tended to conclude that if we did something, it caused the next thing to happen—thus blaming our self (or taking credit) for whatever happened; however, these connections could have been distorted. Perhaps we concluded that if we wished grandpa would go away and then he died, our wishing it so had made it happen. We might then have incorrectly believed that his death was our fault.

As we grew to be school-aged children, we more likely concluded that bad things happened because we misbehaved and broke the rules. If grandpa died when we were nine, perhaps we concluded that he died because we made too much noise and therefore hadn't been a good girl.

By the time we became adolescents, we were developmentally able to think abstractly so that we could see our situation more objectively. If grandpa died when we were sixteen, we were more able to understand that he died because of heart failure, which was not our fault at all.

My own grandfather lived with us until I was five years old. I felt loved by him, but I also remember him molesting me. Many years later as an adult, I became aware of three different core beliefs regarding why he had hurt me that demonstrate the typical reasoning skills of a preschool child. I believed that he had hurt me because I played too much, because I "let" him love me, and because I had pretty naturally curly hair. These reasons made perfect sense to me as a preschooler. As a result, I begged my mom to cut my hair so that I would be ugly, I quit playing and became a very serious child, and I quit "letting" people love me—all so that the trauma I had experienced would never happen again. My five-year-old conclusions following my trauma became driving core beliefs about how to live my life.

As an adult, once I became aware of what I had concluded from my childhood experiences, I could understand that my conclusions were my best effort to explain why it had happened and what I could do to prevent it from happening again. But these conclusions were only what I could have understood at such a young age. The real reason I got molested was because I had lived with a child molester and he had picked me. It wasn't my fault at all. I couldn't have done anything to make him molest me—and I couldn't have stopped him.

As this updated, more accurate belief settled inside of me and replaced the old childhood core beliefs, I became able to let my naturally curly hair grow long and curly again. I became able to allow myself to play and to let others love me. This is the healing power of flashbacks when we utilize them to update our core beliefs.

The Power of Brainwashing

Another way in which we adopted core beliefs has to do with whatever we were told repeatedly. We could take the smartest woman in the world, isolate her, and tell her over and over that she is stupid. For the first fifty times, she would likely be able to argue back, "I'm not stupid!" After maybe a hundred times, she would likely question her own intelligence and begin to look for examples of her own stupidity. Sooner or later she would begin to truly believe that she is stupid and quit trusting her own perceptions.

This is basic brainwashing. We have all learned whatever we were told repeatedly. Perhaps we were told that we are going to get hurt, that we can't do anything right, that we had better follow the rules of others, that we can't trust our own choices, or that we are very smart, a talented musician, or good at playing basketball. Brainwashing is not innately bad; it works either way. In any case, being told anything repeatedly tends to create core beliefs.

Raven got caught masturbating by her older brother, who called her "a creep." The term stuck in her family and unfortunately she heard it over and over as she grew up. When I met her as an adult, she was hooked on Internet porn and believed she truly *was* a creep for enjoying sex. When searching for the origins of such a powerful term, she realized she could still hear her brother cruelly yelling, *"Ewww! You're such a creep!"* Becoming aware of this term as merely childhood brainwashing rather than the truth about her, she became able to identify her obsession with sex as an addiction that had resulted partially from believing that she was a creep. She then became able to update the core belief to this: "Being sexual is normal. I actually am a good person."

IDENTIFYING OUR OWN SPECIFIC CORE BELIEFS

Our core beliefs seem hidden, tucked beneath the rules and roles we learned early. They usually feel so much like *the truth* that we have never questioned them. These beliefs drive our automatic choices— the ones we don't even think about. They are the rules we have always followed, the rules that leave us feeling uncomfortable if we don't follow them. They often fuel habits that are difficult to change. They function like the truth about life in general when they are only our own unique childhood conclusions.

Becoming aware of our own specific core beliefs is not easy. When we are ready, we can listen carefully to our thoughts and the words we frequently use. Do we say we are selfish, making a mess, doing something wrong, taking up too much room, being stupid again, fat, or lazy? Noticing the things we automatically do and the words we automatically say leads us toward discovering our own core beliefs. Comments that start with "I," likely have been our own conclusions.

Jade had such a confusing childhood with her mother's unpredictable mood swings that she concluded, "Something is terribly wrong, but I can't figure out what it is." For years she had felt powerless, confused, frantic, and rather crazy. When she finally caught herself making this statement out loud one day, she could see it as a result of her childhood confusion. She came to believe instead that if something was terribly wrong now as an adult, she would most likely know what it was and be able to do something about it to help herself.

Jenny hated it when her body hurt. She had been beaten severely as a child and believed she might die on many occasions. As an adult, her body hurting from illness, an injury, intense feelings, or fibromyalgia could send her into a devastating suicidal crisis.

One day she spontaneously said out loud, "The pain is so severe that I think I'm going to die!" Then she paused, suddenly hearing what she had said to herself on many occasions. This time, however, something clicked into place inside of her, telling her that this statement was not true about her current pain even though she had believed it to be true many times as a child. She laughed a bit, updating her belief almost instantly when she said, "I guess I'm not likely to die from fibromyalgia." While she remained uncomfortable with both physical and emotional pain, she understood that she wasn't likely to die from it. Updating this one core belief helped her let go of her persistent urge to kill herself whenever she felt pain.

In contrast, comments that start with "You . . ." may be words that we often heard from someone else. We are often so used to them that we no longer even notice them—until we listen.

Raven became aware that she still heard her mother's voice telling her she was so stupid that she couldn't do anything right and would never amount to anything. Needless to say, this all-encompassing core belief had greatly affected her career and relationships. When she became aware that she had adopted her mother's opinions as true and updated the belief to knowing that she was actually quite smart, she was able to physically feel the shift inside her body. Stupid was only her mother's opinion of her, and she no longer valued her mother's opinions about her more than her own truth.

The following open-ended questions may help you to identify some of your own core beliefs:

♦ What things happen over and over in your life? How do you explain them?
♦ What are you never supposed to do? Why?
♦ What should you always do? Why?
♦ What particular words or phrases do you frequently speak and think?
♦ What was said to you repeatedly as a child?
♦ How does your family describe you?
♦ What do you believe other people say about you?

Attending family and high school reunions is nearly always fertile ground for discovering core beliefs. I felt inferior at my high school reunion when I was reminded of my core belief that I needed to keep quiet to please other people. Inside I heard a familiar statement: *Keep your mouth shut!* Even my body shifted to accommodate this core belief. My thoughts, feelings, behaviors, and bodily sensations combined to show me how I used to live life based on this core belief. While uncomfortable, the experience helped me to realize that I now knew it was both impossible and unnecessary to please others by trying to be silent and invisible. I updated my belief to knowing that I am equal to all others on the most basic spiritual level, that we are all what I have come to call *spiritual equals*. While my new belief took a while to stabilize inside of me, I knew that I didn't have to please everyone anymore. I didn't have to go one-down and defer to all others anymore. I didn't have to try so hard to get everyone to like me anymore. I didn't have to try to be perfect anymore. I no longer needed to be a good girl. I only needed to be *me*. I sigh and feel my shoulders relax even now as I remember making this shift.

LISTENING FROM A DEEPER PLACE

We can tell when we finally discover the exact words of a core belief by how true the words suddenly feel inside us. The precise words seem to click into place inside and may all of a sudden explain a number of related things in our life. Often, we know at once that our old core belief is not really true because our now-adult brain— the rational neo-cortex part—immediately tells us so. This moment of simultaneous awareness that something is both true and not true sometimes feels rather weird, as you may surmise from the examples given in this chapter.

So what do we do with our core beliefs, once we have discovered the precise words? We listen from a deeper place inside to discover a deeper truth that more accurately fits us now. We reinterpret the data as adults and come to a different conclusion. Sometimes, this shift happens spontaneously when we find the exact words of our old belief. If not, we can pause and wait a few moments until the words of the new belief come to us. Rarely are the new words merely the opposite of the old ones. We can't anticipate what the new belief will be, but when it comes, it tends to click solidly into place.

In Olivia's childhood, "honor thy father and thy mother" meant to obey her parents always and immediately without question. Her parents reminded her of this commandment from the Bible often and told her that it meant that she was to do whatever they told her to do. The few occasions Olivia tried to argue back brought her abusive consequences. She learned to do what she was told, of course, as we all would have.

As an adult, though, Olivia's mother was still telling her what to do and she still felt compelled to do whatever her mother said. One day, the exact words tumbled unexpectedly out of her mouth surprising us both: "I must do whatever they tell me to do or I will die." This core belief had driven her behavior nearly her entire life. It explained her inability to stand up to them and gave her an opportunity to update that old core belief to what fit her better now: "I no longer have to do everything other people tell me to do."

"Honor thy father and thy mother" has been misused and mis-interpreted in many families. To *honor* means to treat others with respect—to be courteous, kind, and appreciative. Parents do not have the right to use and abuse their children to meet their own needs—not even under the pretense of obeying a commandment from the Bible.

As I began to write this chapter, I was surprised to run into my own old vortex of rules and roles, and it temporarily stopped me. My writing became convoluted and confusing as I wandered around unable to focus my thoughts. I eventually discovered that I was break-ing my own childhood rule to respect all authority figures, which I had apparently interpreted to mean never saying anything bad about parents—not even to choose a path that fits *me* better. I had tapped into my old core belief: never blame the parents. It was a brick wall I hadn't previously been able to see until I was writing about flashbacks and core beliefs. It was an inner law I struggled to be rational about but couldn't. My fear of breaking this old rule tensed my body so much that, for a while, I even wondered if I would need to give up writing this book.

Finally, after struggling for a few days, my breakthrough came when I wondered if honoring thy father and thy mother and respect-ing our elders could simply mean this: "Hey, thanks for the launch. I really appreciate what you did for me when I needed help, but now

I can find my own way, take care of my own needs, and live my own life. I'll take it from here." I laughed at how simple it could be. I found that line between respecting parents and sacrificing *me* to meet the needs of parents. I reminded myself that there is enough room to meet the needs of both parents and children. I reinterpreted the data and updated my core belief to this: "We are each responsible for our own choices—even parents." And I redefined good parenting to mean fostering a child's sense of self.

Problematic words and phrases don't always mean what we were taught or what we concluded they meant when we were children. There are many ways to reinterpret the data. When we find what fits *me* now, the old outdated core beliefs lose their power over our life.

REBUILDING OUR TRUE SELF

When we listen from a deeper place, we hear a deeper truth. Core beliefs leftover from childhood experiences and returning as flashbacks are not usually our deepest truth. When we recognize the vortex of rules and roles returning to us through flashbacks, we see the opportunities available at the Y in the road to reinterpret the old data to better fit us now. And when we listen for our deeper truth in all three ways—emphasizing choices, cherishing time alone, and updating core beliefs—we also rebuild the strength of our true self. And our true self begins to blossom.

Some Things Matter

There is a me—
Of course there is,
And I matter.
My needs matter.
My feelings matter.
My truth matters.
My true self matters.
Of course they do!
How could I think otherwise?
There's something significant here
In my existence,
Something important about my birth
Into this lifetime.
I'm not always sure what it is,
But I know it's important,
That it matters,
That I matter.
And yes,
I finally now genuinely matter . . .
To me!

PART IV
RETURNING HOME TO OUR TRUE SELF

RETURN:
go back to
coalesce, fuse, or integrate
coordinate into a functioning whole

When we claim without judgment what genuinely fits our true self and let go without judgment of all that does not fit, the boundaries that surround and protect us naturally develop and slide into place. We discover what we can trust completely.

"And the time came when
the risk to remain tight in a bud
was more painful than
the risk it took to blossom."

—Anais Nin

Claiming What Fits Me

What Is My Deeper Truth?

I loved Boulder. It drew me to it like a magnet, and I almost moved there—almost. I had long dreamed of living in a small college town and the timing felt perfect to begin an exciting new chapter of my life in this community that seemed to nourish my true self and reliably invite my aliveness.

I had already begun to see clients in Boulder two days a week in an effort to begin building my private practice. I participated in a monthly support group there that I greatly appreciated and had made a few good friends. I even had a buyer waiting to purchase my house and was in the process of looking for a new one to buy in Boulder. I felt cautious yet willing to take out a huge new mortgage that wouldn't be paid off until I was over seventy. Somehow, it all seemed perfectly right—until that one day. . . .

I was visiting my good friend Alice. I had been at her home for several days, eating her wonderful cooking, taking naps, enjoying her companionship, reading, and taking glorious long walks on the nearby Pacific beach. I had completely collapsed in exhaustion on her doorstep, and she was lovingly nourishing me back to my usual good health and sanity.

On the fourth afternoon, downstairs where I had been sleeping, I suddenly began crying those heavy, heaving sobs that shake the whole body and feel as if they will never end. I just kept sobbing with this uncontrollable, whole-body outburst of truth, listening to my body and letting it do its natural thing. I didn't even know what I was crying about, but I could hear myself saying, "I can't do it any more" over and over and over. What was "it"? Was this another NO MORE moment?

After sobbing heavily for perhaps twenty minutes—which felt like an eternity—everything began to become clear. I couldn't keep driving that hundred miles to Boulder every week. I couldn't keep seeing clients in two offices. I couldn't take on the pressure of a huge new mortgage. I couldn't keep pushing myself so hard, so ferociously. I couldn't. I just couldn't. I cried and cried and cried some more, surrendering to my sobbing body.

Couldn't slowly morphed into *didn't need to,* and I began to understand. I didn't need to push myself so hard. I already had what I wanted, what I needed, what I had been looking for in Boulder— exactly what fit *me* perfectly! I didn't need to move at all! I simply needed to go home and claim the house I had already been living in for ten years as my home. I already had my home. I already had my life. I already had what genuinely fit my true self.

Back at home, I see everything with fresh eyes. I see my house as if it were for sale and I could choose to buy it. I notice the neighborhood and my neighbors with surprising fondness. There are some interesting folks here. I notice with renewed respect and appreciation the hundred-year-old ash and elm trees in my yard and down my street. They seem to know just how to embrace each home to protect it. I notice the beauty of my big backyard full of the flowers and bushes I have personally planted, one by one, a few more each spring.

I enter through the front door and walk slowly from room to room. I notice the unique, old plaster walls with a few cracks here and there. The Victorian woodwork softens my heart, as it always has. I notice some things that need repair and make a mental note to take care of them soon. All of the little rooms connect cozily to each other rather than to a hallway. I walk from room to room noticing, acknowledging, experiencing throughout my body my newly aware truth that yes, I love my house. This is the home that fits *me* perfectly—such as it is and such as I am. This is where I belong. I have found my home, my precious, safe, nurturing nest. Once again, I hear a long sigh of relief.

THE ESSENCE OF CLAIMING

Claiming means to recognize and acknowledge as mine what fits *me* now as I am. It can be as simple as a young child saying "mine" about her toys or as complex as discovering something we truly need to do, even if we are terrified to follow through with it. What fits could be a new job we are excited about or a fabulous trail to hike. It could be a painful decision to leave a particular friendship. It could be finally acknowledging the truth about a long-denied childhood trauma. It could be feeling connected to a new puppy or a certain child. It could even be buying new jeans after trying on numerous pairs to select the ones that best fit.

Claiming what fits *me* means to listen to our deeper truth about our safety, our body, and our feelings—the three essential self-skills that reconnect us with our true self as described in Part II. It means to pay attention to our choices, our time alone, and our core beliefs—the three powerful ways to rebuild and strengthen our sense of self described in Part III. It now also means claiming our home, our experiences, our relationships, our family, and our personal qualities.

Claiming what fits *me* is a lifelong process that honors who we are. We are constantly evolving from one segment of life to the next and then the next through various relationships, jobs, homes, events, and challenges. Our sense of self is the part of us that continues through all these changes. Living from our true self is a way of living that connects who we are now with who we have always been and who we are still becoming.

So we claim whatever fits, whenever it fits, however it fits. These are the parts of us that no one else can take away or destroy. By claiming, we surrender to the truth that is already within us, for there is no longer any reason to ignore, deny, or hide it.

This chapter shows how solid we feel when we claim what genuinely fits us and suggests additional things we might want to claim to fully return to our own complete truth and integrity. Special attention is given to creating and claiming a secure home base from which to live. As we become able to let go of judging our own truth—whatever it might be—we find it easier to fully trust that inner reference point we call our true self.

HOW IT FEELS TO CLAIM WHAT FITS ME

When I claimed the house I already owned as my home, I felt enormous relief. Did you hear my long sigh? The pressure and weight lifted from my shoulders. I didn't have to do so much anymore. I didn't have to push myself so hard to meet the expectations of others.

I didn't have to drive that hundred miles every week anymore to keep two offices going. I could simply be *me*.

Whenever I came home, whether from a trip or errands, I felt welcomed into my safe little nest. I slept well there. I knew at a deep level that it was truly safe to be there, safe to call it my home—and to be *me*. I could be grubby or dressed up, fancy or not, have fun or cry. It didn't matter, because I was in my own home, my own space. I felt free. I sigh again now as I remember that awakening moment.

Over the next couple of years, I cleaned and redecorated my home. I wanted to fill my entire home with what fit *me*. I got new carpet, changing the color from red-orange to blue-green. I repainted most of the walls to soften the whiteness, purchased a new couch, put up new antique lace curtains to go with my antique furniture, and added more light. I rearranged the furniture and grew more plants. I selected each change carefully, adding much more aliveness and color, and then the softness surrounded and nurtured my own aliveness in return. I loved it! It fit *me* and I fit it. We felt like a team. I wanted to take care of my home and sometimes I didn't even want to leave it. For several years, my very best vacations became those days I took time off from work to stay home with myself in my precious home.

Relief is one of the best clues that we have found what fits us. Something clicks into place inside, like a puzzle piece that has found where it belongs. Something settles. Our shoulders drop. We can breathe more fully. We become mentally and emotionally more clear. We feel free.

Sometimes we feel as if we are taking more room on the planet and that doing so is actually okay now. As we step into our rightful place after feeling confined and shut down in the Good-Girl Jail, we often stand taller and feel bigger. We need more wiggle room. We might want to sprawl, spread our things around more, and make a mess we don't clean up until we are ready to. We might talk more and perhaps even a little more loudly, take bigger steps when we walk, and laugh more often. We might even want to be silly and begin to tease and tell jokes. We feel safer now, making bigger risks possible. We notice this change without judgment, without stopping it, just letting it be okay. It is a sign that our sense of self is becoming more solid.

Sometimes claiming our truth feels outrageous or scary to acknowledge. Maybe we discover that we like something wilder than we have ever before worn and wonder if we will dare to wear it. Maybe it feels right to break an old rule we have lived by for years. Maybe we get clear that we need to leave a job or a specific relationship.

Jenny, for example, had tried hard to keep the peace between her mom and dad for many, many years. She had become the family scapegoat and had taken much of the blame for their relationship difficulties. While she felt considerable terror at the possibility of not meeting these expectations of her parents, she also felt tremendous relief one day when she suddenly got clear that her mom and dad's relationship was *their* issue, not hers. There was nothing she could do to fix their relationship. They needed to work it out themselves. They needed to make their own choices, whether good ones or not.

With that awareness, Jenny claimed her truth that she was powerless over her parents' rocky relationship. It was an awakening moment for her. She shifted her focus from what her parents were doing wrong to what she wanted to do with her own life. It was a big step that gave her more wiggle room. She felt immensely relieved.

WHAT TO CLAIM

New things come into our life and to our attention every day. We start to claim what fits us wherever we can. Nobody else can tell us where to start, of course, as no one else can possibly know either what fits us or what we have not yet claimed.

You may have already at least partially claimed your sense of self, your fears, your need for safety, your body, your feelings, your choices, your time alone, and your core beliefs as you read the previous chapters.

Now, can you imagine fully claiming some of these things?

Your favorite colors	Your creativity
Your belongings	Your personal mess
Your friends	Your opinions
Your inner beauty	Your physical and emotional pain
Your career	Your character defects
Your name	Your past, whatever it may be
Your humor	Your financial responsibilities
Your skills and talents	Your parenting responsibilities
Your family	Your spirituality
Your sexuality	Your smile
Your voice	Your playfulness
Your joys	Your dreams for your life

After a while, we have accumulated a long list of things we have claimed that fit *me*. What we claim and the order in which we claim things varies immensely from person to person, but each quality we claim helps us fully return home to our true self.

CLAIMING A SAFE HOME BASE

Whatever we have claimed gives us a reliable foundation to return to in times of stress and confusion—a safe home base inside that never disappears, that no one else can ever take away or destroy. As our sense of self strengthens, it gradually becomes our safe home base. Earlier in the claiming process, though, our safe home base might be our physical home, as it was for me.

Where is our home? Is it where we grew up or where we live now? Do we still call our parents' house our home even though we have grown up and lived in six other places? Do we say we've "come home" when we get to the ocean, even though we live hundreds of miles inland in the mountains or desert? Do we get that homey feeling when we walk in the forest, even though we live in the city? Do we try to have more than one home?

And what defines our home anyway? Is it wherever we "hang our hat"? Is it where we sleep? Is it where we keep our underwear? Where we store our stuff? Or is it a feeling—that homey feeling we get in certain places where we feel comfortable and relaxed, where we seem to naturally fit and belong, where we feel safe?

We can learn to create and develop our physical home base to both express our self and nurture it. There are houses people just live in and then there are homes that people thrive in. Transforming a house or an apartment into our home is both an art and a skill, but it is not about having the most expensive house and furniture, living in a high-status neighborhood, or hiring an interior decorator to coordinate colors to impress others. Instead, creating our home now is about claiming what fits us. It's about what works and what is comfortable—for *me*.

On a physical level, our safe home base is a place to sleep and keep our belongings as well as a place to live from, a place to leave from, to go to work from, and leave on trips from. More than anything, home is our anchor, our place to come back to when the day is done, where we feel "at home." It is part of our truth.

Our home base can also be a place inside our body, an image or particular feeling that brings us security. It might be a particular truth or belief, perhaps our connection with God or Goddess, a meaningful book, or an imaginary place. Remember the teddy bear phenomenon? It doesn't matter what our safe home base is, as long as it creates that solid connected feeling we need when the winds of everyday life toss us about. The important part is that it is available when we need it.

Remember Rubianne, who experienced her sense of self as a rock in her tailbone? Whenever she felt angry, scared, or confused, she could return to that spot in her body and feel her rock to calm and return to her ordinary clarity and safety.

Remember how June said she knew only one thing about herself—that she liked the color green? Whenever she became overwhelmed by her fear or too much to do, she recuperated quickly by reminding herself that she liked the color green. Green brought her home.

Remember Sirena, who walked to her certain tree every morning for a hug? She said it grounded her for the day. That tree was her safe home base.

Elissa anchored herself every morning with prayer. She was in a twelve-step program of recovery and had learned to turn her addiction over to the care of God, as she understood God, and ask for help and guidance for the day. God became the center of her life and anchored her in sobriety.

Others have found those deep core home places in statements like "Oh, yeah, I'm Italian," "I'm healing," "I'm making progress," "I'm in recovery," "I really am a good person," "I'm taking good care of myself," "I like my hands," or "I need a walk every day."

This process of claiming what fits *me* creates that effective, safe home base to return to when we need an anchor inside from which to live our life—and it does so without any judgment.

CLAIMING WITHOUT JUDGMENT

Claiming our truth about our self is considerably easier when we are not judging what fits us as good or bad, worthy or unworthy, right or wrong. If we don't like a certain truth, we can perhaps choose to grow beyond it or claim a deeper truth, but the task for now is to accept our truth as it is at this present time—*without judgment.*

One morning not long after I had claimed my home, I went for another long sunrise walk in the foothills. Enjoying the momentary peacefulness, I stopped to sit on a big rock by the stream. As I was lying back on the rock listening to the tumbling water, I looked upward toward the sky. I had often noticed the brilliant azure blue of the clear morning air, but this time I also noticed all the tall trees reaching for that blue. I noticed each individual tree. Some seemed extra tall and powerful. Many of them were ramrod straight. Some had pine cones. Most looked healthy and green.

Then, as I continued to let in the full experience, I noticed the other trees. Some were dying. Some were crooked. One had somehow lost its top and was beginning to grow a new one. They seemed to be sharing the sunlight, each occupying its own space and taking up the amount of space it needed. There were many kinds of trees with differently shaped leaves. And there were little trees perhaps hoping for enough room to keep growing.

I kept lying there, soaking in the experience and feeling the peace of the moment. Then it came to me: nobody judged the trees in the forest—nobody! Nobody said the forest was growing in the wrong place or that those trees weren't growing right. Those trees were simply doing what they needed to do. They were just growing in the best way they could. They didn't give up. They wound themselves around as necessary to get the light and nourishment they needed to keep growing and to live their own life. They didn't seem to judge each other either. All were equally valued. Each one had an equal opportunity to grow. There was no need to judge any of the trees. They just were. All were simply living their tree life—just as I was growing and living my human life.

Suddenly I realized that I didn't need to judge myself in any way for not moving to Boulder. Several of my friends thought I had merely lost my courage to move, but I knew courage had not been the issue. In that moment with the trees, I knew what was true for *me* and honored it—without any judgment. It was okay that I stayed to live in the house I already owned. I didn't have to do more or do something bigger or something more important. I didn't have to live where others thought I should or where anyone else wanted me to. It was important to live where I fit.

Sirena had a different kind of awakening moment that helped her let go of judging herself. She said she woke up suddenly one night feeling scared and more than a bit crazy. Not knowing what was going on inside of her, she got up, went to the bathroom, got a drink of water, came back to bed, and asked her partner to hold her.

As her fear calmed, she became aware that God was right there in her, near her, and all around her—not judging her at all. Sirena had grown up in a fundamentalist Christian family but had left the church behind as a young adult to live her own life as a gay woman. Now here was God, many years later, coming to her once again but with no judgment at all—none whatsoever!

Sirena said it was the first moment in her life that she hadn't felt judged. Her own judgment of herself simply melted away in response. There was suddenly no need to judge herself if God wasn't judging her. Then her judgment of all others melted away as well: "It suddenly made no sense for me to judge anyone if God wasn't judging all of us." She peacefully fell back asleep, knowing deep down that God wasn't judging her and probably never had.

Over the next few days Sirena noticed that she felt more honest. She could share things with friends without worrying about what they thought of her. She noticed that others responded differently to her and seemed more accepting of her. She felt more open to all her relationships and worried less in general. When she shared this dramatic experience with me a few days later, she acknowledged that she didn't have any idea where this revelation would take her, but it felt so real and true to her that she knew she could trust her experience. Sirena had claimed her truth without judgment.

What is simply is. Things are the way they are. There is no need to be perfect in any way. There is no need to do more than we can do. Being who we are is enough. Being you is enough—and really quite adequate.

Claiming our truth without judgment changes everything. It makes claiming what fits us possible. It makes trusting the process of our life possible. It makes returning home to our true self possible. We actually cannot fully claim our own truth as long as we are judging. The two are incompatible.

Judging is part of a particular way of thinking called *duality*. Duality involves separating things into the two basic categories of good and right on one hand and bad and wrong on the other hand. It means that we separate just enough from what we are looking at or thinking about to distinguish these two rudimentary categories. Then we align with one side or the other so that we judge our self as either good and right or bad and wrong, especially in comparison to others. Duality limits our choices to these two extremes, making it difficult to see the millions of other possibilities that actually exist in this smorgasbord of life.

Duality is clearly not the only way of thinking. Listening to what fits *me* without judgment takes us directly to our own internal experience without any comparison to others. While we may have let others determine the truth about us in the past, listening without judgment now allows us to know our own truth. It opens our thinking and makes it possible to go beyond what we have already learned. It calms our confusion and helps us trust our own perceptions.

Listening without judgment leads us toward living from our internal reference point, our home base, our true self. It allows us to integrate the various truths we know and helps us to trust our evolving sense of self.

Rubianne came in for a session utterly exhausted. "Being *me* is such a burden!" she moaned. "Being precious is really hard work! In fact, I think it must be unattainable." She had been trying to love herself. We worked together awhile, exploring what was going on inside her. Before long those words shifted: "It's being the lie of me that's actually the burden; I just need to be the truth of me." Then her judgments began to melt away. She said all those judgments others had made of her were also slipping away and becoming irrelevant. She described her body getting bigger and a bit woozy but feeling solid. She felt her shoulders drop and her energy flow again. By the time she left my office that day, she had claimed her new, evolving core belief, "I *am* the truth of me." She recognized and trusted this process of claiming her evolving true self—without judgment.

CLAIMING OUR SELF WITHIN A FAMILY

To claim what fits us without judgment, we inevitably begin to examine the ways in which we are unique and different from the others in our birth family—and what a challenge this can be.

There are numerous ways in which we are similar to our childhood family. We are "blood," permanently linked genetically to those who by definition share our ethnicity and numerous physical traits. Many of us grew up in the same locality, knew the same relatives and neighbors, and may still share a family surname. We have experienced much of the same history, whatever that may have been.

Of course we are one with the family tribe, whatever that has meant for us over the years, but now in what ways are we different? Every family is composed of individual human beings, each with her own unique and specific genetic make-up, body, personality, needs, skills, natural talents, and choices. No two people in any family are exactly the same—not even identical twins. Is it okay to differentiate from the others in our family? Can we claim our differences? Can we claim these differences even when doing so may upset someone important to us? Can we honor our own uniqueness? To claim what fits our true self includes honoring and valuing these specific differences.

Clues that we may have more claiming work to do regarding family include the following:

♦ Regressing into old safety patterns during family contacts
♦ Feeling afraid or protective in anticipation of contact with family
♦ Feeling young, insecure, bad, inferior, or passive during family contacts
♦ Feeling obligations or expectations from other family members
♦ Noticing that we play a role that no longer fits us in the overall family dynamics

As we begin to claim our uniqueness, we might perceive our family as threatening abandonment. We might think they believe our differences are a threat to the goodness or solidarity of the family, as if we are making the family look bad or wrong in some way. We may think they no longer love us. The vortex of rules and roles can powerfully seduce us back to that promise of love and acceptance—*if only* we will give up this ferocious determination to live our own life.

It is the effect of our fears that we want to notice, keeping our focus on our own experience rather than judging what we believe our family may be doing wrong. Differentiating from family is never about trying to change the family. When we no longer judge family as bad for trying to pull us back in and quit fighting the inevitable power struggles that tend to ensue, we can begin instead to consciously and purposely choose who, what skills, which specific behavior patterns, and qualities fit us now and which do not.

Sirena told her mother one day that she would be welcome to come live with her. Sirena had a basement that didn't get used very much and said it would work really well. She would be glad to have her mother move in. Her mom quietly looked off in the distance and slowly said, "It will be interesting to see...."

Sirena's mother lived in a different community with her husband, whom Sirena described as controlling and critical. As Sirena related this story to me, surprised that she was now able to stay being adult around her mother, she paused and then added emphatically, "I would never stay in a relationship like that!" While compassionate toward her mother's marriage situation, here was a moment of claiming one way in which she was very different from her mother. She claimed this difference and trusted it completely, even as she invited her mother to live with her.

TRUSTING WHAT FITS ME

Was considering moving to Boulder a mistake on my part? Had I been off-track in my life? I don't believe so, not when I trust my own experience.

I felt a draw toward Boulder that I needed to follow to see where it would take me. I couldn't know where it would take me, of course, but I trusted the steps in the process as they came to me. So, I opened an office there and began to look for a house to buy. It had all progressed quite easily—until that one day with that one long, sobbing cry when my deeper truth became clear.

Trusting the steps in the process took me exactly where I needed to go: to the point of choice, to that Y in the road that I had not been able to see and feel before. I learned that I could move to Boulder if I wanted to, but I didn't have to. I learned that I was capable of moving to Boulder if it fit, but it didn't. Seeing that free choice at the Y in the road helped me back off from my friends' opinions about what they thought I should do and instead make the choice that I needed to make. It helped me return to my internal reference point to claim what truly fit *me,* trusting my own truth and my own evolving true self.

Each little truth we claim as we recognize our sense of self, reconnect with our safety, our body, and our feelings, and then rebuild our true self with active choices, time alone, and updating our core beliefs takes us directly toward this deeper process of returning home to our true self.

At first, the various little truths we claim may not fit together very well. They may even seem conflicted. Maybe we don't want some of them to be true, but as we claim each truth as it becomes clear, the pieces gradually begin to fit together. The older I get, the more readily I can see that all the pieces do fit together eventually. Each job, each relationship, each choice, and even each "mistake" contribute to our becoming fully who we are now.

Claiming our various parts and pieces is much like putting together a five-hundred-piece jigsaw puzzle. We may have a general idea what the puzzle is about, but we don't yet know where each piece fits. First we do the edge pieces to see the outer perimeters—the certain limits like when we were born, who is in our birth family, what our body is like, and where we lived as a child. Maybe the picture on the box of the puzzle is a bowl of fruit. Maybe the orange is easy to put together, but the grapes seem more difficult. The bowl is pretty, but the melon is so big and complex that we don't like it. And there are those darker areas that we don't yet know very well. Perhaps they fit together last. If we trust the pieces are all there, trust that we will learn how everything fits together, and trust the evolving process, we eventually see how all the pieces fit together to create the whole.

To integrate means to bring together the various parts and pieces to complete or produce a larger, harmonious, congruent, interrelated, undiminished, functioning whole—like completing a puzzle. When we trust this process of growing and healing, claiming each truth as it comes to us and feels right, we evolve into a more integrated, whole human being.

Rather than feeling afraid and crazy, we come to know our truth. Rather than feeling confused, we learn what's what. Rather than feeling empty and lost, we feel solid and real. Rather than getting triggered into the old vortex of rules and roles, we trust our internal reference point. Our own perceptions, thoughts, feelings, and experiences replace the definitions, roles, expectations, and judgments others may have bestowed upon us over the years. And we return home to our true self.

RETURNING TO OUR TRUE SELF

As we claim what fits *me*—honestly, completely, and without judgment, we trust our true self more and more. We know there is a *me*. We know where we fit and where we belong. We have a home—or rather, we are home again. And as we say *yes* to what feels true, the rest begins to fall away.

There Is a Me!

I used to wonder, is there a me?
And why do I seem to keep hiding in my armpit?
I didn't know; I just didn't know.
But now I know—there really is a me!
I can feel me from the inside
Through every muscle and tiny motion,
I can dance up and down inside my body,
And I feel ALIVE!
I know 'cuz when someone steps on my little toe,
I hurt.
I know 'cuz when my best friend moved away,
I felt sad and cried.
I know 'cuz when someone sits too close,
I want to move away.
And 'cuz I can wear pink wool socks when I want to.
I know 'cuz I have dreams for my life
and 'cuz I care about my kids
and my dog (and lots of other things, too).
I know 'cuz I have my own opinions about all kinds of things
and they don't always agree with yours!
And I have my own memories and my own room,
my own choices and my own skin and bones
that you can't take away.
I know 'cuz here I am in my body,
Alive . . . and fully experiencing me.

Chapter 11

Letting Go of What Is Not Me

What Am I Ready and Willing to Let Go Of?

I am working the seventh step in a twelve-step program, which involves letting go of *character defects*. Character defects are shortcomings—those behavioral patterns we have adopted that perhaps used to serve us in some way but now are actually in the way of continued growth. Often, character defects are specific parts of what I call our safety pattern. I think I have let go of all of mine.

As a final check-in before going on to the eighth step, I take another long sunrise walk in the foothills with my favorite hiker, Elliott, to ask if there are any more character defects I need to let go of. Not getting an instant response, I feel a little cocky about the thoroughness of my work. I come home, change clothes, and head off to my favorite Al-Anon meeting. All twelve-steppers know that *cocky* is not a good sign, but I am not seeing that yet.

I am usually comfortable with the people at this meeting. We meet together in this powerful circle every Wednesday morning, rain or shine. I appreciate their efforts toward recovery and trust their support of my own recovery. I feel safe here.

This morning, however, is different. I feel annoyed and impatient. Instead of focusing on my own issues, I am muttering inside: "Is she still dealing with that issue?" "He talks about that same thing every time he comes." "Her voice is so irritating." "She looks pathetic today." On and on and on I ramble.

All of a sudden, the old light bulb comes on and I get it. I do indeed have yet another character defect to let go of: judging others!

I am appalled! How embarrassing! Judging myself has been somehow acceptable to me all these years, perhaps even considered modest and humble, but judging others? No, good girls don't judge others. How can this be? I have taken great pride (there's that warning sign again) in my kindness toward others, my acceptance of others, and my ability to like everyone—only to now discover both this silent but nasty intolerance and its partner: righteous arrogance.

Well that doesn't last long. I recognize it right away as more judgment toward myself and I thought I had let go of that one! I am confronted in this awakening moment with my judgment toward both myself and others—and how they hook together. I can't let go of one without also letting go of the other.

I feel trapped and suddenly exposed. I somehow manage to make it through the meeting and slink quietly out the door when it is over.

Judging others is a difficult one for me to relinquish. I stay with the awareness for several months, noticing how pervasive and persistent my judging is. I notice how much it affects every relationship and how much it gets in my way of being fully alive. I notice how judging keeps me from my feelings and limits me instead to those muttering thoughts and opinions.

I notice that it keeps my children at a distance and that I can even feel the tight scowl on my face when I judge them. Do they notice that? I wonder if it shows. I notice that my judging isn't merely a hidden internal thought. It often grows into rude behavior toward others. I reluctantly discover that I am not as nice a person as I have always thought.

Even though I'm still in my five-year moratorium on relationships, I ask myself what I am looking for in a relationship and discover a very sad truth. The job description is so long and impossible that no man could ever meet the specifications. He would have to live in the basement and come up upon command! Yes, I am judging everyone it seems—even in my imagination.

I gradually stop condemning my judgment and get to know this behavior more objectively. I trust it has been useful to me at some earlier time and wonder how that could possibly be. As my attitude slowly shifts toward curiosity, I hear a deeper truth and come to understand this old familiar safety pattern of judging others.

I remember that I once concluded that my grandpa molested me because I had "let" him love me. One of my five-year-old solutions to keep safe, to make sure that the abuse never happened again, was to keep everyone at a distance so that nobody would hurt me. Judging others became part of preventing others from loving me—and I'm quite sure that it did.

I comprehend now as an adult, though, that getting molested didn't have anything to do with "letting" my grandpa love me, and I don't want others to stay away anymore. I can see that judging others doesn't keep me safe either, so it is no longer helpful. I begin to experience it as a heavy sandbag hanging on my shoulders, now separate from *me*. It is actually *not me*. It no longer fits the internal true self I have come to know and claim.

Continuing to be curious, I learn to recognize my judging more quickly. I acknowledge my truth about it with a few close friends. I discover that I don't even have to figure out all the reasons why I have become so judgmental. I just need to let it go.

I begin to feel that choice, that familiar opportunity at the Y in the road to let go of this quality I do not value, do not like, and no longer choose because it no longer fits me. Cautiously, I work my way toward becoming willing to let it go.

On yet another meditative sunrise walk, I risk asking my judging to leave—but just for the day. I am so surprised by how much more I enjoy other people that I try it a few more times. I discover that I feel better both physically and emotionally. I like other people more. I even like *me* more.

Then one day when I finally feel completely willing, I talk with my judgment as the separate entity it has now become. I thank it for protecting and helping me feel safer for so many years. I tell it that I am ready for it to leave. I give it back to what I call Universal Supply in the Sky—that source from which all our safety patterns seem to be so generously issued as needed to help us live our early life. When I stop judging my judging as bad and wrong, I see that it might actually be useful to another child someday. I certainly no longer need it. I let it go.

My judging leaves, as requested—almost too eagerly, it seems. And I know now that I will be okay without it.

THE ESSENCE OF NOT ME

Claiming *me* and letting go of what is *not me* fit together in a complementary manner like the Chinese yin and yang. They are parallel intertwined processes, often dependent on each other for completion and wholeness. Knowing what fits helps us to identify what does not fit and vice versa; knowing what does not fit us helps us to recognize what does.

Up to this point, we have focused on learning to recognize and claim what fits *me*. Now, can we see everything that does not fit? Can we see that *other* category?

Not me is all that does not fit our true self—all other ideas, all other things, all other events, all other qualities, all other people and their opinions, feelings, and needs—all of them. *Not me* also includes what used to fit us but no longer does—harmful habits and addictions, character defects, old rules and roles, old core beliefs, homes we have left behind, activities and jobs no longer purposeful, clothes we have worn out, relationships that no longer work, and certainly old safety patterns we no longer need. We may have adopted or merged with many things over the years for all kinds of reasons, but now we sort what genuinely fits our true self from what does not.

These others are the things we can let go of. They are leftovers from previous chapters of our life—excess baggage we carry around and accommodate. When we claim what fits *me* and let go of all that is *not me*, we cut the wheat from the chaff. What remains is our whole undiminished, harmonious, integrated true self—that internal reference point we increasingly trust.

This chapter calls attention to the things that may appear to be parts of our sense of self but that truly are not, whether those things are belongings we no longer need, activities that harm us, or certain behavioral qualities and patterns we may have adopted to feel safer. As we listen now for what is *not me*, we learn to recognize this distinction and begin to know what we can let go of. The sometimes painful process of letting go is described, demonstrating how it leads toward greater aliveness. As what fits and what does not fit both become clear, we find it increasingly easier to return to our true self. We discover that there really is life after letting go.

RECOGNIZING WHAT IS NOT ME

Many of us are aware of at least one thing that is *not me* that we hang onto but believe we need to let go of. Anna knew that she needed to let go of her kids. She was a stay-at-home mom who had devoted her days to her children for many years. They were now fourteen and twenty years old and she was still hovering over them way too much. She said she needed to create something new in her own life so they could be free to live their own lives. After all, she was still doing laundry for her twenty-year-old and waking him up in the morning so he could get to work on time.

Iris knew she needed to let go of her mother. She had taken care of her mom ever since she could remember. She had been there for her mother through her parents' divorce and the deaths of her mother's parents. She saw her mother as weak and vulnerable, unable to deal with life on her own. She called her mother every day to be sure she was all right. She made decisions for her mother, telling her what to do. She wasn't sure her mother could manage life without her attentive care.

Nora was close to retirement, trying desperately to hang on long enough to secure her pension, but her body was giving out. She knew she had to let go of something, but she wasn't sure what.

Clues that identify when we may need to let go of something that is *not me* include the following:

- Dreading a particular event
- Avoiding a particular person or group
- Feeling exhausted for no apparent reason
- Getting "burned out" and losing our passion or integrity
- Feeling overwhelmed by something we cannot control
- Losing our self in a relationship or job
- Pretending to enjoy an activity when we don't
- Resenting that we can't get what we want from someone

- Anticipating that others will respond negatively to us if we change
- Pushing hard to do more than we can reasonably do

Dreading, pretending, and resenting are excellent clues that we are trying to fit our round self into some square hole.

WHAT TO LET GO OF

Life is full of many opportunities for letting go. As infants, we learn to let go of our mommy and daddy every time we have a babysitter. We learn to let go of our teddy bear to go to school. We learn to let go of high school and parents to live on our own. Weddings, graduations, and funerals honor significant letting-go transitions. Pets die. Our children need us less and less frequently as they grow older—and we grow older. We don't always see these events as opportunities, but when we practice letting go with each life change, we build our skills and confidence that we can do so when we really need to.

Just as we learned to make smaller active choices before making bigger ones that became visible to others, it is easier to let go of things that do not show or affect others, such as unseen habits and things no one else will miss. Starting with small things, we can then build our letting-go skills and confidence before we need to deal with the reactions of others.

Some of these small places to begin that probably won't show to others include letting go of old clothes, knick-knacks we no longer value, weeds in the garden, traffic on the highway, a nickname that doesn't fit, and the trash. Purposely saying, "I choose to let go of these old shoes" might be a perfect place to begin.

Things to let go of that will show more to others as we gain more confidence might include certain relationships, old fears, addictions, outdated family roles, and our external point of reference.

Yes, there is much that is *not me*—and a lot of freedom to experience when we learn to let go of the no-longer-needed extras we have been carrying around.

THE ESSENCE OF LETTING GO

Letting go means to allow something to melt away, to dissipate from being with *me* or about *me* to being in that other category I call *not me*. It is a process of unattaching, a transition from hanging onto something to letting it have its own life. It involves a definite internal shift in perspective from believing that something is ours to recognizing and accepting that it truly is not.

Letting go is not the same as abandoning, not caring, pushing away, or getting something over with. It has nothing to do with revenge or control. It has nothing to do with looking good or letting go because we should. Those behaviors focus on others. Letting go is instead an internal process that rarely, if ever, involves others and never requires a particular response from others. In fact, others may not even notice when we let go of something.

Letting go doesn't just happen on its own, though. It requires a choice, our choice at the Y in the road. When a situation feels confusing or uncomfortable, we can examine what parts fit *me* and what parts do not fit *me*. We listen for both. Then we can claim the ones that fit and let go of all those that do not. Letting go moments are the times we clearly make this choice.

Letting go is also more than a choice. It is a process, and the process is the same whether we are letting go of something internal or something external. It is the same whether we are letting go of something small or something gigantic. The letting go process is the same whether it is a natural separation or unnatural. It is also the same process whether the letting go is long and gradual or way too sudden.

There are three basic stages of the letting go process: (1) a beginning awareness that we need to let go of something, (2) the emotional turmoil that typically comes as we are letting go, and then (3) a relieved ending when we become willing to go on with our life without whatever we have let go.

Hanging On to the Old

Since many of us are not skilled at letting go, we tend to resist change as long as possible, fighting it like crazy. We hang on to the old, denying that change is coming and trying desperately to control the outcome. We hang onto all kinds of things—objects, habits, people, the past, outdated beliefs, and useless junk. We store more and more of everything, it seems, rather than risk letting go of something we might need someday. We stay in jobs and relationships we no longer find meaningful. We avoid all kinds of uncomfortable feelings we may need to release. We fight our body to avoid aging. Hanging on to what is *not me* confuses us and can take enormous amounts of energy.

Sometimes, when we must let go of something, we quickly switch to the other extreme to hurriedly get rid of it. "If I have to do it, I'll do it right now," we say. We suddenly clean all our closets and let someone else haul it all away. We start hating someone to get her out of our life. We lose weight entirely too fast. When a loved one dies, we pretend to get through our grief as quickly as possible. Well, letting go rarely works that way either. Throwing something away in a sudden *urge to purge* is the opposite extreme of hanging on too long—and it is not the same as letting go.

We need to be gentle with our self. Letting go is a *process*—a gradual process that begins as soon as we become aware there is something in particular that we need to let go of. Hanging on to the old is part of that emerging awareness. Hanging on to the old is the natural first step in the letting go process.

Surrendering to Change

The second stage in the process of letting go begins the moment we realize we can no longer fight the impending change. Something has to give. Something has to change. Our old way is gone and the new way is not yet in place. Whether this change is a small one or a big one and whether or not it has been our choice, we are in the mire of a transition. We don't yet know what the new way will be or where we are going, but we can feel the falling apart of the old and the inevitable need to surrender to the change.

We likely experience a lot of feelings at this point—fear, confusion, powerlessness, anger, and aloneness to name a few. Our feelings may be mixed up and more intense and volatile than usual as we emotionally bounce off the walls. We don't know what's what. We don't know what to do. We don't know where our life is going. We don't know what will happen if we let go. We often feel lost and vulnerable. Like an earthquake, the ground beneath us is shifting and we don't know when the trembling will stop.

Do we really have to let go? Can we let go? Can we survive? Are we making the right choice? Sometimes it feels as if we are letting go of a precious part of our self. Sometimes we have never known life without whatever we are letting go, so how would we know for certain that we could survive without it? How could we know what our life will be like without it? Life could be better . . . or worse. We can't be certain of much of anything.

The intensity of the fear and uncertainty we feel inside tells us the extent to which we believe this particular thing we are letting go of is somehow related to our deep need for safety. Fears, remember, are not always rational. They may feel childlike. They often serve as signals that notify us when something new and different is coming. While uncomfortable at times, the more thoroughly we work through each and every fear, the easier letting go becomes.

If you are having difficulty letting go when you believe you are ready and willing, it means that you are still attached in some sneaky way you may not yet recognize. Perhaps you don't yet trust that you will be okay. Perhaps you feel resentful that you have to let go. Perhaps a core belief is strangling your thoughts. Or you might simply be having an "I don't wanna ..." moment. Take your time. Letting go is a process, not merely a decision.

Asking these questions may help you to let go:

+ Are you remembering that you have a choice, that you don't have to let go?
+ What are you afraid will happen if you let go?
+ What might you have to face?
+ What do you blame yourself for?
+ What do you wish could be different?
+ What are you trying to control?
+ What will letting go say about you as a person?
+ What else might you need to claim in order to let go?
+ What old belief is keeping you from letting go?
+ What or who are you judging as bad or wrong?
+ What else would help you become ready to let go?

Sonia once wrote out a long list of things she felt ready to let go of, crumpled up the paper, and threw it into a roaring fire in the fireplace. But it wouldn't burn! She yelled at it to burn. She pushed it around with the fire stoker. She considered pulling it back out but then decided once again that yes, she was genuinely ready to let these things go. When she felt that stronger, more solid choice to let go, remembering the Y in the road, the list finally burned.

We cannot possibly be in control during this transition stage. It is often emotional and messy, but when we surrender and take each tiny step at a time, we get through the transition ... and we let go.

Choosing to Go On

Once we realize that our life might be better if we let go and feel fairly certain we can survive doing so, we let go and choose to go on with our life—the third stage in the process of letting go. We take that proverbial leap of faith and step off the imaginary cliff, floating and trusting the air currents like a downy bird feather.

If we want to, we can first experiment with letting go. Perhaps we let go of something specific for a day at a time or even just for a particular event to see how it feels, as I first let go of judging others. We thus try out the change, knowing we can still go back to our old way if we want to. Maybe we feel curious about what letting go might create in our life, and we notice what happens when we do. Doing this emphasizes our choice at the Y in the road.

Iris, who knew she needed to let go of her mom, decided to view her mom as growing up and going off to college. She then experimented with cutting back on those daily phone calls to see if her mom would be okay. Instead of telling her mom what to do, she experimented with helping her mom brainstorm options and then letting her mom decide what to do. She began to visit her mom less frequently. Interestingly, her mother seemed to do well with the changes, and Iris could then let go of the unnecessary responsibility that no longer fit her.

Sooner or later, when we experiment and practice surrendering, there comes a moment of letting go completely. Those heavy sandbags hanging on our shoulders drop away. Our body relaxes. Our mind calms. We feel safer. Like shedding our heavy winter coat when spring finally arrives, we feel lighter. We feel relief. We move more freely—and we often hear that long, relaxing sigh.

Nora, as mentioned earlier, was close to retirement but not yet quite there. She needed to continue working another entire year to secure her pension, but she was beginning to hate going to work. After twenty-nine years of hard work, she was angry that she had recently been demoted. She no longer felt valued by her coworkers. Her resentment was keeping her awake at night and she was getting exhausted. The whole situation was affecting her physical health. She began to wonder if she could actually make it to retirement.

When Nora became aware that she needed to somehow let go of work emotionally before she could physically retire, her transition began. Together we brainstormed ideas and worked out a plan to practice letting go.

In the morning, when she got out of her car, she would say "hello" to work, go in, and do her job. Then at the end of her shift, when she reached her car again, she would take a moment to turn around and say "good-bye," emphasizing the line between work and the rest of her life: "Good-bye, work. I'm done for today. I'll be back tomorrow." Then she would get into her car and spend the time driving home focusing ahead on her evening, rather than on all the things that had gone wrong at work, as she had previously done.

As Nora practiced letting go of work each day, she discovered that she wanted to stop by her sister's shop on her way home. It was fun and brought a sparkle back into her life. She began to look forward to getting there each day. As she became clear that she would spend considerable time helping in the shop after she retired, she began to sleep better again and her fatigue dissipated. She gradually let go of work as the dominant focus of her life.

Even as we feel vulnerable stepping into new territory, we often know that letting go is setting us free. While we can't possibly know where the process of our life will take us, we trust it, somehow just knowing that we are on the right track.

Anna, who knew she needed to let go of her children more, accepted a part-time job that fit her personality and skills perfectly. It was not an easy adjustment for her or her family, but soon she was beaming with enthusiasm. She loved working again, and her children were both doing just fine without her constant attention. She knew she was on the right track.

Once I had let go of judging others, the world looked brighter to me—less dismal, less violent, and less negative. Perhaps it was I who had become less dismal, less violent, and less negative. I began to feel more confident, as if I could let go of all kinds of things. I wanted to clean my closets, cleaning externally just as I had cleaned house internally. Life felt simpler.

Letting go usually feels great. Occasionally, though, when we let go of something that is *not me*, we experience an uneasy void that reminds us of that horrible emptiness we experienced earlier when our sense of self was still underdeveloped. Some vulnerable memories may get triggered, creating an urge to quickly refill that emptiness with whatever we have just let go of—or perhaps with some addiction we tend to use whenever we feel uncomfortable. Perhaps anything would seem to do in this desperate moment to relieve the temporary discomfort.

If we interpret this momentary emptiness instead as a quiet openness that creates room for something new and better to come into our life, we are likely to be pleasantly surprised. If we can sit quietly in this new openness with an attitude of curiosity, perhaps even smiling that little smile that barely turns up the corners of our mouth, we will notice what comes next. While we cannot predict what new thing might come to us, it is likely to be something more alive, something that fits us better now.

LETTING GO WITHOUT JUDGMENT

You may notice that I often add the phrase "without judgment" as I describe letting go. This is a critical point. Judging what is *not me* keeps us attached to what we are trying to let go of, because it keeps us focused externally. Thus, if we are judging what we think we have let go, we have not yet completely let go.

Judging what is *not me* as bad or wrong often serves to protect us in some sneaky way. Maybe we feel right if we define something different from us as wrong. Maybe we feel better about our own ways of doing things when we judge other ways as bad. Sometimes we judge others as better than us in some way. Whether we judge other ways as better or worse, judging sacrifices our ability to accurately assess what fits *me* and what doesn't.

When we are not judging, we can see the object or quality we are letting go as simply *not me*, not a part of *me* in other words. Maybe we no longer need it, but it may fit others. Whatever we are letting go of certainly has a right to exist, and there is no need to prevent others from claiming it as fitting them.

Judging is not a part of our sense of self, and it does not help us grow to trust our self. It is instead an essential, defining part of duality. Duality, remember, is that particular way of thinking that centers on two opposite extremes—what is right and therefore good versus what is wrong and therefore bad. In duality, everything is compared by this basic guideline, applying one end of the duality to *me* and the other end to *not me*. Duality feeds our illusion that we are right—or wrong. It is a way of thinking that severely limits possibilities.

It helps to remember that we were not born thinking in duality. As infants, we could only live from the reference point of our own internal sense of self. We had nothing to compare our self to until we became aware of things outside of us that were *not me*. Rather than simply expanding to notice the external world *in addition to* our internal world, many of us learned to watch outside *rather than* listen to our internal sense of self. That is the traumatic disconnect described earlier in Chapter 3. We learned to judge good and bad, rather than simply choose what fit us and what didn't. Now, as we sort out what fits *me* from what is *not me*, we discover that we must let go of judging to fully trust and live from our true self.

There simply is no need to judge what is *not me*. I like to think that claiming what fits *me* and letting go of what is *not me* is like eating at a salad bar. We take what we want and leave the rest for others. There is no need to judge the beets or cottage cheese as bad just because we don't like them.

LETTING GO WITH LOVE

Relationships with loved ones are often a challenging entanglement of what we need to claim and what we need to let go of. This entanglement shows most clearly when a relationship changes significantly, as when a loved one breaks off our relationship, dies, or moves away. Some of us hang on until the end becomes absolutely unavoidable. Then we might crash and burn emotionally until we can work our way through all the varied feelings involved in the transition. Hopefully, we eventually choose to let go and go on.

In order to freely go on, we claim all that is ours, all that fits us— our fears, our feelings, our loving, our choices, our belongings, our responsibilities, and our own life. And we let go of all that is not ours, all that is *not me*—the other person's fears, feelings, loving, choices, belongings, responsibilities, and life.

We do not have to let go of loving the other person, because loving is a quality of *me*. We can keep our memories, precious gifts, and feelings of warmth and caring in our heart when a relationship ends— whether the ending is our choice or not. For example, we still love our children when they leave home. We still love pets when they disappear. We still love those who die. When we claim our loving as a part of *me*, we can more easily let go of others. Loving and letting go are not incompatible. We can let go of others as we need to—with love.

Lindsay, who knew she needed to leave her husband in order to protect her children from his violence, kept saying, ". . . but I love him." In her mind, loving him seemed to be a reason to stay with him no matter what. She believed she had to stop loving him in order to leave him, and she couldn't stop loving him. Once she could claim her loving as her own quality, she became able to leave the violence that did not fit her. She didn't have to hate her husband to protect her children.

Iris had always loved the baby she had once lost. Letting herself continue to love that little baby helped her twenty years later to finally forgive herself and let go of both her baby and her guilt, knowing the baby's death was not her fault.

When a friend of mine was dying, I cried a lot. I had not yet experienced many deaths and was having a difficult time. One day when I was sobbing about losing her, my wise teenage daughter said, "Mom, you don't have to lose her; you just need to let her go." This may seem like a fine point, but it is an important distinction. We don't have to lose our brain to let go of a thought. We don't have to lose our body to let go of feelings. We don't have to lose our life to let go of an addiction. We don't have to lose a child to let him venture out into the world on his own.

The word *losing* implies failing in some way when we are thinking in duality. Losing suggests that we are not winning. Losing suggests that we had the object or person to begin with and failed to keep it, so now it no longer belongs to us. It suggests that something bad has been done to us or that we lost control over the situation. Do you hear the judgment in these words—losing, failing? Do you hear the external focus on others—done to us, lost control? When we let go, we recognize that we never had control over the situation to begin with. That loved one never belonged to us. It wasn't up to us to keep him or her.

Once I was able to see this distinction, it was easier to let go. I wasn't *losing* my friend. I had never *had* her. It was simply her time to leave us all. Her leaving wasn't about *me*. I felt my emptiness, honored her, cried some more, claimed the gift of having experienced her in my life, said good-bye, and eventually became able to let go—with love.

RETURNING HOME TO OUR TRUE SELF

When we let go of anything that no longer fits, we will likely feel lighter and more alive, but most of us need to learn this lesson from our own experiences. When my mother was dying, I was afraid that I wouldn't be able to deal with her death. In the midst of my struggle to let her go, I had a dream of being a little boat. A big rope connected me with the much bigger mother ship. Feeling little and desperately trying to keep up with the bigger boat, I hung on to that rope for a while, but then I couldn't hang on any longer. The powerful mother ship sailed away into the nighttime fog. I was left there, sailing around in the sea by myself, feeling a bit lost but also surprised that I was perfectly safe and okay.

Over the following few days, I began to see my mother as the individual person she was, living her own life as best she could. I began to trust that she had made the choices in her life that had best fit her. I found myself whispering, "I give you your life. I give you your death. I give you your right to make your own choices," to clearly acknowledge that she wasn't mine to keep. She wasn't part of *me*. She was indeed a separate human being. Eventually, I was able to add "... and I take back my life, my death, and my right to make my own choices," as I also claimed what fit *me*. That simple dream image helped me to let go of her with love. It helped me find the line that distinguished my mother from me. It helped me claim what fit *me* and also let go of what was *not me*.

When she died, I still cried, of course. I felt the loss of that mother ship sailing off into the nighttime fog, but I also knew that I would be okay, even when I felt scared, lost, and vulnerable. She hadn't been mine to keep. I hadn't failed in any way. I hadn't done anything wrong and neither had she. There was no reason to judge the loss as bad. There was no reason to judge her. There was no reason to judge *me*. I just needed to let go. She was *not me*.

As we claim what fits and let go of the rest with love instead of judgment, we increasingly trust that integrated home base from which we now live our life—our true self. And we learn that there is life after letting go—our own life.

Cleaning Out the Closets

Let's collect it! More and more and more!
Store it away for years and years.
Might need it someday, you know.
And maybe more is better, like they say.
Maybe it means something.
Maybe it's important.
Doesn't matter what—just keep it all!
Memories, friends, "just things" from twenty years ago,
Feelings, jewels, letters, books already read and underlined,
Little kids' clothes, worn out shoes,
Broken flowerpots, leftover paint,
Newspaper clippings, faded curtains,
Pictures and presents that never did mean anything.
Hanging on forever.
What a load it comes to be!
No longer helpful,
It sucks my energy like a whining child.
A burden filling nooks and crannies and closets,
Soaking up room in my body, in my home,
Like a pacing elephant—a load too heavy to move.
Slows me down
Like a yoke on an ox, pulling the old wagon
With not-quite-round wooden wheels.
How things change over the years.
Now I want a lighter load—
And I want cleaner closets!

Chapter 12

Honoring Our Own Boundaries

Where Is That Line Between Me and Others?

With no warning, Marni accuses me of being seductive with her boyfriend. She is angry! She says I keep looking at Hank and sitting close to him. She thinks I am trying to steal him from her. She doesn't trust me and wants to know what is going on.

I gasp, feeling embarrassed but also confused. I resist my impulse to run and hide, aware that I have never been accused of such a thing. I am flooded with memories. I try hard to listen to her, but I remember being on the other side of this painful issue years ago when I once lost a man I loved to another woman. It was messy. It was confusing. It hurt a lot. I had come out of that experience promising myself that I would never date a man who was already in a relationship.

Besides, I don't like this guy—at least not yet. I don't even know him. I just met him when this group came together two days ago. Yes, I have watched for an opportunity to have a conversation with him. I did sit close to him in one of our sessions, but not because I was seducing him. I wanted to get to know him because I have heard my friend Marni talk about him. I am curious about what he is like, but I clearly have no interest in stealing him. I check inside again to be sure. No, I'm not even feeling attracted to him. Her accusation is simply not true for me.

I notice that Marni is attacking me. She is not simply asking me; she is accusing me. I feel her arrows of attack flying in my direction, but they seem to fly right on past. They don't come into my heart. It feels unusual.

I also notice that I have lots of questions. Is she purposely trying to discredit me in front of these other people I don't know for some reason? Doesn't she want me to be her friend? What is *really* going on? It doesn't occur to me to ask her these questions—at least not now, because I can't move. I am frozen again. *Hmmm.* . . .

Well then, how am I going to handle this situation? Everyone is looking at me for my response. I don't know what to do, but I have to say *something*. I'm afraid the other people won't like me. I'm afraid they will take her side against me, believing her more than me. I'm afraid I will be humiliated. I don't want to argue with Marni. She already has her own conclusions.

With hesitation and more than a little trepidation, I finally open my mouth hoping something sane will come out and that my voice won't crackle too much.

Fortunately, I don't start off with a meek "I'm sorry . . . I didn't mean to . . ." That would be my old safety pattern talking—just agree with others and slink away to hide and shut down. It's inviting but not a good idea.

And I don't start off with "Are you crazy? I don't even like your boyfriend!" That is also a little tempting but not a good idea. It would be the other extreme.

You wouldn't be getting attacked this way if you had been a good girl. I hear this silently in my head. It's an old core belief rearing its ugly head once again. I thought that one was long gone . . . I recognize it but it no longer fits. I quickly let it go.

No, instead I take a deep breath and simply speak my truth. "I have heard you talk about Hank, and this is the first time I've met him. I just wanted to have a conversation with him to get to know him better. That is all. I am not trying to steal him from you."

The two of us have by now become the center of attention. Marni invites the others to share their observations but no one does. I don't think anyone else has noticed anything. She keeps going on for what seems like an eternity making endless arguments to prove her point. I sit there, calmly repeating my simple truth each time it's my turn to say something in the conversation. I don't fight back. I don't attack her in return. I also don't back down, and surprisingly, I don't get confused. I don't give up. I don't cry. I simply speak my truth, and I notice that I feel increasingly clear and calm as I restate my truth several times. I can feel my precious boundaries in place exactly where they belong. I like this feeling. . . .

Finally, the group takes a break. Marni doesn't pursue the issue any further. Neither does anyone else. It's over for me as well. I don't need to talk about it anymore. I don't need support. I don't need to hide or cry. I have said all that I needed to say. I feel relieved. And I hear another long familiar sigh . . .

DEFINING BOUNDARIES

Boundaries are the borders around us that distinguish *me* from all that is *not me*. They are the lines that separate us and our territory from other individuals and their territory. We do not sprawl all over the place and neither do others. We have edges. Everything does. When we look at a book, it has a skin-like cover around the outside and the story is inside. The whole book is right there. We can see it and touch it. There are more books that may look similar but each one is a book unto itself. Each book has a story, a voice, a style, and an identity that goes with that book that is distinct from other books, and so it is with us.

As we repeatedly claim what fits and let go of what does not fit, our boundaries naturally evolve and increasingly differentiate us from that vast other category of *not me*. At some point, we begin to feel them quietly and effectively surrounding our body like silent soldiers on sentry duty, gently and reliably protecting us.

Perhaps a woman cries and we see her tears, but we know they are her tears, not ours. We feel compassion for her, but we don't feel her feelings. Instead, we feel our own. Perhaps we express a different opinion and doing so feels okay. Perhaps someone gets mad at us, and we realize that we are solid enough now to get mad at. We see it as a sign of progress. The energetic aggressive arrows fly right on by our boundaries rather than pierce our heart the way they used to—just as Marni's arrows flew past me.

Because boundaries are a developmental issue related to the sense of self, it is difficult to even comprehend the concept of boundaries until we begin to feel them in action. When I first heard others talk about boundaries, I had no clue what they meant. I took an assertiveness training class and decided that boundaries meant being able to say "no" to others. I tried and tried to set boundaries as the class had suggested, but that didn't work very well for me. I just didn't have the solid energy behind my "no" to mean it and be able to follow through. Later, when I could feel my boundaries in action, I could say "no" when I needed to and also follow through.

As we begin to sense our own boundaries strengthening, others often do, too. If we have been too passive and others have been walking on us a bit, their experience might be like a rug getting up off the floor to start walking around. Maybe they don't want the rug to start walking around, so they attempt to get it back on the floor where they think it belongs. Others, however, will see us as more real, more honest, more open, more courageous, more available for a deeper relationship, and perhaps even more fun to be with. These people will appreciate our growth and the opportunity such growth offers to better connect with us. We just can't expect everyone in our life to be excited for us and supportive of our developing boundaries.

This chapter distinguishes two levels of personal boundaries. It describes how we know our boundaries are present and identifies specific ways to honor our own boundaries. Honoring the boundaries of others then follows quite naturally.

TWO LEVELS OF BOUNDARIES

It is interesting that we refer to *boundaries* as plural rather than *boundary* as a single entity. At some level, we all apparently realize that there are two levels of personal boundaries. The first—the boundary we call our skin—is more concrete and easier to recognize. It distinguishes what is inside our physical body from what is outside. We can touch our skin, see it, feel it, smell it, and even taste it, so our skin boundary is clear to most of us. We can readily identify whenever this boundary has been violated. We hurt physically when a knife cuts our finger, germs invade to make us ill, a stranger pushes us in a crowd, or as a more extreme example, we get beaten or raped.

Our second-level boundary is somewhat outside our skin and admittedly more difficult to recognize. It completely surrounds us on all sides, protecting us just as our skin does, but it is invisible like a transparent bubble. It is this boundary that naturally surrounds our body to protect us when our sense of self develops sufficiently. I call it our *space boundary*.

Perhaps you can feel your space boundary with your hands. I invite you to try it by putting your hands up close to your chest with your palms open and turned outward. Closing your eyes may help you focus on the energy in your hands. Now very slowly move your hands outward away from your body until you sense a subtle change in the energy in your palms. Of course you can push right on through it, but can you feel the change? That is your space boundary. The stronger your sense of self becomes, the easier it will be to feel.

We also feel our space boundary in action when something *not me* is violating *me*. This is the line that feels crossed when someone sits too close, yells at us, betrays us, or plays loud music that we don't want to listen to. This is the violation we describe as feeling used by others to meet their own needs. Perhaps a salesperson aggressively works on us to close a deal, someone steals from us or doesn't return something borrowed, or another insults us or calls us by a derogatory nickname. This was the attack I felt when Marni accused me of something I had not done.

These invasions don't necessarily hurt our body, but they bother us. We feel the intrusion, the transgression against our will. Our concentration gets interrupted. We say that person hurt our feelings, that she doesn't have a right to treat us that way, or that something wasn't fair. We want the invasion to stop. We might pull away, feeling small, insignificant, wrong, inferior, ashamed, or invisible. We often feel angry and resentful. We might want to attack the other person back. Or perhaps we feel crazy, not understanding the violation at all.

We feel violated because our space boundary has been violated. Something *not me* has entered our *me* territory without permission and we notice it now—because we experience our evolving boundaries.

RECOGNIZING OUR OWN BOUNDARIES

We experience challenges to our boundaries every day. Other people ask us to do things to meet their needs and sometimes talk to us longer than we want. The phone rings. The traffic is heavy. Construction workers make too much noise. The kids need lunch. The dog needs a walk. Bills need to be paid. The news is upsetting.

Before we deal with others, though, let's take a look at what we might be doing to our self. We violate our own boundaries whenever we do something inconsistent with our true self. This may include one or more of the following:

- Hurrying too much
- Pushing to do more than we can reasonably do
- Not doing what we really want to be doing
- Shutting down emotionally
- Not taking time alone when needed
- Owing others too much money or too many favors
- Not listening to our body
- Absorbing the stress and emotions of others
- Losing our self in a relationship or work
- Attaching to phones, computers, and social media in ways we don't value

When we focus on external demands that do not fit our true self, we often end up feeling scattered, exhausted, and overwhelmed—back in the Good-Girl Jail. We lose our boundaries. We lose our internal reference point. We lose the connection with our self once again.

Consider a day, perhaps a Saturday, when we have no commitments to others, no pressures, and no interruptions. It is a morning we can wake up asking, "What do I really want to do today?" When we allow room to choose our own priorities, we feel solid and calm inside. Our deepest needs get met. We stay connected with our precious internal reference point and our boundaries remain clear.

How different we feel inside! The primary difference is recognizing and honoring our own boundaries. While every day cannot be a Saturday, can we begin to honor our own boundaries enough that our external behavior and choices fit our true self? Can we do it more often?

BOUNDARY SKILLS

Let's consider three specific skills we can develop to honor our own boundaries, further clarifying that line between *me* and *not me*. We can learn to create gentle transitions between activities, resign roles that no longer fit us, and say "yes" and "no" with equal ease.

Creating Gentle Transitions—Boundary Skill #1

When we say the words *hello* and *good-bye* at the beginning and end of an activity, we honor our boundaries for that particular interaction, opening it and closing it. The curtain opens when a play begins and closes when it is over. A movie announces its beginning with the title and its ending with the credits. We say "hello" when we answer the phone and "good-bye" when we end the call. It is as if we are saying, "I'm here and choose to spend this time with you" in the beginning and then "We are finished interacting, at least for now" afterward. It is courteous to acknowledge our boundaries to others in this way. More importantly for our sense of self, however, emphasizing the perimeters around an event helps to keep our own boundaries clear to us as we shift our attention from one activity to the next.

It may be easiest to learn about different kinds of transitions by observing how others transition with us and how we feel in response. One day I went directly from a chiropractic appointment to see my accountant. At the chiropractor's office, I waited a long time for him while vulnerably lying on my stomach on his treatment table with my feet toward the door. He thus entered the room from behind me which made it awkward to greet each other. He moved quickly and talked loudly. He gave me my treatment and left the room just as quickly. There was barely any casual conversation. I didn't have a chance to ask questions. I felt no interpersonal connection. A noisy tornado could have just blown through. I left feeling off-balance, brushed aside as if I were nothing more than a mark on his to-do list on a busy day. It took some effort on my part to reconnect with myself.

In contrast, when I entered my accountant's office, I was greeted warmly. She made eye contact and chatted with me for a just a moment, relating to me as an equal person. We talked and laughed as we reviewed my taxes. I had time to ask questions. At the end, we chatted casually a bit more as she walked me to her door, easing the "good-bye" transition for us both. I had participated in setting the pace, the agenda, and how much I shared. We had both worked to create a good connection with gentle transitions in and out. My boundaries had easily remained intact throughout the appointment. I walked out of her office feeling respected and whole—and still connected with my self.

Since that day, I have discovered other places to purposely create gentle transitions to honor my own boundaries—before and after traveling, before and after having company, moving into and out of relationships, driving to and from work, easing in and out of sleep, and healing from an illness or accident.

We can tell we are creating gentle transitions when we feel like the same centered person as we move through our day going into and out of various activities. We remain connected with our true self, our boundaries left intact.

Resigning Outdated Roles—Boundary Skill #2

Resigning outdated roles is a second skill that honors our own boundaries. With our sense of self stronger now and our boundaries becoming clear, we can relate to others directly from our true self.

Rather than relate through the filter of an adopted role that no longer fits, we can let go of the role.

As part of the Good-Girl Jail, many of us adopted a specific role that made it possible to fit into our unique family and community. Perhaps the role was a way to meet the needs of others or a way to keep safe. That specific role probably became part of our safety pattern, and we may have related to others from that long-outdated role ever since.

It can be difficult to identify what our role has been, because it feels so automatic and normal. Sharon Wegscheider-Cruse identified four basic roles that children in alcoholic families tend to adopt:[31] (1) *the hero*, whose role is to achieve to make the family look good, (2) *the scapegoat*, whose role is to take the blame for everything that goes wrong, (3) *the lost child*, whose role is to remain quietly good and invisible, not needing anything from anyone, and (4) *the mascot*, whose role is to distract everyone from their problems, often by making them laugh. All four are ways to fit into a family by meeting the needs of others more than our own needs—also known as a *role* by definition. Whether or not we grew up in an alcoholic family, many of us have adopted some sort of a role.

Jenny saw her role as *the crazy one*, a specific form of the scapegoat. All of the family problems were blamed on her craziness, which left the rest of the family feeling completely innocent. Jenny's role was to carry all the responsibility for everything that went wrong for the family, even after her parents divorced and she had grown and left home. She found it difficult to live her own life as an adult, because her family still needed her to be the crazy one and she was used to taking the blame. To resign this outdated role, she gradually and quietly decreased contact with her birth family and increased contact with friends, thus creating her own non-crazy life with others who had no need to blame her for whatever went wrong. While it took considerable effort on her part, she no longer automatically accepted her family's blame. It was a huge achievement for her.

Living from a role hampers our efforts to trust our sense of self and live our own life, but once a role is identified and we choose to honor our own boundaries, we can quietly resign. It may not be easy, but we can let it go. It is not ours. It is *not me*.

Saying "Yes" And "No" with Equal Ease—Boundary Skill #3

While not an easy skill to learn, becoming able to say both "yes" and "no" is indeed a critical third skill to develop to honor our own boundaries.

Children's compliance is highly valued in our society and most of us were taught as children to do whatever we were told to do by adults. Some of us were punished severely for saying "no." We may have learned to think of the word *no* as defiant, rude, or perhaps even mean. Indeed, *no* has been trained out of many of us as part of the Good-Girl Jail.

Anna says it feels safer to have stronger boundaries, but she never feels completely safe when she needs to speak up to say "no." She can do it now, but it is not yet comfortable. I think she speaks for many of us.

At the moment we realize we want to say "no," we have come to a Y in the road. We have choices and can sit at that juncture as long as we need to, saying "maybe" or "give me a moment" until we know for sure whether we need to say "yes" or "no."

When we choose to say "no," some effective, respectful ways to say it to others include the following:

- "No, thank you."
- "I'm really not interested."
- "That doesn't fit for me, at least not now."

- ♦ "This isn't working very well for me."
- ♦ "What if we did something different?"
- ♦ "Let's see if we can find a better way."
- ♦ "I really can't do this."
- ♦ "I really do need to say no."

These are polite, kind, gentle yet assertive ways to say "no." They work well because they are words that are easy to say in a matter-of-fact tone of voice and difficult for others to argue with. We are simply speaking our truth from our internal reference point, as I did with Marni when she accused me of stealing her boyfriend. We are not trying to hurt anyone. We are not being rebellious or rude. We are not saying we don't like the other person or don't care about that person's needs. Instead, we are remembering that we have a choice. We are choosing what fits *me*—and letting go of what is *not me*. We are honoring our own boundaries.

The most difficult part of learning to say "no" is to stay focused on our own truth rather than on the other person's possible reactions.

Whenever I have difficulty saying "no," I think about what I would want a good friend to do if we had made plans to go to the movies together, but when the time came to go, she needed to stay home for some precious time to herself instead. I would want her to trust our friendship enough to be able to tell me her truth and say "no." I wouldn't want her to go to the movies with me just because she had given me her word days earlier when it seemed like a good idea. I might be disappointed, but her welfare and her ability to say "no" in our relationship would be much more important to our long-term friendship than seeing the movie together on that particular day. We could always go another time or I could still go by myself or with someone else. Then I would also feel permission to say "no" to her at some other time, if I needed to.

It is easier to say "no" when we simultaneously say "yes" to an alternative that better fits us. When we say "yes" to what fits *me* and "no" to whatever does not at the same time, we can see that "yes" and "no" fit together in a complementary manner that honors our boundaries.

Learning to say "yes" is thus just as important to honoring our own boundaries as saying "no." And as our "yes" grows stronger and grows into "YES," we are saying "YES" to our true self, our internal reference point, our truth. We are saying "YES" to our own life, our needs, our feelings, our body, and our integrity. We are saying "YES" to coming fully alive.

HONORING THE BOUNDARIES OF OTHERS

Does all this emphasis on returning to our internal reference point make us unbearably selfish, unable to be kind to others or even to notice them? Quite the opposite turns out to be true.

As our boundaries develop, we also readily notice and more easily sense the boundaries of others. The more solid our sense of self becomes, the more we are able to see others as individual beings just like us with their own needs, bodies, feelings, and core beliefs. They make their own active choices and spend their time alone as they want. We comprehend that others have the same right to claim what fits them and let go what does not. They have the same need to honor their own boundaries. As we learn to listen for our boundaries, we also listen for the boundaries of others. The two naturally develop together.

Iris had a history of hurting her own body in various ways on purpose. She had been learning to process through her feelings rather than hurt herself and was making good progress honoring her own boundaries in this particular manner. One day, she began to weep a gentle but deep, heartfelt sadness. When she could talk again, she said, "Oh, I have hurt so, so many other people. I wish I hadn't. I regret that." As she had become able to recognize and honor her own boundaries, she also recognized and respected the boundaries of others.

BOUNDARY CONFUSION

Sometimes our boundaries become entangled with the boundaries of another person. All of a sudden, we sometimes wonder whose needs are going to get met here—yours or mine? These moments are invitations at the Y in the road to return to the vortex of rules and roles to argue about who is good and right and who is bad and wrong. These invitations into duality can be surprisingly seductive and are crucial moments to honor everyone's boundaries.

Boundary confusion sometimes occurs when we ask someone to help us meet our own needs. We have many needs that are more easily met with the assistance of others and we always have the right to ask for what we need from others. In fact, we can ask anyone for anything.

Asking, however, doesn't mean that we always get what we want. Other people are not obligated to meet our needs just because we ask them to. We never have the right to expect or demand that others meet our needs. This is the point at which we sometimes run over our own edges and begin violating the boundaries of others. Others always have the same right we do to say "yes," "no," or even "maybe"— because they have boundaries, too.

Another common area of boundary confusion involves giving gifts. Sonia, for example, struggled for years to find good Christmas presents for her aging mother. She had tried giving expensive gifts. She had tried giving simple gifts. She had tried giving things that Sonia herself would enjoy. She couldn't find anything that her mother seemed to appreciate. Finally giving up, she impulsively sent her mother a silly little stuffed Santa. Well, her mother loved it! She saved it and showed it to everyone. Sonia was genuinely surprised.

What Sonia learned that Christmas was that giving wasn't about trying to get a specific response from her mom to meet her own need to feel like a good daughter. That approach had been violating her mother's boundaries. Giving was instead about giving what fit her to give—and then letting the gift be her mother's to do with as she chose. She learned to let go completely of both the gift and her mother's response. Attempting to control the response she wanted wasn't what gift-giving was about.

Boundaries can also become very confusing when a loved one is dying. Kathy struggled with this as her husband was slowly dying from cancer. She had been his primary caregiver throughout the entire process. One day, she said, "I feel like I am dying right along with him." Her comment caught my attention instantly. Could she find that line between her and her husband? Could she honor her own boundaries while also honoring his through this difficult process? She didn't have answers to these questions in that moment, but when I saw her again a couple of weeks later, she looked much brighter. She was less exhausted. She had thought about my questions and had found that line. He was dying, but she was not. She had her own life to claim and live. She let go of what was not her. She honored his boundaries as well as her own by letting him go with love—and no judgment.

LETTING GO OF OUR NEED TO CONTROL

It can be quite a challenge to honor the boundaries of those around us while also honoring our own boundaries. It becomes possible only when we let go of our persistent need to control.

One December, when my son was twenty and my daughter was seventeen, they had planned to drive with their dad to spend a few days with their grandparents. When their dad had to cancel the trip, they decided to go anyway. I was concerned but trusted their driving abilities.

What I didn't know was that they were driving at night across a sparsely populated area when it was twenty degrees below zero. The car spun out on ice going around a corner and landed upside down in the ditch. They managed to find their jackets in the dark and walk to the nearest farmhouse to ask for help. The farmer took them in, let them sleep, and fed them breakfast.

Then they called me. I heard my son tell me what had happened. I heard him say that they were safe and had not been hurt. I heard that they were getting the car fixed and would drive back home when it was done.

Then, when I got off the phone, my thoughts erupted. They could have been killed in the accident—both of them! Or they could have been injured and died from hypothermia before anyone rescued them. There could have been no one around to help. The farmer could have been an ax murderer. Finally, I sobbed as my fears ran wild.

Both of my children could have been killed—just like that, in that instant. I could not have done anything to prevent it even if I had known what was happening. All those years of looking after their needs, of believing that I knew what they needed, of assuming they would live beyond me, of trusting they would be okay . . .

Something very deep shifted inside me with that phone call. I began to grasp that I couldn't even keep my own children alive. Their lives were not within my realm of control. I did not know what their lives were all about or what they needed in this lifetime. My children, I discovered in that awakening moment, were *not me*!

That shift in perspective changed everything. I realized that I didn't know what anyone else needed, even when I felt certain that I did. I couldn't get other people to do or think or feel what I wanted them to. I realized that I wasn't in charge of sunrises and even if I had been, I wouldn't have thought of creating some of the most glorious ones I had observed. I recognized that I couldn't control my gradually aging body or what feelings and thoughts came through me. No, my perspective on how the world works shifted dramatically. I was not in control and could not be in control—no matter what I did. It wasn't even my job to be in control.

Life goes on. We can fight it all we want to and try our best to control the world to make it stop or change for just a moment here and there, but in the end, there is much over which we have no control at all. While we highly value control in our Western culture, it is not a bad thing to not always be in control. Clearly we can take action to meet our own needs, make our choices, and choose our own behavior, but we are not responsible for all that we cannot control. Realizing this distinction, we can experience sunrises without controlling them. We can ask for help without controlling the other person's response. We can give gifts without controlling the receiver's feelings. We can stand in our own truth without trying to change anyone else's perceptions. We can even be amused or puzzled by the behavior of others without trying to change them. The overall result is that we honor our own boundaries *as well as* the boundaries of others.

There is actually no need to try to be in control—once we let go of judging others as bad or wrong in some way. Judgment and control are the two basic elements of that way of thinking called duality, but we are now no longer limited to the two options of good and right or bad and wrong. We may never fully understand why some people make the choices they do, but we accept that they have the same options we do at the Y in the road and the same right to claim what fits them. As I sometimes say, "There are many ways to wash the dishes." There is room for all of us.

RETURNING HOME TO OUR TRUE SELF

When we see the entire smorgasbord of possibilities available to us, claiming what fits and letting go of all that does not fit, thus honoring our own boundaries as well as the boundaries of others, we actively participate in our life. When we recognize that control is neither necessary nor desirable in most situations and let go with love instead of judgment, we honor that line that distinguishes *me* from all that is *not me*. We comprehend that others have their own sense of self and boundaries just as we do and that we can't judge or attempt to control them without violating our own boundaries as well as theirs. We comprehend that choosing is not the same as controlling and that being fully alive is never about being in control.

Life is easier with well-developed boundaries. We no longer need to push beyond our natural limits. We say "no thank you" more easily whenever we need to. We feel more confident relating to other people. Others seem to treat us more respectfully when we stay more consistently with what fits *me*. We feel safer and trust our sense of self more, knowing that our boundaries will alert us if we need to take any action to protect our self.

As we grow to trust this inner reference point I call our *true self*, we complete our return home to our inner truth. We are saying "YES" to our amazing aliveness. Now, do you dare to live from your true self?

This Moment

This moment I'm here.
This moment I know that
I am safe,
In my body,
Aware, alive, and calm.
With nothing assaulting my senses,
I'm fresh and rested.
That line between me and not me is clear.
With no need to judge,
No need to control,
And nothing controlling me either,
There is nothing I have to do.
This moment I simply am.
Yes, I am.

PART V
LIVING FROM OUR TRUE SELF

LIVING:
being active, spirited, vibrant
being naturally full of energy
thriving

We have listened from a deeper place to hear our own deeper truth. We have worked through the 4 R's to Recognize, Reconnect with, Rebuild, and Return home to our true self. We now open to new possibilities and discover surprising new adventures that fit our true self perfectly. We have grown beyond the Good-Girl Jail and now dare to live from our true self.

"We have to dare to be ourselves,
however frightening or strange
that self may prove to be."

—Mae Sarton

Chapter **13**

Standing in Our Truth

Am I sure?

The man hands the official paper to me at my door and asks me to sign for it. I sign. My trembling legs feebly carry me to a chair nearby. It's a subpoena. Another woman has sued my therapist and has called me to be a witness. I will have to testify in court.

Everything in me screams *Noooooo!* How am I going to do this? I don't want to. I shouldn't have to. I can't do this. How could this be happening? Things have been going so well. Why this? Why now? Why me?

I just want the entire ordeal to go away. I want things to go back to the way they were yesterday. I am grateful I have found a good therapist, and I don't want to lose her. Besides, how could anyone sue her? My therapist couldn't have done what she is accused of ... could she?

I'm overwhelmed. I have doubts. I have questions. I want to understand what my therapist has done and why. I want to know the truth about what happened, but I also want to protect her. I am ashamed that I have trusted my therapist so much when perhaps she has been harming someone else. Would I have let her hurt me in the ways she is accused of hurting this other client? I don't think so . . . but I wonder.

I feel vulnerable, weak, sad, and scared. I am angry that I have to get involved. I feel like David going up against Goliath. The tidal wave of feelings confuses me. A lawsuit seems so sudden, so extreme, so completely out of my control. I just don't wanna . . .

Ah, I hear clues that I am at another Y in the road. It's time to do my emotional work. It is not easy. I journal and take a long walk alone. I listen inside. I climb back into my body. I flow. I work through my fears one at a time. I notice, claim, and release my feelings. I finally begin to see more choices and begin to claim what fits *me*. Gradually I hear my own truth, which is that I can't know for sure what has happened between the two of them. I find that line differentiating me from my therapist and sink solidly back into my internal reference point. Ah yes, this feels so much better.

I begin to realize that this lawsuit is not mine. The battle is between the two of them. My therapist's integrity is at stake, not mine. I haven't done anything wrong. I notice that I have no real need to protect my therapist after all. I also have no need to attack her. In fact, I discover that I have no need to take either side—my therapist's side to defend and protect her or the other client's side to join with her to make our therapist wrong. It is not my issue. My boundaries have not been violated. This is not my war. I let go of all that is *not me*.

The attorney tells me why I have been subpoenaed. I groan, knowing that I definitely will have to testify. I have a specific piece of information that is relevant to the case. This one little piece is mine to claim. Yes, I will testify. It fits *me* to do that. A time has come to fully speak "my whole truth and nothing but the truth," as the oath states.

I begin to comprehend that this court situation is an invitation for me to return to duality and the old vortex of rules and roles. As in all court situations, there are two opposing sides. One side wins; the other side loses. I have worked hard to grow beyond duality to open to all possibilities, not just the two standard ones regarding who is right and who is wrong. I have grown to trust and live from my true self. It has been hard work and a long road. I have valued my progress. But now this! It feels like some weird kind of Good-Girl Jail final exam.

I remember that I don't have to accept this seductive invitation back into duality. I remember that there are always more than two options. I keep claiming what fits *me* and letting go of the rest. I choose not to fight for either side of the lawsuit to help either one win the power struggle. In fact I choose to stay out of the power struggle completely and simply stand in my own truth, fully 100 percent. It isn't easy, but it works.

Because I have not invested in any particular outcome, I feel clear and free when the lawsuit finally settles. I have participated in the ways that fit *me* and only in those ways, maintaining my boundaries and integrity. I have claimed my own truth and let go of the rest— without judgment. I haven't tried to control the outcome and I haven't lost my sense of self. I feel whole, undamaged by the experience. I know what's what. I feel relieved.

I hear that now-familiar sigh once again. But also, something I don't fully understand has shifted deep inside me. I wonder what that is.

DISCOVERING INTEGRITY

We have come to Recognize, Reconnect with, Rebuild, and Return home to our true self—and there is still more. Can we now live consistently from that deep core that is our truth? Can we open to the many possibilities beyond what we have learned from others?

This chapter describes the authentic integrity that listening to our self develops and the unique challenges that come with this choice. As we actively stand in our truth, we have courageous conversations when we need to. We let in the goodness that comes our way. While we continue to slip and slide at times as we dare to live from our precious true self, we discover that there genuinely is life beyond the Good-Girl Jail. And some of us will experience the big ARE YOU SURE?

Integrity is a state of being a harmonious, undiminished whole. When there is no longer any need to maintain an external reference point to feel safe, what remains is our precious inner truth. And when we live from our inner truth, we experience integrity—our true self in action, fully alive, and no longer shut down in the Good-Girl Jail.

Integrity means being seen for the whole human being we truly are. What shows on the outside fits what we feel on the inside. The various parts of us work together, complementing and supporting one other. What our head thinks and what our body experiences fit together. We are the same person on Thursday that we were on Monday. We feel like the same person at work, with friends, with our children, when we are home alone, and even at high school reunions. The words *integrated* and *congruent* fit us now as the walls separating the various categories of our life begin to soften.

The various truths about our sense of self that have been evolving begin to fit together. We see that who we used to be has contributed to who we are now. We see that all our awakening moments have shaped us the way a funnel channels a mass of splashing water into a steady stream.

At some point we cross a line, actively choosing to return home to live from this integrity. This may be as smooth and easy as making the choice to step over an imaginary line on the ground—or it might be rather rocky and dramatic, as mine was when I needed to testify. Crossing that line is often uncomfortable. After all, we may be seriously breaking the old vortex of rules and roles set for us by others, and we were never supposed to do that. We wonder how crossing that line will change our life. We may be scared we won't be able to go back, if and when we want to.

Shifting to live from our integrity, from the truth of our self, is a choice at the Y in the road—and it is more than a choice. We cannot make this choice until we are developmentally able to do so, until we sufficiently strengthen and reclaim our self and let go of the rest. When we reach this particular point of our development, shifting to live from our true self begins to feel essential. We now see this choice as safer for us than living from our old safety pattern with its external reference point. This choice may even feel mandatory to some of us, as if needed for our soul to survive.

While we may have shut down to follow others and violated our own boundaries for many years, we have also experienced a strong drive to find our own path and live the way that best fits us. This particular path we have sought is living from our true self while listening to the deeper inner truth we call integrity. It isn't always an easy choice. It isn't always an easy way to live.

When we stand in our truth, though, we know for certain that we exist. Remember Eva coming to this awareness in Chapter 1? She simply stated, "I am." There is no need to justify our existence, no need to apologize for or forgive our existence. Our existence is part of our inner truth.

When we fully claim *I am*, all else slips away. We are home. We feel aligned and on track. We are neither pushing nor holding back. We are flowing. There is nothing to prove. There are no battles to wage or win. We are in our body, fully experiencing our life.

Integrity feels right—not because we are being good girls follow-ing the rules, but because we have become one with our true self. It feels right—not because others say we are right, but because we are living what fits *me*. Integrity is never just a *should*. It *feels* right. It fits our own values and priorities.

The way I chose to handle testifying felt right in the sense that I felt solid inside. I could live with myself afterward. I didn't wish later that I had done something different. It was nothing to brag about as an achievement and equally nothing to be blamed for or ashamed of. I stood up to the plate, as we say, actively accepting full responsibility for my part—nothing more, nothing less. I did what I needed to do. I had grown to trust my sense of self. I had listened to my truth. I had grown into my own integrity. I felt whole. I felt real.

This is what lies beyond the Good-Girl Jail.

Active Responsibility

Being a good girl involves what I call *passive responsibility*. When we're being good, we follow the rules. We generally do what is expected of us. We try to please others so that no one will get angry with us or hurt us. We try to stay out of trouble and not get caught doing anything wrong.

Passive responsibility may make us look good to others, but it is based on an external reference point. We determine what we do based on what others want us to do or what others tell us we should do. Passive responsibility is a significant part of the Good-Girl Jail and keeps us shut down until we can grow beyond it.

Listening to our inner truth—living from our true self—means going a step further. *Active responsibility* means being responsible *for our self* rather than responsible *to others*. We are generally less responsible to others than we believe but considerably more responsible for our self and our choices than we think.

Active responsibility means participating in our life. It means taking initiative for what needs to be done and following through, not just setting the wheels in motion. It means staying with our internal reference point to do what is right by our own standards. Active responsibility means honoring our deepest inner truth by living from it, making the active choices we need to make.

I could have given a weaker testimony, minimally answering the questions and passively meeting the legal requirement to testify. Years earlier, while still living from an external reference point, I would have done exactly that to avoid the wrath of both parties in the lawsuit, essentially hiding to protect *me*. It certainly felt risky to speak my full truth, but speaking my full truth felt less risky at that point in my life than leaving my sense of self once again. This awareness helped make it possible to stay with my integrity.

When my daughter was in middle school, I stopped one morning to get gas at a station near her school. There were students there buying snacks on their way to school. When the clerk accidentally gave me an extra dollar in change, I simply handed it back to her and went on my way.

When my daughter came home from school that day, she had heard that I had given the clerk back the dollar. The other students had recognized me and were surprised that I would do such a thing. What a golden parenting opportunity to talk about listening to our own truth to do what feels right!

We rarely get rewarded in such grand ways when we live from our integrity. Our reward, usually, is a simple inner feeling of being on track in our life and honoring our own truth when no one else may even notice. If we didn't still focus outside our self for validation at least a little, wouldn't being on track be enough?

COURAGEOUS CONVERSATIONS

Standing in our truth also includes having *courageous conversations* —a term aptly coined by Connie, one of my clients. These are the conversations we need to have but want to avoid because we dread the other person's response. Perhaps we are afraid the other person will get angry or end our relationship if we speak our truth or ask tough questions. We may need to speak up more assertively than usual to say something that is difficult for us to say. The other person with whom we need to have these courageous conversations is usually someone important to us, someone we want to continue a relationship with— perhaps a partner, a friend, a boss, an employee, a parent, a child, or a therapist.

To not speak our truth at these times would create shutting down moments that would violate our integrity. Having these courageous conversations, when needed, thus becomes an essential part of living from our true self.

When Connie was leaving her marriage, she learned to take one courageous conversation at a time, one issue at a time. She worked to become clear about each individual topic and how to tactfully, truth-fully, respectfully, and fairly say what she needed to say to her husband. She worked to let go of her expectations regarding his responses. She put her emphasis instead on saying what she needed to say to him and asking for what she needed from him. Even though each conversation felt risky because she feared her husband's anger and retaliation, she wanted him to know who she was at that point in their marriage. She wanted him to know her truth about their relationship.

By the time they divorced, Connie knew that she had done her best. She had asked for what she needed, even though she didn't always get it. She had expressed opinions that differed from his. She had shared her truth and had said what she needed to say. She carefully honored both her own and his boundaries every step of the way. She stood in her truth. In the process, she learned exactly why they had become incompatible. After numerous courageous conversations, she became able to respectfully let the relationship go with honesty and closure.

When I was learning to speak my truth to better ask for what I needed, I worked to get clear exactly what I needed to say, sometimes even writing it out and practicing it out loud to build both my clarity and courage. Then I said what I needed to say to the other person, feeling grateful that I could speak up more than usual.

Sometimes, however, the issue didn't settle inside me afterward, even if the other person gave me what I asked for and wasn't mad at me. I felt confused rather than clear and relieved. I kept thinking about the person and the issue. I kept rehashing the entire scenario, wondering why speaking up in courageous conversations wasn't working for me.

What I eventually learned was that I was speaking up but saying only 90 percent of what I needed to say. This was more than my usual 50 percent and felt like progress, but I was still avoiding that last sentence or paragraph—usually the most crucial and powerful part of the conversation and the most difficult to say. I was still holding back! I learned to ask, "Is there anything else I need to say?"

Once I learned to speak 100 percent of what I needed to say, completing the courageous conversation, the issue settled inside me and felt finished—whether or not I got what I wanted. I only needed to have my full and complete say in the matter and that last 10 percent was often a crucial part of standing in my full truth. I also learned that speaking 100 percent was never about telling others what they were doing wrong. What I needed to share was only about *me*—my feelings, my thoughts, my needs, and my responses.

Active responsibility and courageous conversations are critical parts of integrity, and there is still more.

LETTING IN GOODNESS

One of the surprising difficulties for some of us as we dare to live once again from our true self is letting in all the goodness that comes our way. Life brings hurdles to jump and rivers to wade. We already know this to be true, but some of us need to learn that our inner truth also includes goodness—things like love, joy, fun, and abundance. We don't have to do more. We simply need to let in more, and we tend to get confronted sooner or later with whatever upper limits we may have about letting in goodness.

Letting in goodness is often the point at which we recognize the immense significance of shifting back home to live from our true self. All of a sudden, it seems, all this goodness leads us to realize that we have completely shifted the point of view from which we live our life—*and we can't go back!* And it is true. We cannot *unlearn* what we have learned. We cannot *ungrow* ways in which we have grown. We can no longer pretend. We can no longer violate our own boundaries without realizing that we have done so. We comprehend now that this shift back to living from the inner truth of our sense of self changes everything—every relationship, every value, how we work, how we play . . . *everything*. It is indeed a paradigm shift. I call it a *grassroots revolution*, as it is happening one woman at a time.

Remember how NO MORE marked an earlier transition when we could no longer tolerate old ways? *I can't go back* now dramatically marks this return to living from our true self.

Elissa had received her six-month chip in Alcoholics Anonymous and felt solid in her recovery from addiction. She felt more alive than she had in a long time. She had plenty of support for this significant change in her life and was diligently working the twelve-step program with a sponsor. She still had thoughts about drinking but accepted this as normal and had learned to call for help whenever she needed it. She believed she was well on her way. "Life is really good," she said.

Elissa just had one question for me: "Why do I still have contact with my old boyfriend who is drinking and drugging and wanting to get back together with me?" Contact with him felt risky to her yet also like some weird sort of security blanket that she didn't understand. When I asked what would happen if she went back to her relationship with him, she immediately knew that she would sooner or later return to drinking. Still, she did not see how she could end all contact with him. Here was an invitation back to her old life that she could accept at any moment she chose—a significant Y in the road.

When I asked Elissa if she could allow all this current goodness she experienced to continue in her life, it struck a familiar chord inside her. She said she had always sabotaged her successes. Nothing good had ever lasted. She couldn't do anything right. Do you hear her quick judgment of herself? Do you hear some old core beliefs? When I reminded her how the Y in the road sometimes shows up to help us strengthen our choice to live from our true self, she immediately saw the choice in front of her. Letting go of this old boyfriend was part of her deeper choice to come fully alive. Allowing goodness was crucial to making the choice she wanted to make. Perhaps this was also her big ARE YOU SURE?

THE BIG ARE YOU SURE?

A rather interesting phenomenon sometimes happens after we have been living from our true self for a while, enjoying the clarity that doing so brings. It often feels a bit like a final exam after learning many lessons in a class. It is that something extra that I felt shifting inside me after testifying in court.

That something extra is a bigger-than-usual Y in the road that definitely gets our attention. It is a challenging moment of doubt when we begin to comprehend how much our life is changing and we seriously ask, "What have I done?" This moment is indeed a turning point. I have come to affectionately call it the big ARE YOU SURE?

Jenny called for an emergency appointment one day saying that she couldn't eat, sleep, or even clean her house. She was furious with everyone and her body physically hurt all over. She had pushed everyone out of her life and was panicking about what she was going to do. She didn't trust her judgment about anything and was considering suicide—an option she had considered frequently in the past but not recently. She believed she had completely lost her mind and was dying. She was desperate.

Jenny had learned early that she must never say the word *no*. *No* had been forbidden in her family forever, and the consequences were often severe.

Now, as an adult, she had become aware that some people were teaming up to take advantage of her. She was getting emotionally depleted, losing her connection with her sense of self, and even feeling the old NO ME LEFT she had experienced much earlier in her growth. She was trying hard to work with these people but felt tremendous turmoil inside herself. She believed that she had to say "no" now or she would die. That is exactly what it felt like to her. She had to say "no," but she also felt trapped, unable to say "no" to anyone. Something had to give. She didn't really want to kill herself. She thought she had let that option go, but in that moment, she couldn't see any other options.

Once Jenny identified the situation as a bigger-than-usual Y in the road—a choice of whether to obey an old childhood rule to shut down her aliveness or to live from her true self now as an adult—she could see that she didn't need to kill herself. She took a moment to pause at the juncture of the Y in the road—to see it and feel it. Yes, there were other options. She took her time. She began to claim the pieces that fit her and let go of the rest. Although still unsure what to do, she felt relieved and free again as soon as she could feel the reality of having a free choice to do whatever she needed to do. She had returned to that point of choice at the Y in the road. No longer in danger of suicide, Jenny went home, ate, and slept well that night.

The next morning she said "no" to the people who had been taking advantage of her. She ended those relationships but kept the other people in her life who were important to her. Her words to me that next day were "I'm not dead!" She had said *no* out loud and had not died. She had chosen to listen to her own deep inner truth and yes, she was sure.

While Jenny's experience was intense and sudden, some of us experience this same phenomenon of a bigger-than-usual ARE YOU SURE? over a period of weeks or months.

Rubianne asked to come back to therapy after several years, saying that either something huge was coming up or she was completely crazy. She said she was suddenly seeing the whole world differently and she couldn't figure out what was what or what to trust. While she had never been suicidal, she was panicking now because she couldn't tolerate what was happening inside her.

She was in a power struggle with her budding teenage daughter, trying hard to manage her daughter's emerging independence. As she began to let go of her outward focus on her daughter and began listening inside herself again, the pieces began to make sense to her. She was learning that she just needed "to be real." She said she was "being taken to a new and different level in her growth by God."

One day in my office, Rubianne experienced herself talking to her old familiar safety pattern as if it were distinctly separate from her. At first it seemed to be far across this deep chasm from her, but then it came closer and spoke to her. It told her it had worked hard for a long time to protect her and was relieved that she was now willing to take back the responsibility for living her life. It needed to rest and gently melted into the background. She then felt a distinct physical shift inside toward living from her true self instead of from her safety pattern. She felt no judgment about either part of her. There was no good or bad. It was simply time to make the shift and she experienced it in quite a vivid way. She said she knew her safety pattern would always be there in case she ever needed it again.

As her reference point shifted back home to her true self, Rubianne said she *just knew* she was back on track. Her crisis had not been about dying. It was about living her life. Almost as a sidelight, she began to share more of her experiences with her daughter rather than trying to control her, and they then quickly became more of a team again.

A month or so later, Rubianne rather matter-of-factly commented that she was dying. She had no obvious illness and wasn't suicidal. She just knew that she was dying. She had written her will and was getting her affairs in order.

Once again, I encouraged her to listen inside to her self. This time she realized that it was duality that was dying for her—not her body. She could see that duality was important to teach us what fits us as well as what doesn't. "We just don't need to stay there," she said. "We need to keep growing to find our own way." Then she had an image of the two extremes of duality coming together like zipping a zipper. Something larger encompassed all the extremes of duality, and she felt absolutely no reason for fear. She completely trusted the experience of her own life, wherever it took her. She said, "yes" to her life. In fact, she called it "the big yes," wiggling and giggling every time she said that phrase out loud.

Both Jenny and Rubianne listened inside to their truth. It was not *the* truth for the whole world, of course. It was simply their deeper inner truth to live from. They discovered what their truth was by listening inside. They learned that their panic wasn't about letting go of life. It wasn't about going back to old ways. It wasn't about being in control. It was, instead, about coming fully alive. It was about choosing to live from their integrity, from their true self. They had both answered a resounding YES to the big ARE YOU SURE?

THE POWER OF
THE LITTLE WORD "AND"

Sirena experienced the big ARE YOU SURE? and also discovered the power of the little word *and*. In a crisis of deep confusion, Sirena suddenly didn't know what to trust. She had difficulty describing what she was experiencing and simply said, "I'm in a foreign place." She was aware that she suddenly saw people differently and that she needed a lot of time alone. She was very uncomfortable. She tried to stay with the discomfort but wasn't sure she could. She said it felt like carrying fifty pounds when she was used to carrying only twenty-five. She was aware she wanted out of her body so that she wouldn't feel the pain. She was full of doubt and swinging back and forth between doubt and trust, saying that without doubt, we don't learn to trust. "I should be happy, but I'm sad," she said. "I'm scared how all this is changing my life." Do you hear her struggle with duality? Do you hear her asking, "What have I done?"

Then she had a significant dream. In the dream, she was in a hospital but walking out of it on her own. Two friends were arguing but she kept walking past them, not getting involved. Even when she encountered people discussing a purple gorilla, she again just kept walking past and feeling fine about doing so. While she was surprised that she kept walking through all these events in her dream, she also saw the choice she had whether to go on with her own life or get caught up in distractions along the way. To her, the choice was to live her life—or let herself die. She felt the presence of God completely accepting her and whatever choice she made in this bigger-than-usual Y in the road that was asking her ARE YOU SURE?

The word that finally came to Sirena to tie her experiences together was *wholeness*. She poetically wrote that wholeness described "when extreme opposites war in my soul, when ends simultaneously feel like beginnings, when fright becomes freedom and doubt becomes trust, the truth that stays the same throughout is that I am whole. I am whole even when all I feel is broken." She had discovered the power of the little word *and*.

And—that one little word—changes everything. It is inclusive, creating room for more than one thing. It adds something to what already is and ties things together. *And* allows for differences. It is the circle that encompasses the two extremes of duality. It is what makes room for all of us on the planet.

We don't have to decide who is right and who is wrong. What is right for one person may be wrong for another. We cannot tell what is either right or wrong for others. There is room for your way *and* my way. There is room for each of us to stand in our truth. There is room for what fits *me and* what doesn't. One person's junk is another person's treasure, or as I have said before, there are many ways to wash the dishes.

Jenny, Rubianne, and Sirena describe the big ARE YOU SURE? crisis vividly. It is experiential and internal. Words fail us. Doubt and confusion abound. We may question everything in these moments. We might feel at least a bit crazy. We may believe we are slipping backward in our growth, not understanding what is happening.

Jenny, Rubianne, and Sirena also describe the outcome perfectly. Duality melts. It just doesn't matter so much anymore. It doesn't grab us in the same old way. We feel no fear. We shift gears. We cross that line into integrity. There simply is nothing left that has the power to shut us down. While we may notice duality every day, something larger encompasses the two extremes. Something else becomes more important. Difficult as it might be to wrap our brain around both ends of duality, we see that the little word *and* has the necessary power to encompass it all.

And is the wholeness Sirena experienced. It is the zipper that Rubianne felt. It is this wholeness that allows enough room for each of us to dare to live from our true self.

With *and*, we see life differently. We feel a deep sense of genuine choice about fully being our piece of the larger puzzle we call this universe. Standing in our truth is no longer hard work. It simply is. As Rubianne says, "It feels like opening the prison gates after being wrongfully accused." Standing in our truth frees us to live beyond the Good-Girl Jail.

CONTROL BREAKS

Even as we progress through the big ARE YOU SURE? we occasionally slip and slide when duality and the old familiar vortex of rules and roles seductively sneak back in. Maybe we venture back to our old familiar safety pattern to see if it still brings us that teddy bear sense of safety and security that it used to. Maybe we hide or run from life again or we try our old addictions just one more time.

Opportunities to feel right and in control are indeed tempting and sometimes we just seem to desperately need a *control break*—just a moment here and there to stop and control *something*, even when we are certain we will no longer choose to stay there. We can learn to watch for these moments and develop the tools to return to our true self when we are ready to go on. We might even see some humor in our efforts to search for something we can control.

When I feel that familiar tug to momentarily control *something*, I have learned to take a few minutes to allow the break. I run an errand, plan dinner, wash a load of clothes, or pull some weeds—all of which feed my illusion that I can control *something* for just a moment or two.

Allowing a control break reminds me that feeling in control—even for that moment—is not the same as being fully alive. Control is not my truth, but whenever I try to hide from my truth, I return to controlling. So I take my control break and then again look for the Y in the road. I take some time alone. I notice, claim, and release my feelings. I claim what fits *me* and let go what does not until my boundaries again feel clear and I return to listening to my sense of self. It often feels like returning home after another slight but seemingly necessary rebellion. Allowing these control breaks emphasizes that it always is a choice to live from my true self. It is a way of creating an ARE YOU SURE? moment when I need to remind myself that yes, I am sure.

Sometimes when the world is sneaking back in to dominate everything as it so often does, I ask myself, *What's important here?* When I get an answer like *Getting this chapter written, Seeing clients, Getting the house ready for company, or Buying groceries,* I ask, *And what is more important than that?* If need be, I keep asking what's more important until I get back to *Knowing that I will be okay no matter what* or perhaps *Experiencing my life fully in this moment.* I come back to claiming what fits *me* so that the rest can fall aside into that other category of *not me.* I come back to the gentle truth of listening to my true self.

LIVING FROM OUR TRUE SELF

While we can neither predict nor control the content of this journey we call our life, we can learn to slide beneath the specific events to live from our true self through it all. When we live from this inner reference point, we trust what feels right inside, what feels alive in that deeper sense that feels on track. We follow that, rather than bend to the winds that seem intent on veering us off course. That is our truth. That is how we come to know that we will be okay—no matter what. That is growing beyond the Good-Girl Jail.

We don't always know what an experience is about when we are in the middle of it, but we can trust that each step along the way will take us where we need to go. We begin to see that each challenge in our life also brings gifts that help us with later life events.

When I learned to release my feelings, those skills later helped me leave my battering relationship. When I learned to trust my strength to leave a battering relationship, I strengthened my confidence to choose integrity when I later testified in court. When I managed to stand in my truth while testifying, I came to know that I could live from my truth through whatever came into my life, like my mother's death and writing this book.

Just as each skill or lesson learned helps us with the next challenge life brings, each choice for integrity at the Y in the road takes us closer to consistently living from the inner reference point of our true self. The real challenge is to become willing to go on—without being able to know where we are going, not knowing the outcome, and not knowing how to do what lies ahead of us.

I believe it is more important to trust each step on the path toward aliveness than to set a goal to get there. I believe it is more important to claim our own life to live than to determine the meaning of life in general. I believe it is more important to experience each moment than to attempt to make specific things happen in the future. And I have come to believe it is more important to return to our internal reference point than to be a good girl trying to meet the expectations and follow the rules of others.

When we trust our true self, living from our integrity becomes possible. We surrender to life itself, not knowing what might be next, yet trusting that we will be okay—no matter what. The world looks anew to us, just as it must look to an emerging butterfly who now has beautiful wings and can fly. Saying YES to standing in our truth creates room for the new as we open to the many possibilities we cannot yet even imagine.

Finally Safe

Am I really safe yet?
After a lifetime of being on guard,
Watching the door and lying low.
Watching, watching,
Always the alert guard dog
Protecting the sacred and vulnerable me?
Now I know that Grandpa,
Long dead and gone,
Can no longer get me.
My chances of being raped are slim
And my chances of getting pregnant nil.
I finally know what's essential:
I finally know I am loved for being me.
I finally know, too, that I am loving
And that I can openly share my loving
With my cat, my lover, my friends,
And my garden.
I feel at home in my precious nest.
My sunrise walks alone are glorious,
Bathing me in that peachy-pink neon glow.
As I awaken my soul, eager for another day,
I feel tenderly cradled in the Great Mother's arms.
Oh yes, life is good
And dying will be all right.
I am okay—just as I am.
I breathe.
I sigh.
I laugh.
I cry.
Oh yes, I am finally safe.

Chapter **14**

Uncorking
Our Voice

What Do I Really Want to Do Today?

By the time I wander next door to my old friend Maury's for the bluegrass party, the house is full of people chatting and eating and the musicians are already playing. The party has certainly begun without me.

Maury has played fiddle for nearly three quarters of a century. He just beams all over whenever people join him to play those lively old tunes like "Ragtime Annie" and "Orange Blossom Special." I had never been around bluegrass until I moved next door to him, but there is no missing the beat or the radiant energy when these long-time friends pick up their precious instruments.

I fill my plate with baked beans, potato salad, and chicken from the summer potluck and discover that there is only one chair left. It is so close to the musicians that I can almost feel them breathing.

Not minding me at all, they enthusiastically jump from one tune to the next. I eat and listen to the old songs, not paying a whole lot of attention to what is going through my mind. I'm just eating my dinner and enjoying the music.

When I set down my empty plate, though, I discover that I can't move. *Hmmm* . . . I've had this sensation before. I pay attention.

The music is suddenly rumbling through my soul, vibrating the air I breathe. I am right there, completely engrossed, barely noticing the slight trembling throughout my body. Something about that music has grabbed my whole being.

I am looking around the circle, slowly checking them out—the instruments, not the musicians. *Guitar? Fun but no; it's too big to hold. Fiddle? Too hard to learn. Mandolin? Too high-pitched. Banjo? Maybe; pretty interesting.* At the end of the circle is the bass. *Bass? Hmmm* . . . I am mesmerized by that low, resonant beat, seemingly inside that big, wooden, acoustic instrument. I feel my body keeping the rhythm, seemingly anchoring the music to the earth. I am fully there, not thinking at all, simply flowing and one with that big old thumping bass.

Suddenly Izzie, the bass player, cries out in exasperation, "Doesn't anybody else play bass?" No one answers her. No one else plays bass and she wants to play her mandolin instead. What is she going to do? Then, as if she is mysteriously guided to be there just for me, she asks what I later call another magical question, "Does anybody here want to *learn* to play bass?"

My hand is in the air! She sees it. I see it, too, but who put it there? I swear I didn't do that, decide that, or even think about putting my hand in the air, yet there it is—the only hand up in the air. She says something quick and direct like "Come here." When my body jumps over there on its own, she puts her fingers on those giant strings and says, "Do this, and when I say to change, do this." Wow! Two chords!

We play a few simple songs in the key of G. Well actually, I stumble through a couple of songs with her direction and considerable kindness on the part of the other musicians.

I don't know what I am doing, but I know I absolutely love doing it! Goosebumps are crawling all over my body. I *want* to do it! It is exhilarating! It is fun! I am uncontrollably wiggling and giggling. I don't even seem to care if I am doing it right or what anyone else is thinking about me playing bass. All that doesn't matter. It just doesn't matter. I am playing bass and I trust it absolutely.

WHAT IS OUR VOICE?

Once we have claimed what is *me* and let go of what is *not me*, once our boundaries have evolved to protect us so that we no longer need to be in control to feel safe in the world, and once we have returned home to live from the integrity of our true self, our voice comes knocking at the door that has long been protectively closed. Our *me* is undeniably here. This is the "more" that has long been coming.

Our voice is our true self now coming to the surface, sharing with the outside world the way the birds burst into song on spring mornings. It now feels safe to be both seen and heard. Uncorking our voice means no longer hiding, no longer keeping unwanted secrets, no longer holding back, no longer shutting down. It means being real, being honest, and becoming genuinely known. It means becoming willing to share who we are, what we have, and what we have learned. It means letting our light shine—"with no dimmer switch," as Rubianne likes to say.

Uncorking our voice is a way of being in the world that includes expressing our truth—or more accurately, living and breathing our inner truth. It is our integrity in action. It means honoring our natural deep need to acknowledge our self. It means experiencing life fully rather than interpreting life through the filter of an outdated role or safety pattern. It is permission to grow as much and go as far as we need to—or want to.

Uncorking our voice is another invitation at the Y in the road, should we choose to accept it, to live the way we now want to. It is being home after a very long detour. We see a bigger picture, and that greater universe unquestionably includes permission to fully live our life. It is our freedom to be—at last.

Our true self seems to be shouting to us, as if gratefully knowing it will now be heard. We hear it saying, "Listen to *me!*" And yes, we are now listening—as if with fourteen ears and seventeen eyes—to whatever needs to be expressed.

This chapter describes the clues that our voice is emerging, illustrating some of the common ways we still sometimes fight and minimize the importance of what is emerging. Making peace with powerlessness opens the door to all kinds of expressing, especially playing, creating, and loving. Guidelines for knowing what to trust help us fully uncork our voice to release it in whatever ways it comes through.

CLUES OUR VOICE IS EMERGING

No one else can tell us what we need to express or how we need to do it, as our answers come from deep within us. So, we notice the gentle taps on our shoulder, ideas that surprise us, things that draw us to them like a magnet, and other *whispers from the edge of aliveness.*

Sometimes our sense of self coyly invites us out to play. Sometimes it simply keeps nudging us gently over the years, not quite fully coming forth and yet never quite fully going away either—the way this book has patiently waited until I was ready to write it. At other times, our self eagerly demands to be fully expressed and won't take "no" for an answer—the way playing bluegrass bass came to me that one day.

The following list includes more clues that our sense of self is emerging to find expression:

* Urges that seem silly but secretly fun
* Activities that seem unusually or surprisingly interesting
* Discovering skills and talents we have never fully used
* Visions of how things could be different that pull us toward them
* Times we are no longer willing to shut down
* Invitations that just won't go away
* Moments when we care more than usual about something or someone
* Moments it no longer matters what others think of us
* Whatever answers "What do I *really* want to do?"

Sometimes boredom feels as if nothing at all is happening, as if nothing is coming forth to be expressed, but boredom can be a pause, a pregnant stage of anticipation and readiness, a knowing that yes, something is definitely coming. We just don't know what it is, and we can't make it happen faster. Yet, when we are patient with boredom, turning toward it and opening to all possibilities, something always comes. Something more alive always seems to slide into place.

However our voice comes, we listen. We begin to experience our aliveness stirring from deep within, needing release to the outside world to dance and play, to wiggle and giggle. We can trust that our voice is never, ever about hurting others and never about being in control. It is never about becoming numb. It is never bad for us or evil. Our voice is probably not about accumulating expensive toys or looking good. It is rarely about what we *should* be doing or about getting our to-do list done. Some surprises are often in store.

At age forty-five, Olivia let her hair grow long for the first time since her mother had cut off her long hair as punishment for not being able to adequately take care of it when she was only five. Growing her hair long again became a symbolic and powerful expression of her emerging aliveness. She said she felt softer. She felt free.

Remember Marsha, who finally left a violent thirty-year marriage that had kept her painfully shut down? When she listened to her voice, she moved to a different town and got a job she thoroughly enjoyed. She developed several good friendships, and nobody could any longer keep her from fun with her friends. She absolutely loved living alone and felt more alive than ever.

Kathy began to be more playful, laughing and teasing her friends. She had shut down her playfulness as a child when others criticized her for being a brat. She said she wasn't being mean; she was playing. She loved being a brat. She loved being expressive. It was fun—and her friends loved her rediscovered playfulness.

Gillian bought a brand new white convertible. She had learned to drive in a white convertible as a teenager and had driven one ever since—except for the past few years. She hadn't known what was missing from her life until one day, when she saw the exact white convertible that fit her. She hadn't been looking for it, yet she recognized it when she found it. She said it "just felt right"—like coming home, like just being. I could see her big smile as she told me about seeing this car. She petted the steering wheel. She felt energy when she touched the car. It calmed the questions inside her about what life was all about. She said some others thought she was crazy, but that didn't really matter very much. She concluded that what others think is their business and not her problem. She knew how alive she felt driving it. She knew it was her voice.

If we have difficulty recognizing our voice when it comes forward to express, we might erroneously interpret what's coming through as manic, evil, crazy, or even psychotic—as if we are losing our mind or being taken over by some dangerous force. Others might say we are "having a mid-life crisis" or "going off the deep end." They are entitled to their opinions. Some might even try to get us to settle down again, attempting to get that rug back on the floor. Perhaps we are simply beginning to listen and honor what has long been inside of us needing a freedom channel for expression. The voice of our true self is never manic, evil, crazy, or psychotic. It is real.

When Raven was unemployed, she wanted to start a business she had dreamed about for years, but her mother thought she had gone berserk. She didn't believe her daughter had what it took to run a business and thought she should be more practical and just go find herself a regular job. Her criticism left Raven seriously questioning what she was doing, as if perhaps she truly was crazy. Eventually, she trusted the way in which her business idea had long been a dream. She reinterpreted being unemployed and unable to immediately find another job as an opportunity to follow her dream. She willingly worked other temporary jobs to help pay the bills as she developed her business, thus also being practical but focused on that dream coming from inside her that gave her a reason to get up in the morning. She trusted the way in which the dream had come to her. She trusted that it made her feel so alive. She trusted her emerging voice.

HOW EXPRESSING FEELS

When we engage in the expressive activities that lead us toward feeling alive, our body seems to paradoxically both relax and have an enormous amount of energy. Our energy is flowing. We are flowing. We feel on track, settled, connected, and integrated. We feel good. We feel free. We may feel bigger, as if we are taking up our full space on the planet. We sense that whatever we are doing is right for us, that it nourishes us, even if it might feel scary.

Evelyn began to write a book about healing from her traumatic childhood, fully telling her truth and refusing to keep her secrets. Then her voice kept growing even bigger beyond her book to educating all kinds of people about the long-term effects of child abuse and what it takes to heal. She described her growth as "finding her calling." She beamed and wiggled ever so slightly as she told me about this step-by-step process that had led her to come more and more alive.

NOURISHING OUR VOICE

Sometimes expressing is simpler than we expect it to be. Years ago, when I was still in my doing-things-perfectly stage, my getting-things-done-to-please-others stage, I would turn my day over to my higher power in the morning and ask for guidance. "What do I need to do today?" I expected one of the seemingly profound items on my to-do list, but more days than not, the answer was simply "Smile." *Smile—ha! Where does that get me? I have too much to do to smile.*

While I believed smiling was ridiculous guidance, when I actually honored it, even though I didn't understand it, I learned that smiling softened me, opened me to new things, and took me exactly where I needed to go. Smiling is a simple choice, a small behavior we can choose to do anywhere and anytime. It opens everything inside, and it certainly expresses *me*. Smiling is an excellent place to start. It was the perfect place for me to start.

Other simple places to encourage your voice, if you choose to, include the following:

Wear brighter colors	Change your hairstyle
Sing a little louder	Stretch or do yoga
Dance wildly to music	Write a bigger signature
Plant more flowers	Paint the front door red (or purple)

Take up more room in bed	Scribble or doodle mindlessly
Be silly	Honor yourself on your birthday
Stand taller	Learn to play an instrument
Breathe deeper	Buy flowers just for you
Learn something new	Take longer walks
Take two weeks off instead of one	Make a mess, get dirty

I also like chuckling. We can chuckle at our own foibles, at our own wild ideas that we may or may not choose to follow, at our own playfulness, fears, or rebellion—simply because it feels good. Without judgment, chuckling doesn't humiliate anyone and it lightens the load on our shoulders. We can even chuckle quietly when it is not appropriate to be chuckling out loud. Being amused helps us to detach from power struggles, judgment, controlling, old familiar safety patterns—and the seriousness of others.

Sonia had recently ended a relationship that no longer fit her but that was painfully difficult to leave. While reviewing the whole situation with a friend, they started laughing about what they had both done in relationships over the years—weird things they had done to please their partners, how much they had given to hold their relationships together, ways they had allowed their partners to discount them, how much they had ignored their own needs, and on and on. For three hours Sonia and her friend chuckled at themselves and finally laughed uproariously—without any judgment at all. Laughing helped Sonia see the relationship clearly at long last, and it helped her let it go.

LITTLE DITTIES

It is easy to dismiss the importance of some of these early voice expressions. Some of us have done all we can do to allow them in the first place. Allowing them to have any value is an even bigger step.

For years, I called my poems *little ditties*. They were just little explosions I couldn't stop. I had to write them down, it seemed, but I just stuffed them away in a drawer somewhere. I never read them and I certainly didn't share them with anyone. They didn't seem worth sharing. They were just those little ditties. Can you hear my old familiar judging sneaking back in?

Then some songs started coming through. Those were harder to dismiss, because they seemed louder and therefore more difficult to hide. I didn't share them very much either, but neither did I want to forget them.

"First Birdie" was one of those songs. I remember lying in bed early one spring morning soon after it had become warm enough to sleep with the window open. This one bird wanted to sing way too much and too early for my comfort. It was waking me up *again*—and I was resenting it *again*. But pretty soon I let go of my obvious judgment and began to listen. Suddenly, I realized that I *was* that little birdie, singing to wake everyone up to enjoy the dawn. A song began to flow through me about being the first birdie of the morning, honoring the way I'm up early every morning letting my light shine and "trusting the rhythm and the rhyme."

I also did some painting during my ditty stage. My paintings seemed mostly irrelevant to the world because they were not *good art*, but they meant a lot to me. I never called them ditties, though. This, I thought, was progress. I saved them all, because they represented moments in my healing. One of them was an unusual symbol I had never seen before. I first painted it very small and then I needed to keep painting it over and over. Each one needed to be larger than the previous one until the final one filled the entire page. I could feel my true self growing bigger and bigger as I painted that unusual symbol. In fact, I could barely breathe. It felt a little scary, but mostly, it felt freeing and fun.

And I began to write—*just handouts for my clients*, I told myself, once again minimizing my voice, but my handouts gradually grew bigger and longer. I wrote a monthly column for a nationally distributed newsletter. I began presenting at national conferences and created more workshops and weekend intensives, which kept getting stronger. Eventually, I began to comprehend that I needed to write this book because it would not leave me alone! That was the best clue that I had something deep that I truly needed to express—that it wouldn't leave me alone.

My experience is that we can dismiss our little expressive ditties all we want to, but sooner or later, they demand more time and attention. They gradually settle into a form that appears to make more sense to us. They also seem to want to grow bigger all on their own, as if they have a life of their own—and they do. These ditties are our voice, expressions of *me* and our inner truth. They are the long-hidden passion of our true self, now exuberantly exploding.

MAKING PEACE WITH POWERLESSNESS

As our voice continues to grow more expressive, many of us inevitably come face-to-face with feeling powerless. When I bring up the subject of powerlessness, my clients and workshop participants usually groan and want to run away—or perhaps throw something at me. Powerlessness is indeed an unpopular subject. It is uncomfortable for nearly all of us—until we grasp its real meaning.

Any experience that leaves us feeling powerless can certainly trigger flashbacks to that moment of 100 percent powerlessness we once felt immediately prior to some past traumatic experience. At that moment, there was only safe and unsafe—perhaps the origin of duality—and most of us came to believe that we somehow needed to be in control to be safe. Maybe we even vowed never to feel powerless again, but it was not powerlessness that made the bad things happen. We got hurt because someone chose to inappropriately use their power over us. Our powerlessness has never been the cause of getting hurt, and feeling powerless no longer necessarily means that we are about to be devastated by an attack from others.

One early summer morning when I was outdoors watering my marigolds, I discovered the distinct difference between generic powerlessness and that threatening kind of powerlessness. I could choose to dig up the soil, plant the seeds at exactly the best time, water them every morning adequately, and fertilize them abundantly. Still, I could not make those little seeds sprout and grow, and I certainly couldn't make them grow faster and any more beautiful than they already were. I could use the best knowledge I could find about gardening and make responsible gardening choices, but something else beyond my control was most certainly responsible for their growth. I was powerless over this force that was *not me* that carried no personal threat whatsoever.

It is the same in all areas of our life. We can make informed choices that will likely produce the results we need and want, but we cannot control the actual results of our choices. We cannot control the thoughts, feelings, choices, and behavior of other people. Neither can we control our own thoughts, feelings, or aging body. We are powerless over the sun coming up every morning, over our children growing up, and over the worms tunneling through our garden. No matter how much we have learned to value being in control, we cannot control how beautiful the sunset is this evening or whether or not the raccoons will wander through our yard tonight.

Noticing such examples helps us make peace with powerlessness so that we can let go of any remaining vestiges of our old need to be in control to feel safe. Powerless truly is not bad. It just is. And making peace with powerlessness opens the door to a whole list of joyful activities that require powerlessness to fully experience, including laughing, falling asleep, loving, feeling, recovering from addictions, having an orgasm, and being musical.

RELEASING OUR VOICE

As we become more comfortable with feeling powerless, we relearn to play, create, and love—three key components to uncorking our voice and expressing our true self.

Playing

One day, when I was busily planning some fun, my fourteen-year-old daughter Sarah burst out laughing. "You don't plan to have fun, Mom. You just do it!" I had no idea what she was talking about at the time, but I began to watch her to see what I could learn.

A few days later, she needed to clean her room and invited her best friend over to help. They shut the door, turned on some music, and came out only once for a snack. I could hear them giggling, singing, talking, and moving things around. I really didn't know if that room was getting clean, but three hours later it was spotless from top to bottom—and they had spent the afternoon together playing rather than working at it. Yes, my daughter knew how to play. She could make any activity fun if she wanted to.

Playing is a child's natural way of being in the world. It is also our natural way of living from our true self. Children don't distinguish play from work the way adults do. We think we need to either work *or* play. We say we can't play until our work is all done. Do you hear duality?

Playing is a stance toward life, an attitude that greatly affects how we approach activities. Playing nourishes us, while working more often depletes us. Working often turns a task into a chore to just get done. Playing can make that same activity a joy.

Playing is thus how we do an activity, rather than what we are doing. We are playing when we enjoy the activity we are doing. We are playing when we proceed at our own pace and do the activity in our own way. We are playing when the process of doing something is as important as getting the job done—or even more so. We can still complete a task when we play, but we also enjoy the activity along the way. Our focus is internal, rather than external.

Some of us might be afraid something bad will happen if we play too much. Perhaps that core belief came from past experiences when we got punished for giggling at the dinner table, had birthday presents taken away, or believed we got molested because we played too much. Now we can separate the past from the present and let in goodness in all its many glorious forms. Playing is part of the *more* to life that we have been missing.

We were born with a natural human ability and desire to play. We can tease, horse around, tell funny stories and jokes, make faces, laugh at the funnies, play with words, dance freely, tickle our lover, poke fun lovingly at a friend's odd little habits, watch funny movies, and even sing loudly off-key on purpose if we want to.

Of course it is okay to play! Playing is all about joy, and we deserve joy simply because we are alive. Now is the time to let life be fun— even if our work isn't yet all done.

Creating

Children are also naturally creative. As young children, we tried everything we could think of, just to see what we could do and what would happen as a result. Experimenting was our way of learning, our way of living, and sometimes our way of getting into trouble. If we were punished for being creative as children, like when we colored on the walls or got into mom's nail polish, perhaps we shut down our natural creativity.

Now as adults daring to live from our true self, we may find a lot of creativity that has been squelched for a very long time. It may burst forth through music, painting, clay, poetry, woodworking, writing, gardening, sewing, cooking, making jewelry, building birdhouses, blogging, wrapping gifts, home decorating, starting our own business, or any of a multitude of other activities.

Creative expression is not about doing something *right*, such as hitting the right note on the piano at the right moment with the right finger or drawing a tree exactly the way it looks to the eye. Doing something *right* in this manner is about being in control enough to follow the rules. It is part of an external point of reference—and often part of the Good-Girl Jail.

In contrast, being creative is about listening internally to whatever needs to be expressed in whatever way we need to express it. We don't have to be trained in correct techniques, we don't have to already know how, and what we express is not necessarily practical and logical—or even reasonable. The process of expressing our voice thus becomes more important to us than how the final product may look.

My good friend, Alice McClelland, is a professionally trained artist in Taos, New Mexico. She teaches *process painting*—a way of painting that starts with listening inside. What needs to be painted? What color does it need to be? What's next? What else is needed? Asking questions rather than telling our hand and mind what to paint and what technique to use takes us directly to being authentically creative rather than imitating the object painted and following the technical rules. Process painting is an entirely different way of painting, a re-learning process about expressing whatever needs to be expressed.

When I was learning to play my bass, I learned that same lesson in a different way. I was lamenting one day to a guitarist friend, "I'm so new at this that I'm not sure I am doing it right." He very kindly pulled me aside and softly whispered the best bass lesson I ever received: "Instead of trying to play the music right, see if you can just let yourself be musical."

Uncorking our voice is about being musical, about painting what needs to be painted, about writing what needs to be written. We are all naturally creative. Creative expression is part of being fully alive, part of listening to *me*, and part of living from our true self.

Loving

Children are also naturally loving. Loving is another quality we may have shut down years ago to follow the rules to please others or to keep safe. Now when we live from our inner core and listen to our voice, we can once again allow our loving to flow forth.

Loving is not the same as falling in love, being loved by others, or forgiving others. It is not about being sexual. It is not even a mutual activity. There are no expectations of the one we are loving and certainly no expectations that another person will change because of our loving. There are no attached needs. Being loving does not include "I love you; therefore you need to do what I want you to do."

Loving is a way of being in the world—an opening of our heart. Loving is a feeling that comes through us whenever it comes. We love whomever or whatever we love. Like playing and creating, becoming loving is more important than the end goal. Also like playing and creating, the experience is internal and incompatible with controlling. We cannot live from our safety pattern attempting to be in control and be genuinely loving at the same time. It is not possible.

Loving means feeling warm inside when we care about another— with no need for any particular response. After all, we can be loving toward strangers, those who have died, others who may have hurt us, and those we choose to no longer be around. While it may be nice to experience a loving response from those we love, a response is not a necessary part of being loving.

June, who lived alone, began deeply loving her cats instead of merely taking care of them. While she had always had cats in her

life, listening to her voice to shift toward freely and completely loving them left her feeling much warmer and softer inside—and less
afraid to be home alone.

Corinne moved back to her childhood home to help care for the
ailing father who had once abused her. It felt right to her to bring a
loving closure to their rocky relationship. She felt grateful that she
finally felt so loving toward him. She listened to her voice, even when
doing so surprised everyone else.

TRUSTING OUR VOICE

When we watch young children freely play, create, and love, we
can't help but notice how much they smile and laugh. When we smile
even a tiny smile, when we chuckle or laugh out loud, and especially
when we are curious, we open to whatever is next without attempting
to judge or control it. As we grow toward freely playing, creating, and
loving, the world opens to us—or rather, we open to the new that
appears to be coming to us. The possibilities seem endless when we
view them from our true self.

Trusting our voice means that we now trust our self more than we
trust the influence of others. But some of us wonder, can we trust our
voice—*really*? Can we trust this fullness that is coming into our life?
Can we trust these silly things we seem to need to express?

Many of us feel considerably safer now being fully *me* than living
from our old safety pattern. It is this surprising sense of deep safety
within us that teaches us what to trust inside us rather than whom to
trust on the outside of us. We trust the calm, peaceful feeling inside
that tells us when we are on track. We trust the energy that flows
through us and feeds us when we listen to our true self. We trust what
stays with us and what makes sense. We trust that *me* inside who is
always there with us and for us no matter what.

This perspective gives us something powerful to live for. Like Raven starting her new business, it gives us a reason to get up in the morning, and to smile and wonder what might be next. She says this trust feels to her like kayaking down a river, not knowing what she will find beyond the next bend but completely trusting that the flow of the river will take her where she needs to go.

Some describe this trust as reconnecting with a higher power, as it indeed feels spiritual and sacred in nature. Perhaps it is God, as we understand God, in action, giving us encouragement and permission. Different people use different language, remember, to describe this phenomenon. The language used may be unique to the individual but the experience is certainly universal.

When we are wondering if we can trust what is surging upward inside us, these questions may help:

+ What is my deepest truth?
+ Does this fit my integrity?
+ Does this feel right for who I am and who I am becoming?
+ What do I genuinely care about?
+ What are my dreams for my life?
+ Where is my passion?
+ Does this bring a deep sense of relief inside even if I feel scared?
+ Has this been coming for a long time?
+ Is my intention to express *me* rather than to hurt or control someone else?

Jade experienced a delicate situation in her life that made her question whether or not she could trust her internal guidance. Her birth anomalies had required numerous surgeries and extra effort over the years. Now they brought her a great deal of pain, but her husband refused to move to get her the medical care she needed.

In the middle of trying to figure out how to better meet her medical needs, Jade met a man she really liked, but she wasn't sure she could trust her attraction for him. She didn't want to be having an affair, as that did not fit her integrity.

After much confusion and soul-searching, she began to trust this change in her life. She knew her old safety patterns were ferocious self-sufficiency and enduring whatever needed to be endured. She had been learning to accept help more graciously and trusted feeling drawn toward moving to take better care of her body.

Jade finally made the difficult choice to leave her husband in order to get the medical care she desperately needed. When she also then chose to accept this other man's help and friendship, she felt a deep sense of relief and could feel her energy flowing again. She couldn't know, of course, if the new relationship would last, but that wasn't the issue. For her, leaving her husband, moving to get the medical care she needed, and accepting the help of this new friendship all independently answered "YES" to the above questions.

Sometimes we know we have to leave something before we know where we are going next. The challenge is to trust our self, one step at a time. So, we write just the next word of a letter, poem, or book. We paint just the next stroke. We say just the next thing we need to say.

We may seem to be going against all the rules we were once taught and the roles once expected of us, perhaps even against the grain of our entire society at times, but we feel a purpose to this shift that is occurring deep inside us as we uncork our voice.

LIVING FROM OUR TRUE SELF

Could I trust that seemingly sudden impulse to play the bass? Let me share the rest of the story.

I found an upright acoustic bass within a few days when others had told me it could take months to even find one for sale. I recognized my bass instantly. It was the right sound, right color, right feel, right everything. It felt just perfect for *me* and Maury was right next door, eager to provide people to play with me as I learned.

It seemed pretty wild and certainly a bit crazy to start playing bluegrass bass at the ripe age of fifty, but it was so much *fun!* I didn't consider the cost or how I was going to learn to play it or what I was going to do with it all. I just knew I needed to do it. While there was no need to hurry, the time simply felt right. I recognized this experience as yet another awakening moment in my life and trusted that deep knowing inside that I couldn't ignore. The pieces fell easily into place, and I couldn't ignore that either.

I have continued to thoroughly enjoy being musical with my bass, playing with different people and different groups. I now play in a women's bluegrass band, but my playing is not about becoming famous or being the world's very best bass player. It certainly is not about doing it perfectly. It is completely about fun. I *play* where and when I get the chance, surrendering to the wiggling and giggling that still rolls through me. That deep thumping now comes from *me*. I am the one who anchors the music to the earth—and it in turn anchors *me* to the earth. Playing bass keeps me expressing what needs to be expressed and keeps me uncorking my voice.

While we never know where this energy flow of our aliveness will take us, we trust this powerful but sometimes strange guidance we mysteriously receive along the way when we listen inside. When we trust our voice emerging through us, we come to know that we will be okay—no matter what seemingly silly thing may need to be expressed today.

More

Is it possible?
Can't be. Too much to do.
But how can that be?
Kids are grown. Career is solid.
Life is good, and I am happy.
More keeps knocking at my door.
"What is it? Who's there?" I ask.
It's More.
"More? I can't do any more," I sigh,
Exhausted by the possibility.
Yes, More.
You can have it all, More says.
"But I can't do it all," I say.
There's a difference. . . .
Gasping, I begin to get it. . . .
"I can have it all?"
Wow! Oh, my gosh!
I have been doing when all I need to do is have?
All I need to do is let it in?
All that goodness in my life—
Just let it in?
Let myself have it?
Just open to the possibilities—in all directions.
Open. Open. Open. . . .
Is there room?
What will happen?
Can I allow so much goodness?
I really don't know,
But I smile, wondering. . . .

Chapter 15

Dancing in Daffodils

How Can I Let This Moment Be Even More Alive?

I have to tell. He is hurting me. It is not right. She needs to know, and I need to tell her.

My little body is trembling. Do I dare? I have to—but he said not to. I have to. I *have* to! I need help. Somebody big has to help me. Okay, I'll do it. Mommy will help me. Should I wait? No, gotta do it now—quick before she leaves.

I am three years old. I am staying home with Grandpa while my mother goes to a meeting. She's in a hurry to get there.

Ooh, I hope I can do this. I really need some help. I don't like getting hurt. Oops, she's already at the door. I run into the dining room.

"Mommy!" I pull on her skirt, "Mommy, Mommy, don't leave!"

"I have to. I have to go to this meeting. I told you that."

"Don't go. Please don't go."

"Stop that. Grandpa will be here with you. I have to go now."

"But Mommy, he *hurts* me. . . ."

There I said it. Now she knows. My little body sighs in relief. I finally did what I needed to do. I spoke my truth. I know my mom will take care of it. She'll protect me from him.

But instead, she grabs my little hands, pulls them firmly off her skirt and pushes me away. "Stop that! Now go away! Go away and leave me alone!" She slams the door, leaving me standing there stunned and immobilized in disbelief.

How could she just leave? I told her and she left anyway. I don't understand. I was so sure . . .

The house is suddenly quiet, very quiet. I hear the snow blowing outside. I hear my own tears. What do I do now? I don't know what to do.

I climb up on the loveseat sobbing. I am so confused. I thought telling her would work, but it didn't. My tummy is shaking. I don't know what else to do.

Oh wait, she did tell me what to do! She said, "Go away and leave me alone." I told her my truth, and she told me what to do. Desperate to be a good girl, I sit there all alone in the utter silence and do my best to go away, like she said, so that I can leave her alone. I wish to be invisible with all my heart, but I can still see those little hands she pushed away. I try to fly away, but my arms flapping don't seem to do the job. I try to hide under the cushion. Nope, that doesn't work either.

I want to go away. I want to disappear. I want to be a good girl and please my mommy. I want to do what she says . . . but I can't figure out how to go away. I'll have to just leave her alone. I can at least do that part. Yes, I'll leave her alone. I'll be a good girl and leave her alone. . . .

It is the moment I land in the Good-Girl Jail.

WHAT MOTIVATES US?

This is the part of my story that motivates me now to go on with my life, to let myself be fully alive. I remember being courageous and clear enough to speak my truth about something really important when I was only three years old.

As I remember it now, I feel a slight trembling inside that tells me that little girl moment is still important to me. The trembling isn't fear any more. It used to be fear when I remembered Grandpa molesting me and not finding a way to stop him. The trembling isn't anger any more. It used to be anger when I remembered the parts about my mother not listening to me that time I desperately needed her help. It is no longer about leaving other people alone to be safe—the seemingly necessary conclusion I came to that snowy evening. And it is no longer about being a good girl, trying to please my mommy.

When I recall this story now, I connect with the *beginning* of the story—the courage and truth I knew and trusted at that young age of three. I knew that what my grandpa was doing was wrong. I knew he hurt me. I knew I didn't like it. I knew I needed help to stop him. I knew I needed to tell—and I did. I spoke my truth courageously. I stood in my truth that day and expressed it clearly 100 percent with no holding back. The fact that my mother didn't listen or perhaps didn't understand did not negate my clarity.

It is that inner core strength that I now reconnect with, that I remember, that I know "all the way to my toenails." Remembering my truth in that poignant moment before I landed in the Good-Girl Jail readily reconnects me with my true self. It is the same energy I reconnected with to leave my battering relationship, testify in court, and play in a band. It is this same energy that motivates me now to fully live my life—and finish this book.

I write this book because child abuse is the one thing I genuinely cannot tolerate. Child abuse is never a necessary part of parenting, yet it affects more of us than we can allow our minds to comprehend. Child abuse permanently changes everyone affected and often dominates life for decades after the traumatic events are over. It bothers me when we don't listen to children. I hate that we don't honor their needs adequately and don't comprehend how much children require their sense of self to live an alive, safe, full, meaningful life—their own life. Once traumatized as a child, it takes an enormous amount of work to return to living from our true self. It takes effort to finally feel safe again, to feel solid inside again, to enjoy life again—to live from the inner strength and truth of our true self once again.

Healing from childhood trauma is not easy and it can take a long time, but as this book indicates, it is indeed possible. Those who make the effort to heal deserve a lot of credit. I feel fortunate and grateful for my own healing experiences as well as for the opportunities I have had to witness many others grow to again feel whole and safe in the world.

But I ask you now, how can it take twenty years to write a book? It is embarrassing but true. I have been writing this book for nearly twenty years. Or is it thirty years now? I think I have lost track. Perhaps it has taken my entire lifetime.

I first believed this book was about parenting in a way that strengthened a child's sense of self. Then the focus shifted to developing one's own sense of self, which is, of course, the best way to encourage children to retain their inner reference point and honor their own true self.

Fifteen years ago I outlined this book and wrote three pretty good chapters—and then quit. I gave workshops about healing from trauma that included developing our sense of self, relating to others from our self, and relating to the sense of self in children and clients—and then quit. I even developed the concept of *spiritual equals* to describe how to relate from our true self to the true self in others. Ten years ago, when I began training other therapists at national conferences about strengthening the self, I discovered that people actually liked hearing my poetry. Finally, about three years ago, I admitted to myself that I was writing this particular book about each of us returning home to live from our true self. That piece came together at a workshop I attended one weekend in Santa Fe.

It was a warm spring afternoon with the trees bursting forth their amazing leaf buds and the birds cheerfully chirping as they tend to do. The New Mexico sun warmed our hearts and souls as we spent the weekend tapping into our deepest life dreams and giving ourselves permission to follow them.

I kept seeing images of huge fields of daffodils. I had often said that I come alive in the spring with the daffodils. They had become my favorite flower and the symbol of my own personal aliveness. That particular weekend I kept hearing all these thousands of little daffodil spirits just chattering away, completely excited that I had finally discovered them. They were ever-so-eager to help me write this book. As strange as the experience seemed, I listened. I welcomed them and their assistance, as I believed I needed all the help I could get for such a momentous project.

Then came the closing ceremony—another awakening moment. We walked a labyrinth while Ashana, an angelic soprano from Santa Fe, sang her gentle yet powerful songs accompanied by her keyboard and the droning sounds of toning bowls. The whole scene took me to feeling fully alive and in my body, moving as I wanted to—and

I wanted to dance in those imagined fields of daffodils! I let myself dance in the daffodils on and on and on, feeling more free and alive and integrated and whole than I had ever felt in my entire life—all the while knowing and claiming that I was writing this book. Dancing in daffodils thus became my personal image of letting go absolutely to come fully alive.

MORE SLIPS AND SLIDES

But of course, I couldn't stay dancing in those daffodils. Some days I didn't want to write this book. I fought it, not believing I was an author or afraid that publishing a book would alter my life in ways I wouldn't like. I tried pushing myself to write many times—and then gave it up again and again in overwhelming confusion. I learned that aliveness never comes when I push. I let numerous day-to-day events take over my deeper need to write, feeling relief sometimes and frustration at other times. I tried to distort my creative writing energy into playing more bluegrass music and sewing beautiful velvet jewelry bags, both of which seemed much more socially acceptable. That didn't work. I even wrote a different book about growing through the death of a parent. That didn't work either.

I have wrestled this book to the ground, beaten it up, stuffed it in the closet, twisted it into what I wanted instead, and shot it in the head . . . but it will not go away! And that is exactly the point: IT WILL NOT GO AWAY! My sense of self, my *me* will never, ever go away!

No, this book has become mine to write. No one else has already written this book and indeed, I had hoped someone else would let me off the hook. It seems to need to get written and somehow I have been elected to do the job. Or more accurately, writing this book has become part of fully living my life, part of uncorking my own voice to come fully alive. It is certainly a central part of daring to live from my true self. When I don't understand exactly why I need to write this book, I remember that little girl whose mom didn't listen to her in a crucial moment of need. That reminds me to listen inside to *me* and I then remember clearly why this particular book is mine to write.

I can see now that almost every experience in my life has led me toward writing this book the way that a funnel brings splashing water toward a central stream. Each awakening moment has helped me reach this point.

My friend Susan asked me that magical question: "And what have you been doing lately, Sandy?" I heard the voice in the cave inviting me to deal with my anger. I began to acknowledge my own fear after seeing fear in a friend. I learned to take action for my own safety. I learned to pay attention to my body. I learned to notice, claim, and release my feelings. I noticed my choices and how I spent my time alone. I updated old core beliefs as I became aware of them. I almost moved to Boulder but claimed my own home instead. I recognized my own judging and gradually let it go. As I let go of all that was not me, I discovered my evolving boundaries. I learned to stand in my truth, even in risky situations. I could even play bass in a women's bluegrass band—and have fun. As life brought me these awakening moments, I made my choice at each Y in the road. I learned the 4 R's—to Recognize, Reconnect with, Rebuild, and Return home to my true self.

Still, through it all, this book has just sat there over to the side, waiting ever-so-patiently for me to surrender to it—waiting for me to surrender to coming fully alive, fully living my own life, fully expressing me, and fully daring to live from my true self.

So I surrender—or at least think that I do. Then some more words flow onto paper—until I take back the reins and shut down again. Sometimes I set a deadline to get the darn thing done, but then can't write at all. Occasionally, I refuse to include a certain story, and then again I can't write at all until I surrender to sharing that particular story.

So here I am, once again up at 2:00 AM writing this story that I didn't want to include because it embarrasses me (do I still hear judgment?). I'm awake when I would rather be sleeping, surrendering once again to this book that simply will not leave me alone. I love it and resent it at the same time. I am inviting my aliveness, yet also still wanting it to be convenient and socially acceptable. Will I ever be able to let go absolutely?

Because this book refuses to leave me alone, I have finally come to trust this seemingly crazy process of writing, for it confronts me with my endless attempts to try to please others at my own expense. It forces me—or rather invites me—to see how attempting to be in control can never lead to feeling fully alive. I experience lesson after lesson about how these two basic paths at the Y in the road are so completely incompatible. And each time I come to that Y in the road, I let go, sooner or later saying "yes" to my precious aliveness. Do I really need so many opportunities to answer the big ARE YOU SURE? Apparently I do.

As I continue to invite my aliveness, writing this book is consistently the primary channel through which it comes. I really do want it, you know. I want the aliveness that consistently courses through my veins when I allow this freedom channel, where there are no rules or roles and where I can flow at my own pace and in my own way. It is what I call *dancing in daffodils*.

So, I humbly surrender once again to trusting the powerful, natural wisdom of my true self. I surrender to expressing whatever deeper truth needs to be expressed from my core today. And I once again notice that ever-so-slight trembling that reminds me how alive I feel when I listen to *me* and choose to live from my true self.

LETTING GO AGAIN . . .
AND AGAIN

How do I let go again each time I catch myself slipping back into the old vortex of rules and roles that I call the Good-Girl Jail? How do I let go when I again want to be socially acceptable so that I don't upset anyone else? How do I free myself when I am trying to be in control again or fighting yet another unnecessary power struggle or feeling afraid or in another flashback? How do I reconnect with my sense of self when I feel that painful separateness once again?

I use any and all of the tools I have described in this book. I ask myself any or all of the fifteen questions listed at the beginning of each chapter—open-ended questions that lead to a flowing paragraph about what is really going on inside:

- ✦ What do I know about my self?
- ✦ Am I listening to my awakening moments?
- ✦ What am I afraid might happen if I come fully alive?
- ✦ What would help me feel safer?
- ✦ What body sensations am I experiencing?
- ✦ What am I feeling right now?
- ✦ How many possibilities can I see?
- ✦ What would nourish me today?
- ✦ What do I really believe about my self?
- ✦ What is my deeper truth?
- ✦ What am I ready and willing to let go of?
- ✦ Where is that line between me and others?
- ✦ Am I sure?
- ✦ What do I really want to do today?
- ✦ How can I let this moment be even more alive?

I ask the questions—and carefully listen to the answers I hear. I come back into my body, allowing my feelings, especially any fear I might discover. I take some time alone. I look for that point of choice at the Y in the road. I claim what fits *me* and let go of the rest—without judgment. I listen until both the expectations of others and my own need to control begin to melt away once again. I listen until the daffodil spirits return and I again dance with them, flowing to the music I hear inside. I listen until the words flow once again onto the pages and I again feel alive—and I care.

THE SIGNIFICANCE OF CARING

We are built to care. We need to care. Caring warms our heart and reminds us that we are alive. Caring inspires us to take action to meet our needs, to make active choices to keep growing. Caring is our passion. It is what creates joy. Caring keeps us loving and gives us the courage to listen deep inside. Caring is our reason to get up in the morning. It is a part of our self that will never completely go away. It is part of what we return home to. It is how we know we have returned home to live from our precious, alive true self.

Sometimes we feel stuck in what we have been told should be meaningful to us or what might be meaningful to others—things like family, children, a nice house, social status, money, and church. But what is genuinely cared about varies a great deal from one person to another. What we care about is whatever we are consistently drawn toward or willing to fight for. Sometimes what we care about shifts over the years as our circumstances change or we begin to listen from a deeper place. Sometimes we need to search a bit for what is genuinely meaningful to us, but it is nearly always there somewhere.

When Elissa got into solid recovery for her alcoholism, she remembered an old dream to teach school that she had given up because of her drinking. She realized that she still really cared about children—especially about protecting them from child abuse, so she chose to return to school and created a new career for herself as an elementary school teacher. She then watched carefully for children who might be getting mistreated. She also taught her students to ask for what they needed and to make active choices—skills she believed would help to keep them all safe as they grew up. Teaching school became the vehicle through which she could express her caring. Elissa's life became genuinely meaningful when she rediscovered caring. She still had her addiction and trauma to tend to, of course, but her passion had been rekindled. Caring gave her a reason to go on with her life. It was part of returning home to live from her true self.

INVITING OUR ALIVENESS

As we discover what we truly care about and align our activities to fit, we open to deeper and deeper layers of our inner truth. We increasingly claim what fits us and let go of what does not without any need to judge or control. We live from our precious *me* and choose to go on with our life. As we begin to realize that there are no upper limits, we invite our aliveness more and more.

Sooner or later, we begin to wonder what could happen if we *let go absolutely* with no holding back. We begin to wonder what else might be possible in our life. We might begin to remember the dreams we have always had for our life.

Maybe we have wanted to live by the ocean as Nora did, even though she was living in the mountains. Maybe we have dreamed of standing on top of a fourteen-thousand-foot mountain as Evelyn did, even knowing she had asthma and would not be able to tolerate the altitude. Maybe, as June did, we always wanted to live again in our childhood home and pass it on to our children but lacked the financial ability to buy it.

Our long-held dreams do not always fit us now, but if we let them come up in our thoughts for consideration, we can either choose to follow them or let them go as things that may have fit us in the past but no longer do. Or we find a way to include the dreams in whatever ways are possible. Nora chose to live close to her children and grandchildren in the mountains but worked part-time in her retirement to save enough money to take a vacation to the ocean once a year. Evelyn climbed a fourteen-thousand-foot mountain as far as she could and got a grand view for over a hundred miles that she will remember forever. June found ways to hike near her old family home, take pictures of it, and tell stories about it to her children and grandchildren.

When we take risks to invite our aliveness, we can never know what will happen or how it will all turn out. We make the active choices that best fit *me* at each step of the way and then see what is next. It is the way life works when we dare to live from our true self.

Rubianne had a vivid dream in which she experienced God reassuring her about the future. God said, "You don't need to know what is going to happen. You only need to know that I am here." She awoke calmly aware that she didn't need to know the outcome up front. She only needed to trust each moment and then open to the next. Whether we believe in God or not, we can trust this moment and open to whatever is next.

Some of us have spent years wondering about our life purpose. I find the word *purpose* troublesome. If we believe we have a specific purpose and should know what it is but don't, we tend to judge our inadequacy. We then spend our energy searching for our unique purpose—usually something grand, like changing the world in some specific way. In my experience, being fully alive is much simpler and more fulfilling. I believe we already have all we need to experience meaning and that we naturally experience meaning when we dare to really listen to our true self. We don't have to "get there." We don't have to get anywhere. There is meaning in the process of living fully all along the way. There is meaning with every choice at the Y in the road. There is meaning in being *me*.

What we want is to experience aliveness, and it comes in many glorious forms unique to each of us. Aliveness is our true self bursting forth as we listen to our own personal dance in daffodils. Aliveness shows us what we genuinely care about. Aliveness is our reason to go on with life, our reason to get up in the morning, our reason to smile.

LIVING FROM OUR TRUE SELF

Many of us have lived hard lives. There is no denying that fact. Maybe we were abused as children. Maybe we have lived in dire poverty, with medical problems, unreasonable challenges, or great losses. We may wonder if it is possible to be happy. Is happiness just that myth we grew up with—that Cinderella story about marrying Prince Charming and living happily ever after in a castle on the hill? Or the myth about how winning the lottery will make our life easy? Or the one about someone taking care of us forever?

I believe it is possible to enjoy life and aliveness every day, perhaps even nearly every moment, but not in these particular ways. There is no one particular solution that brings happiness forever for everyone—like money or love. But let's look at this issue more closely. Aliveness is not the same as happiness.

Happiness is a feeling, a pleasurable emotion that is momentary and usually a result of something specific that we value. We might feel happy when we open a gift that pleases us, when we eat a double-dip ice cream cone in our favorite flavor, or when a child we adore comes to hug us.

Aliveness is a more general, pleasurable term. It doesn't come and go as quickly. It isn't nearly as vulnerable to what others say and do. We feel alive when we quit fighting what is and what has been, when we accept and claim what fits *me* and let go of all that does not. We feel alive when we feel grateful for the gifts in our life, the lessons we have learned, and the awakening moments that have brought us reconnection with our true self. We feel alive when the way in which we now live our life fits with what we value. And when we experience aliveness, we can smile and say, "Life is good"—and mean it.

Aliveness does not mean that everything is rosy and easy. We may feel alone at times, but we no longer feel empty and panicky when we do. We may feel powerless, but we no longer feel threatened when we do. We may feel scared sometimes, but we know we will be able to work our way through our fears and go on. We may even feel a little crazy at times, but we trust that we are following our own path and have the tools we need to return to our body, our inner truth, and our integrity. We may even occasionally get lost on another detour, but we know we will choose to go on with our life. We may be nervous about new adventures and relationships, but we know we will ultimately be okay—no matter what.

Eva, the woman who risked her life to leave a cult with her young children, says this: "Life is not about surviving the storm; it's about learning to dance in the rain."[32] She describes aliveness perfectly.

Aliveness comes when we grow beyond the Good-Girl Jail. It comes when we listen inside and reconnect with the strength of our deeper truth. It comes when we trust our sense of self and live once again from our integrity. Aliveness comes when we dare to live from our true self and find our own way to dance in daffodils.

Dancing in Daffodils

Coming fully alive
As the sun peeks over the edge
And spring creeps around the corner,
The daffodils poke through the crust.
They can do no other
For it is their personal mission
To brighten the earth
As the cold gray melts away once again.
It's what they do,
Because it's who they are.
Then, when the time is just right,
Those dainty sun-yellow teacups
Burst forth their healing glow,
And the daffodil spirits begin
To wiggle and giggle and smile.
And I dance,
Dance in the daffodils,
With my long flowing arms
To the music I hear.
It's what I do,
Because it's who I am,
And I can do no other.

RELATED READING

Belenky, Mary Field, Blythe McVicker Clinchy, Nancy Rule Goldberger, Jill Mattuck Tarule. *Women's Ways of Knowing: The Development of Self, Voice, and Mind*. New York: Basic Books, 1986.

Bradley, Marion Zimmer. *The Mists of Avalon*. New York: Ballantine Books, 1982.

Bradshaw, John. *Post-Romantic Stress Disorder: What to Do When the Honeymoon Is Over*. Deerfield Beach, FL: Health Communications, Inc., 2014.

Brown, Brene. *Daring Greatly: How the Courage to Be Vulnerable Transforms the Way We Live, Love, Parent, and Lead*. New York: Penguin Publishing Group, 2015.

Brown, Stephanie, PhD. *A Place Called Self: Woman, Sobriety, and Radical Transformation*. Center City, MN: Hazelden, 2004.

Cameron, Julia. *The Artist's Way: A Spiritual Path to Higher Creativity*. New York: Penguin, 2002.

Herman, Judith Lewis, MD. *Trauma and Recovery: The Aftermath of Violence—from Domestic Abuse to Political Terror*. New York: Basic Books, 1992.

Hobbs, Carolyn. *Joy No Matter What*. Berkeley, CA: Conari Press, 2005.

Huber, Cheri. *There is Nothing Wrong With You*. Mountain View, CA: Keep It Simple Books, 1993.

Johnston, Nancy L. *Disentangle: When You've Lost Your Self in Someone Else*. Las Vegas, NV: Central Recovery Press, 2011.

Kidd, Sue Monk. *The Dance of the Dissident Daughter: A Woman's Journey from Christian Tradition to the Sacred Feminine*. New York: Harper Collins, 2015.

Larsen, Gail. *Transformational Speaking: If You Want to Change the World, Tell a Better Story*. Berkeley, CA: Celestial Arts, 2009.

LeFrancois, Guy R. *Of Children*, 9th ed. Belmont, CA: Wadsworth Publishing, 2001.

Markova, Dawna. *I Will Not Die an Unlived Life: Reclaiming Purpose and Passion*. Berkeley, CA: Conari Press, 2000.

Masterson, James F. *The Search for the Real Self: Unmasking the Personality Disorders of Our Age*. New York: The Free Press, 1988.

May, Gerald G. *The Wisdom of Wilderness: Experiencing the Healing Power of Nature.* New York: HarperOne, 2006.

Mohr, Tara. *Playing Big: Find Your Voice, Your Mission, Your Message.* New York: The Penguin Group, 2014.

Mountain Dreamer, Oriah. *The Call: Discovering Why You Are Here.* San Francisco: HarperSanFrancisco, 2003.

_____. *The Dance: Moving to the Rhythms of Your True Self.* San Francisco: Harper-SanFrancisco, 2001.

_____. *The Invitation.* San Francisco: HarperSanFrancisco, 1999.

Powers, John R, PhD. *Odditude: Finding the Passion for Who You Are and What You Do.* Deerfield Beach, FL: Health Communications, 2007.

Prather, Hugh. *Notes to Myself: My Struggle to Become a Person.* Moab, UT: Peal People Press, 1970.

Pruett, Kyle D., MD. *Me, Myself and I: How Children Build Their Sense of Self.* New York: Goddard Press, 1999.

Robinson, Rita Marie. *Ordinary Women, Extraordinary Wisdom: The Feminine Face of Awakening.* Alresford, UK: O-Books, 2007.

SARK. *Succulent Wild Woman: Dancing With Your Wonder-Full Self.* New York: Fireside, 1997.

Schaef, Anne Wilson. *Living in Process: Basic Truths for Living the Path of the Soul.* New York: Ballantine, Wellspring, 1998.

Wadre, Bronnie. *The Top Five Regrets of the Dying: A Life Transformed by the Dearly Departing.* Carlsbad, CA: Hay House, Inc., 2012.

Weinhold, Barry K., PhD and Janae B. Weinhold, PhD. *Developmental Trauma: The Game Changer in the Mental Health Profession.* Colorado Springs, CO: CICRCL Press, 2015.

Wilber, Ken. *No Boundary: Eastern and Western Approaches to Personal Growth.* Boston: Shambhala, 2001.